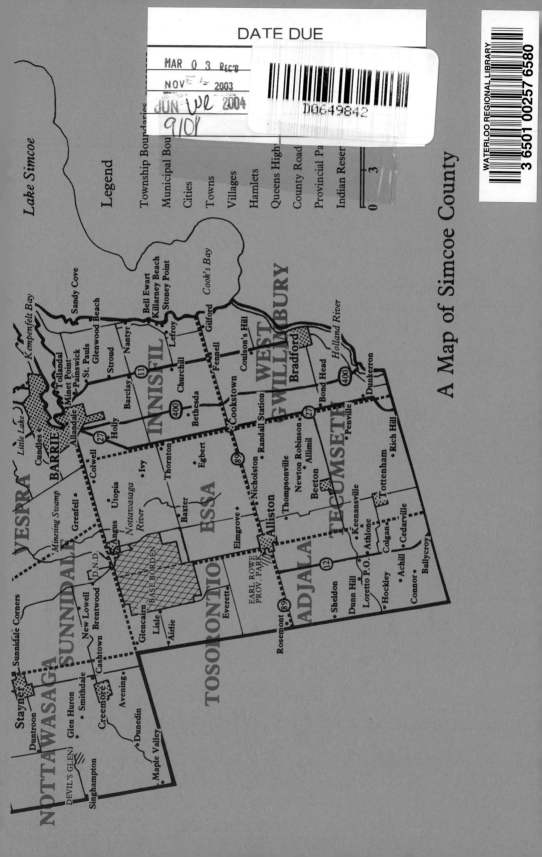

A Map of Simcoe County

Lake Simcoe

Legend

Township Boundaries
Municipal Bou...
Cities
Towns
Villages
Hamlets
Queens High...
County Road
Provincial Pa...
Indian Reser...

0   3

Kempenfelt Bay
Sandy Cove
Bell Ewart
Killarney Beach
Stoney Point
Cook's Bay
Glenwood Beach
St. Pauls
Nantyr
Lefroy
Gilford
Coulson's Hill
Fennell
Holland River
Tollandal
Minet Point
Painswick
Stroud
Churchill
Bethesda
Cookstown
Bond Head
Dunkerton
Barclay
Thornton
Randall Station
Penville
Rich Hill
Little Lake
Cundles
Allandale
Holly
Ivy
Egbert
Nicholston
Beeton
Tottenham
Colwell
Utopia
Baxter
Elmgrove
Thompsonville
Newton Robinson
Allimil
Keenansville
Colgan
Cedarville
Angus
Alliston
Athlone
Achill
Ballycroy
Grenfell
Nottawasaga River
Earl Rowe Prov. Park
Sheldon
Dunn Hill
Loretto P.O.
Hockley
Connor
Minesing Swamp
D.N.D.
Camp Borden
Everette
Rosemont
Grenfell
Glencairn
Lisle
Airlie
New Lowell
Brentwood
Cashtown
Avening
Creemore
Glen Huron
Smithdale
Dunedin
Maple Valley
Devil's Glen
Singhampton
Stayner
Duntroon
Sunnidale Corners

VESPRA
BARRIE
INNISFIL
WEST GWILLIMBURY
Bradford
TECUMSETH
ESSA
ADJALA
TOSORONTIO
SUNNIDALE
NOTTAWASAGA

11
27
400
89
27
12
89
400

NON · SIBI SED · PATRIAE

Simcoe County
The Recent Past

John Craig

Illustrated by
Margot Anderson

The Corporation of the
County of Simcoe

ISBN 0-9690698-2-0

Printed and bound in Canada.

Managing Editor: Helen Nolan
Designer: Carl Brett Design
Printing and Binding: The Bryant Press Limited
Typeface: Plantin
Paper: Publishers' Choice
Cover: Bayside Linen

Contents

Foreword

Since the beginning of the century, the County of Simcoe has had the wisdom and foresight to publish three major works on the County's history. As the Warden of this fine County, I have the privilege of introducing the fourth book, *Simcoe County: The Recent Past.*

I am pleased to have this opportunity to thank the author, Mr. John Craig, for his informative and enjoyable chronicle of our more recent past. Simcoe County is indeed fortunate to have this well-known author write such a human and factual account.

As well, we are indebted to Mrs. Irene Perri and Mr. Jay Cody for their contributions in compiling the necessary research. The 1975, 1976, and 1977 Simcoe County Councils are to be commended for their initiation and support of this entire project. To all others, especially Mrs. Helen Nolan, Managing Editor, my grateful thanks.

Simcoe County can be truly proud of its heritage, traditions and accomplishments. Bounded by waterways and connected by major transportation routes, the County has served as a crossroads for Central Ontario development. Tourism, agriculture and commerce have all benefited from its strategic location. Because of our forefathers' resourcefulness and providence, Simcoe County is today a good place in which to live.

Allan Glassford

Warden, County of Simcoe, 1977

Preface

Although it could be considered a minor sub-division in the overpowering vastness that is Canada, Simcoe County is, nevertheless, a very substantial piece of real estate. Encompassing more than a million acres, it is larger than most of the Caribbean and Pacific islands and could comfortably accommodate at least one European country within its boundaries.

It is not its size, however, but the variety of its terrain that is most impressive—ranging from the delta flats of Holland Marsh in the southeast, across the sand hills of the interior, to the rugged escarpment fringing Collingwood in the northwest, and, diagonally, from Tottenham's sheltered valley to the sometimes storm-lashed shores near Victoria Harbour.

Yet, for all its length and breadth and geographic diversity, there is a feeling of common identity among most of its present-day population of over two hundred thousand—something which, to borrow an Orillia term, might be called "the Simcoe County spirit."

There is also a very strong sense of history. Awareness of the past is everywhere in evidence—in the County's several fine museums and County Archives, in the unusual number of active historical societies, in the painstaking reconstruction of old Huronia, in the interest of County librarians, in the compiling of Tweedsmuir histories by branches of the Women's Institute, and in the historic plaques that dot the landscape.

It is conjured up, too, by the place names. Many are Indian in origin, predating the coming of Champlain and the

Jesuit martyrs: Nottawasaga, Medonte, Washago, Minesing, Penetanguishene, Waubaushene, Tosorontio, Matchedash, and others. Holland Marsh is named, not after the Dutch market-gardeners who came there in the twentieth century, but for Samuel Holland who surveyed the area early in the nineteenth century. Both the County and the great lake which forms much of its eastern boundary honour the family of John Graves Simcoe, while three townships, Flos, Tiny and Tay, reflect the affection felt for the pet dogs of Lady Sarah Maitland, wife of a Lieutenant Governor of Upper Canada.

In 1909 Andrew F. Hunter published his *History of Simcoe County*, which recorded the story of the region from the earliest times to the mid-1890s. Hunter, who had been the editor of the Barrie *Examiner* from 1889 to 1895, was a self-trained archaeologist, a thorough researcher and a dedicated and competent historian. His book, which has been kept in print by the Historical Committee of Simcoe County, covers the arrival of the French explorers and missionaries, the fur trade, the old military route to Penetanguishene, the coming of the settlers, the gradual emergence of a stable community, complete with towns and villages, schools and churches, roads and railroads, courts and lawyers, doctors and the first hospitals, commerce and industry, hotels, newspapers, livery stables, fairs, parades, the regular delivery of mail, and the administration of government.

The purpose of this volume is to bring that chronicle up to date—into and through the first three-quarters of the twentieth century—so that the residents of Simcoe County, especially the young, may have a fuller appreciation of their heritage.

It is a rich legacy that they share, one that incorporates all the elements of drama, comedy and tragedy—an inheritance left not only by sons and daughters who achieved prominence in various fields, but also by the thousandfold others who live their live and did their work in historical anonymity.

I would like to express my deep appreciation: to the Simcoe County Councils of 1976 and 1977 for their gracious support; to my enthusiastic and highly professional editor, Helen Nolan; to Irene Perri and Jay Cody, whose earlier research was of inestimable value; and to Adelaide Leitch for her splendid pictorial volume *The Visible Past* which provided so many useful insights and pointed the way to so much valuable material.

I would also like to thank my fellow-chroniclers who have written local histories of towns, villages, townships and parishes within Simcoe County, without whose labours this book would be very much the poorer.

I have met and been helped by dozens of others throughout the County, all of whom have been generous in their co-operation, encouragement and hospitality. To name them all would require more pages than are available; to single out a few would be to slight the many. So, to all, I would like to acknowledge my indebtedness and to express my sincere appreciation.

Inevitably and understandably, some readers will feel that I have paid less than appropriate attention to their particular communities, or their special interests. They will feel that way because they care very deeply. I can only remind them, very sympathetically, that this is the story of the County as a whole—which is different from, and more than, the sum of its individual parts.

And it is quite a story.

Tug, Magnolia, *built in 1898 by
the Midland Towing and Wrecking Co.*

1 Simcoe County, 1895

In the final decade of the nineteenth century, Simcoe County was nearing the midpoint of its transition from the old, pioneer days to what could be called the "Modern Era."

Much of the past was already irretrievably gone. Oxen had been replaced by horses and had all but disappeared. The passenger pigeon, which had once filled the skies, had been ruthlessly slaughtered and was almost extinct—the last two recorded in Simcoe County were seen near Penetanguishene in 1902.

Throughout the County numerous towns and villages had become virtually self-sufficient in terms of satisfying the needs of their citizens and those of the farm families spread out around them. For example, Stayner, which had been incorporated as a town in 1888, boasted of such businesses and services as a hardware store, a milliner's shop, a tailor, an implement shop, a butcher, two general stores, a bakery, an apothecary, a dentist ("Guaranteed Painless Extractions"!), a tinsmith, and many other establishments. The legislation which transformed Stayner from an incorporated village into a town had been rushed through because of a rumour that Simcoe County was going to set up two centres of government—one in the south and one in the north. The proposal never went through, but it made Stayner the smallest town in Ontario, a distinction which still applied far into the twentieth century.

Even crossroad hamlets like New Flos became prosperous and important centres—their main streets lined with stores, emporiums, professional practices and commercial enterprises.

Some establishments were common to almost all towns and villages. One was the livery stable, such as the one operated in Beeton by D. W. Watson, which provided a kind of taxi service, rented horses and buggies, boarded horses, transported passengers to and from the train station, and picked up and delivered the mail. The Beeton livery was a busy place and four men were required to handle the mail alone. Buggies, wagons and sleighs could be rented for $1.50 a day, and on a sunny Sunday all available equipment would be snapped up long before noon.

There was almost always a blacksmith, a harnessmaker, a seed store and a combined furniture store and undertaker's, where the cabinet makers fashioned caskets as well as tables and chairs, and the mortuary was usually in the cool basement.

Hotels sprang up like mushrooms as commissionmen, drummers and other salesmen flocked into the County on the daily trains. A favourite name was the "Commercial Hotel." Many of the hotels offered much in the way of comfort and gracious living. Beeton's Queen's Hotel, for example, consisted of three stories, was built of solid brick, and was surrounded by neat, well-tended lawns. The main floor consisted of an ornate lobby, dining room, large parlor, tailor shop and saloon—the latter dominated by a forty-foot bar with brass footrail and spitoons, where weary travellers could ease their thirst with five-cent schooners of beer or shots of whiskey. On the second and third floors a total of forty-eight spacious and comfortable rooms were available for overnight guests.

Most villages and hamlets, as well as towns, had had post offices for some time. The one in Crown Hill, for instance, dated from 1878. The mail was usually delivered by train or picked up by stage coach from the nearest rail point.

There were many weekly newspapers. In Orillia the *Times* began publishing in May, 1867, and the *Expositor* published its first edition in 1872. In 1873 Peter Murray amalgamated the *Expositor* with the *Times* and, after a brief period of being known as the *Orillia Times and Simcoe County*

Expositor, the name was shortened to exclude any reference to the *Expositor*. Meanwhile, the *Packet* had been published since 1870 by William and George Hughes Hale. Much later, in 1926, the two weeklies amalgamated to become the Orillia *Packet and Times* and, to complete the history, it became a daily newspaper in 1953.

In Barrie, during the nineties there were three weeklies, the *Northern Advance*, the *Examiner* and the *Gazette*.

The *Elmvale Advocate*, soon to become the *Chronicle* and shortly afterwards the *Lance*, first went to press in 1891. As was often the case, the name of the paper changed with each successive owner.

The *Beeton World*, an ambitious weekly which liked to editorialize that the boom was just around the corner for Beeton and Simcoe County, employed twenty journalists and printers (some part-time) by the mid-1890s.

Apart from church on Sundays, the principal meeting place in most communities was the local general store, especially on Saturday evenings. There the women exchanged family news, gossip, recipes and home remedies as they shopped for their families' needs for the following week; there children played together and ate long-looked-forward-to penny candy; and the men sat on nail kegs around the potbellied stove to discuss politics, the latest farm machinery, and the outlook for that year's crops.

The general stores sold, not just groceries, but almost everything else necessary for existence during that period: hardware, dishes, coal-oil and wicks for lamps, clothing for the whole family, school supplies, ink, tanglefoot for catching flies, boots and shoes, lye for making soap, material for making curtains and dress-goods, oilcloth, and a thousand other items. A constant miracle was the ability of the storekeeper to almost always come up with what was wanted from his crammed shelves or backroom storehouse.

There were almost no prepackaged goods, and virtually all grocery items, from raisins to molasses, tea to spices, rolled oats to brown sugar, were available only in bulk form, stored in casks, boxes and bins. The merchant would scoop out what he judged to be close to the amount specified by the customer, weigh it and state a price, add or take away a little as required, and then pour the agreed-upon quantity from the scale-pan into a brown paper bag or other suitable container.

General stores were heady with the sights and smells of many products imported from faraway lands and from industrial centres like Toronto, a day's travel to the south. One of the most tantalizing sections, especially for children, was the row of glass-fronted bins containing fancy biscuits and cookies.

Typical of the general stores was that opened in 1865 in Minesing by the Ronald family; it contained the Post Office (and still does), and continued to do business into the fifth generation, until Mrs. Grace Ronald McKee sold it in 1975.

Prices in 1895 were incredibly low by today's standards. Eggs sold for about 12¢ a dozen; butter was 25¢ a pound; bread was a nickel a loaf; good beef steak was about 15¢ a pound (often with some free liver thrown in); potatoes brought 50¢ for a ninety-pound bag. A pair of chickens went for about 40¢, spring lamb for 9¢ a pound and flour for $2.85 a hundred pounds.

Hotel dining rooms offered full-course meals—soup, main course with vegetables, bread and butter, dessert and coffee— for 20¢. Haircuts cost 15¢, and a shave was only a dime. A cord of prime hardwood, cut to stove-length and split, would be delivered for around $3.

Of course wages were low, too. A good craftsman such as a cabinet maker or blacksmith would consider himself fortunate to take home $8 to $10 a week, and unskilled labourers were paid considerably less.

To make a living most storekeepers had to put in long hours, opening their doors at 7 A.M. and closing at 7 P.M., except on Saturdays when they remained behind their counters until 10 P.M. or later. For them a work week consisted of from sixty-six to seventy-two hours, plus extra time for keeping the books, uncrating stock and replenishing their shelves.

Although less common than in earlier years, the barter system was still used extensively. Farm wives brought eggs, chickens, and butter to the general store and exchanged them for such staples as tea, sugar and spices. Most merchants were lenient in extending credit until the farmer could market his fall crop of grain. Similarly, wheat was exchanged for flour at the local grist mill, wool for yarn and blankets at the woolen mill, and milk for cheese at the cheese factory.

Cheese factories were common throughout the County. There were four in Oro Township alone. Dairy farmers put the large cans of milk on wooden stands at the end of their driveways, where they were picked up by wagon or sleigh. Some had the whey from the previous day's milk returned with the cans to be fed to the hogs being fattened for market.

A few communities had libraries. Stayner, for example, made the collection of books owned by the local Mechanics' Institute into a public library in 1895. Dr. Charles Jakeway was the first librarian. The books were housed in a room above the hardware store. A bell tinkled when a borrower came through the door, thus summoning the librarian from the back room where he resided.

There was also a literary society at Minesing. Its members held discussion groups and sponsored annual picnics at Wasaga Beach.

A major undertaking each winter was the cutting of ice from lakes and ponds to provide refrigeration for the summer months. The ice was cut into 50-, 100- and 300-pound blocks. It was brought to shore by sleigh, and stored in ice-houses, where each tier and the cracks between blocks were carefully packed with sawdust. There, with proper ventilation and reasonable care in removing each successive block, the ice would last with very little loss of volume throughout the hottest days of July and August.

The ice cutting was originally done by hand, later by steam-driven saws. Either way, it is hard to imagine a more bone-chilling occupation than working out on a wind-swept, open lake on a sub-zero February or March day.

By the mid-1890s ice cutting had become a commercial operation. Ice cut in Kempenfelt Bay was shipped from Allandale by train. Three ice companies operated out of Belle Ewart. The Belle Ewart Ice Company began operations in 1891, and four years later was joined by the Burns' Company Ltd. and the Lake Simcoe Ice Company. For a few weeks each winter Belle Ewart was the scene of much industry, and added prosperity, as two to three hundred men poured into the community to harvest the ice, swelling the boarding houses to the point of bursting and spending their wages on whatever amenities were available.

Most towns and cities had some kind of street lighting, at least in their downtown sections. Collingwood had recently replaced its kerosene Edison lamps with electric lights. Barrie had carbon-arc fixtures at its most important intersections. The Johnson brothers of that town had a contract to go around by horse and buggy each day, replacing burned out carbon sticks. In Alliston, where the electric current was supplied by a small local plant, the lights were thriftily turned off at 11 P.M. each night—an hour when, as the Reeve noted, "all honest people should be in bed, and rogues had no business being up."

In all communities, towns and villages alike, the main streets were still plain dirt roads and became quagmires of ankle-deep mud in spring or after a heavy rain. Many had wooden sidewalks, and long, wide planks were stacked at strategic points to help pedestrians across the wide stretches of mud.

In villages and hamlets, and to a lesser extent in the towns, livestock was still permitted to roam the side streets almost at will. Many non-rural families kept a horse or two, perhaps a milk-cow, often a few chickens, and sometimes a number of pigs to be eventually slaughtered for bacon, sausages, roasts and chops. Eventually, early in the twentieth century, Stayner passed a by-law limiting each family to one free-roaming cow. As early as 1886 Beeton established a pound for stray animals and empowered James Heuchen to round up livestock pedestrians. For assuming this responsibility Heuchen was paid a five dollar annual salary and given a percentage of all resulting fines—which ranged from a dime for a lamb to 75¢ for a bull. In a somewhat similar vein Midland introduced dog licences in 1896.

While most houses were modest, if sturdy, almost every community could claim at least one imposing structure—a church, court house or municipal building. And the towns had some huge and imposing mansions, such as the Williams residence in Collingwood and the Mulcahy and Tait homes in Orillia.

Barrie's magnificient Grand Opera House, one of the most impressive theatres in Ontario, opened its doors in 1895, and subsequently played host to such stage attractions as Madame Alberni, the Coldstream Guards and the Dolly sisters. It was built and donated to the town by Jim Sanford, a flambouyant entrepreneur. Sanford was also the Treasurer for Simcoe County, and soon after the completion of the Grand Opera House a shortage of some $80,000 was discovered in the Simcoe accounts. With the law on his heels, Sanford slipped out of the country and sailed to South America. There he built a fortune from mining investments and eventually paid off his debts in full. Truly, as the Barrie *Examiner* commented many years later, he was "both a scoundrel and an honest man."

By 1895 Barrie had a population of close to 6000, Collingwood had about 5500, Orillia was just over 5000, and Midland and Penetanguishene both stood at just over the 2000 mark. Among the townships, Nottawasaga with a little more than 500 had the largest number of residents. The population of the entire County was slightly over 70,000.

In January, 1897 the village of Allandale, with a population of 984, became Barrie's Sixth Ward. Allandale prospered from the new railway boom of the early 1890s. To accommodate the influx of workers, several dozen frame houses were thrown up west of Essa Road; these were offered for $700 apiece—a seemingly low price until one remembers that labourers were paid $1 for a ten-hour day.

Government officials were no doubt as conscientious then as they are today, although none more so than T. D. Robinson who was appointed Clerk in Medonte township in 1894. To protect the township funds in his home, Robinson used to keep a pistol on his person or under his pillow, and a shot gun on hand at all times, day and night. Fortunately, during the fifty-six years he served the township (longevity of service was a characteristic of Simcoe County officials), he never had any occasion to fire either of his weapons.

In education too, the County was also moving away from the past. However in 1895 many of the one-room, log schoolhouses of an earlier era were still in operation. The cracks between the logs were chinked with clay or, if available, lime. The inside walls were given a coat of whitewash every now and then. Lighting came from coal-oil lamps or candles, and heat was provided by red-hot Quebec heaters, stoked with huge blocks of hardwood. And as pointed out in *The Story of Oro*, "The steaming mitts placed around the stove to dry took the place of the humidifier of today."

In such schoolhouses the pupils sat on backless benches and did most of their lessons on slates. There was often a pulpit in one corner since the classroom doubled as a church on Sundays. The schoolyard was usually the little travelled public road in front of the school, the "washroom" was a privy, discreetly shared by boys and girls. The drinking water was carried in a wooden bucket from a nearby spring and drunk from a dipper which hung beside it.

Teachers' salaries were extremely low—even railway labourers received higher pay. In order to keep body and soul together, many teachers boarded from house to house in their school districts and did chores to help pay for their accommodation. In 1894, for example, the total annual budget for S. S. No. 11, Oro, was $380.43—this included the teachers' pay, wood for the potbellied stove, maintenance and all supplies.

All subjects and all grades were taught by one teacher. According to law, no teacher could be required to be responsible for more than fifty pupils, but in many cases this limitation was ignored. One schoolmaster, faced with a student body of eighty-two, ranging in age from six to sixteen, suffered a nervous breakdown before the completion of his first term.

Most of the teachers were men, many of whom hoped to survive a year or two of rural teaching so that they might continue their professional training in medicine or law.

Women who ventured into the field had to cope, not only with low salaries, but also with stringent rules, such as: you must not marry during the term of your contract; you are not to keep company with men; you must be home between the hours of 8:00 P.M. and 6:00 A.M., unless attending a school function; you may not ride in a carriage with any man, unless he is your father or brother; and, to keep the school neat and clean, you must clean the floor at least once a week with hot water, clean the blackboards at least once a day, and start the fire at 7:00 A.M. so that the room will be warm by 8:00 A.M.

Yet, for all the hardships and degradations imposed upon them, some great and memorable teachers, male and female, contributed immeasurably to the education of the young of Simcoe County. To let one name stand for all the unsung others, Frederick C. Batten of Collingwood, a teacher at S. S. No. 9, Vespra, died of consumption in 1896, while yet a young man. His still younger wife, a victim of the same disease, had pre-deceased him by some two years. Long after his premature death Batten was remembered, mourned and beloved by those who had studied under him.

By the 1890s a trend toward more adequate and modern educational facilities was taking place. Many of the towns established "continuation schools," where children could go from grade one through to grade twelve (or to grade ten in some schools) in the same building. In Essa a new brick building was erected to replace the original log schoolhouse in 1899. In Beeton an even more substantial edifice, heated by two large furnaces, was in operation on Tecumseth Street. Similar replacement of the old by the new was occurring throughout the County.

Three excellent collegiate institutes were offering secondary school education in Barrie, Orillia and Midland, making it possible for Simcoe County boys and girls who sought higher education to acquire the prerequisites close to home.

Penmanship, grammar and spelling were regarded as vital elements in a sound education. Spelling bees were major events, not only in the schools but also at many fall fairs. Mothers and fathers spent a great many hours going over lists of difficult words with sons and daughters who aspired to win the spelling championship of their school or township.

In 1895 parents paid for their children's school books, if any were available. Always in short supply, these texts were greatly prized and were handed down from one family member to the next. In the 1890s a First Reader sold for 4¢, and the Fourth Reader (being much fatter) for about 40¢. To a large extent books were filled with stories and poems which glorified British military and naval victories, instilled patriotism, and extolled the greatness of the British Empire. Kipling was, of course, a favourite.

Most men and women worked from dawn to dusk or longer for six days of the week, but the seventh, Sunday, was scrupulously set aside for rest and for the worship of God. The degree of abstention from considerations of the flesh varied from denomination to denomination, and from individual to individual, but a common denominator was that no unnecessary work was performed on the Sabbath.

Apart from the actual cooking, Sunday dinners were prepared on Saturdays. On that day, too, shoes were polished, shirts and blouses ironed, collars starched, velvets brushed, horses groomed, buggies and cutters cleaned, and baths taken in tubs in front of kitchen stoves. It was considered mandatory (both in the eyes of God, and in the eyes of one's neighbours) to "look your best" at morning service or Sunday School.

After church people spent the rest of the day according to their particular persuasions. Some activities—playing cards, dancing, drinking, loud laughter—were frowned upon by almost everyone. So was the conducting of any kind of business. Many a father retired to a shaded hammock in summer or to a comfortable couch by the fire in winter until his wife announced that supper was ready. Some families used the day for visiting relatives or friends. Others went for walks; the stroll along the boardwalk from Barrie to Allandale was a favourite. Some people read the Bible.

Some parishes could afford a resident minister; others were served by circuit preachers who divided their time among several churches within a limited area. Many members of this fraternity were student ministers, some were lay preachers; all needed to be made of sturdy stuff, physically as well as spiritually, because they were almost as poorly paid as schoolteachers and had to endure considerable travel, often through rainstorms and blizzards, to keep their appointed rounds. Not only were they responsible for Sunday services, but also were on call for weddings, christenings and funerals.

Typical examples of the period were Rev. Theophile Laboreau, who served parishes in Penetanguishene, Port Severn, Waubaushene and Midland, and Rev. G. I. Craw, who ministered to Victoria Harbour, Port McNicoll and Moonstone.

Sermons, usually of the fire-and-brimstone type, were as much subjects of conversation as movies and television shows became a half-century later. They were even "reviewed," as this excerpt from a Flos township newspaper of January, 1894 attests: "Mr. John Coburn preached three sermons on the Elmvale circuit. The boy preacher does not use a note, and he holds his audience in a tight grip."

During the last decade of the nineteenth century a great many new churches were built in the County, while others were renovated, expanded or replaced with more modern buildings. Among many others, the Free Methodist Church at Crown Hill held its first service in 1892; the Van Vlack

Presbyterian church at New Flos opened its doors in 1894;
and the first Presbyterian church in Oro township was built
that same year. In 1896 an impressive brick and stone church
replaced the former frame structure of the Minesing Methodist Church (later, the Minesing United Church).

A remarkable phenomenon was that, thanks to the dedicated efforts of their congregations, most of these churches
were entirely or almost paid for by the time they opened their
doors. In 1890, for instance, a new Presbyterian church was
built in Beeton—an imposing wood and brick structure, with
an abundance of stained glass windows and a forty-foot ceiling adorned by huge brass lamps. It could accomodate three
hundred worshippers and had separate rooms for Sunday
School classes and other functions. There was a bell in the
tower which could be heard for miles around. Members had
raised $2,100 prior to turning the first sod, and through their
continued support the building was mortgage-free when the
official opening took place on May 24, 1891.

The lot of Simcoe County farm wives remained hard during the 1890s, although their isolation was somewhat relieved
by the fact that they could look forward to a weekly visit
to town and to church on Sundays. The general store was
a great boon to them because, thanks to the railways, it
stocked items that were of great importance in turning their
plain dwellings into homes—needles and thread, ribbons
and lace, dry goods, wallpaper, carpets and rugs, and factory-
made furniture. Eaton's catalogue, which first arrived in 1884,
brought still more magic. Women spent countless hours leaf-
ing through each year's edition, marvelling at the endless
items available. All they had to do was fill out and mail a
form and whatever they ordered would be waiting for them
at the nearest railway station a week or so later—provided, of
course, that they had the money to pay for it!

A few primitive gadgets and appliances which were sup-
posed to make life easier for the housewife came on the market. In 1895, for example, Robert Hisey of New Flos was
appointed agent for "the celebrated Whirlpool Washer" and

"the Belvidere Carpet-Stretcher." Whatever the merits of such technological breakthroughs, it remained true that the household work was never done—the sweeping, mending, sewing, cooking and a hundred other chores had to be attended to as part of the daily routine. On Mondays the laundry was still usually done in copper boilers on top of the kitchen stove, the white things were scrubbed by hand on a washboard, and everything was hung outside to dry in the fresh air, not only in summer, but also when the temperature dipped well below zero on January and February days. The next day there was the ironing to do, with sadirons or flat-irons, heated on the same kitchen stove.

The women often did the milking, churned the butter, made soap and cured meat. They kept the fire going with fresh hardwood chunks, carried in water from the pump, and brought vegetables and fruits up from the root cellar. Of necessity their clothes were practical rather than glamor-ous: calico sunbonnets in summer; woolen undergarments, chamois drawers, and bloomers gathered at the knee in the cold months; and up to three petticoats under their long skirts. The only cosmetics used were powder or corn starch and occasionally, among the most daring, a touch of rouge.

In those days there was plenty to eat in summer and through most of the fall, but during the long winters it was more difficult to keep food on the table. From just before Christmas until around Easter, cows produced little milk, and hens almost completely stopped laying. Canned foods had not yet made their appearance, and housewives had to rely on what they had prepared and stored against the months of cold and snow. The cellar was the "frozen food locker" of the 1890s. There were stored the hundreds of jars of peaches, pears, cherries, jams, jellies, pickles, relishes and other preserves that had been "done down" the previous summer and early fall. September was the peak time for pre-serving; women spent long hours peeling, coring, slicing, chopping, mixing, and stirring, while the big pots bubbled away on the cookstoves, filling the kitchens with rich and

13

spicy smells.

In the cellar, too, would be stored the root vegetables: potatoes, carrots, turnips and parsnips, the home-grown herbs, and a variety of apples: Spies, Greenings, Russets, Snows and others, some of which, known as "good keepers," would be reserved for late winter and spring use.

Farming was going through some basic changes during this period. By 1895 a variety of horsedrawn equipment was in use—mowers, rakes, cultivators and disc harrows, for example. The Mercer Bros. & Co. Agricultural Works in Alliston was advertising the merits of their new binder in 1895.

The portable steam engine played an increasingly important role in farming, particularly at threshing time, but also for many other purposes ranging from the making of cedar shakes to the drawing of water. Usually one steam engine, plus a portable threshing machine, served an entire neighbourhood. It was drawn from farm to farm, with all the men of the community pitching in to supply the work force. Similarly, their wives co-operated to keep harvest tables groaning under the weight of hot and cold meats, mounds of mashed potatoes, vegetables, fresh-baked bread, salads, pies, cakes and cookies—no one ever went hungry at harvest time.

With this kind of community spirit, a carry-over from the pioneer days, a substantial barn, perhaps forty-five by eighty feet, could still be raised for a total cost of under $1,000.

A trend away from grain farming and towards the raising of livestock began. County farmers discovered that there was a profitable demand for fattened heavy steers, shipped live to England. More and more sheep were raised, both for their wool and for the market. The growing importance of pork to Simcoe County was underlined by the opening of a packing plant in Collingwood which boasted that it was the home of "Canadian, Pea-Fed Bacon." For some years a train, known far and wide as "the Hog Special," ran three times a week from Barrie to Collingwood. It consisted of six or seven cars of hogs, followed by a single passenger coach, the occupants of which were inclined to leave the windows closed even on the hottest days of summer.

One popular event each spring was Farm Implement Day. During the fall and winter, agents of the manufacturing companies travelled throughout the County soliciting orders for everything from binder twine to large pieces of equipment. The agent notified all his customers to come to town on a certain day in the spring, usually in May, to pick up their orders which would be at the railway station. They were also advised which hotel was to be headquarters for the festivities. On the appointed day the red carpet was rolled out for the farmers who came in to pick up their merchandise. Everything was free (courtesy of the agent's company): horses stabled and fed, a huge dinner in the hotel dining room, beer or whiskey at the bar. Later there was a parade down main street, each farmer with his purchases in his wagon, led by the town band.

At that time the roads of the County, still somewhat primitive, were maintained largely by statute labour, a government requirement by which every able-bodied man was expected to spend a certain number of days each year in keeping up the public thoroughfares in his particular part of the County. This might involve grading, repairing bridges, pulling stumps and hauling out large boulders. The extent to which it was performed, and the degree to which it was performed well, varied considerably from community to community. In the absence of any equipment for the purpose, no attempt was made to keep the roads open in winter. The Ontario Cabinet passed an Order-in-Council in April, 1896 creating a new position in the public service, that of Provincial Instructor of Roadmaking. The first incumbent, christened Archibald William, but soon to be known throughout Ontario as "Good Roads" Campbell, held the post until his death in 1927.

The 1890s were the golden days of railroading. Supplies came by train. So did travelling salesmen, immigrants and politicians, and famous speakers and entertainers from faraway places. Honeymoon couples used the train. Livestock was sent out and bodies were brought home for burial by train. Trains took farmers to and from the Agricultural College at Guelph, brought sons and daughters home from university on weekends, transported hockey and baseball teams and their fans to games in other towns, carried families to fall fairs, delivered members of Orange Lodges to celebrations of "the Glorious Twelfth," and took hundreds of boys and girls to Sunday School picnics.

The familiar sound of a steam whistle drove away some of the loneliness and the sense of isolation on bitterly cold January nights.

Every weekday six or seven trains passed through little Anten Mills, located partly in Vespra and partly in Flos. The agent in Stayner cleared two mixed freight and passenger trains each way, plus weigh-freights and a number of through-freights, every twenty-four hours.

First train from Barrie to Toronto, 1865

In 1888 the Grand Trunk Railway absorbed the Northern Railway and with it the historic Ontario, Simcoe and Huron line, known to everyone as the "Oat, Straw and Hay" railroad.

By 1895 the old "wood-burners" had been replaced by coal-serviced engines, but railroading remained a hazardous occupation. Brakemen still had to scramble over ice-covered freight cars in the frigid blackness of January nights. Fingers were still lost to the old draw-bar couplers. Freight trains often ran only ten minutes apart or less, running "dark" because telegraph operators went off duty at midnight or earlier, after which engineers could only peer along the limited path of their carbon headlights and hope for the best.

Steamships, too, figured prominently in the day-to-day life of Simcoe County, both on its northern Great Lakes frontier, and on the relatively placid, interior waters of Lakes Simcoe and Couchiching. Into Georgian Bay and the upper Great Lakes sailed such majestic, and increasingly palatial vessels as the luxurious *J. B. Maxwell*, a paddle-wheeler with tall stacks, wood-panelled staterooms and grand dining salon, which ran from Midland and Penetanguishene to Parry Sound along the famed and beautiful "inside route"; the majestic *City of Midland*, which sailed out of Collingwood; and later the *City of Parry Sound, City of Collingwood, Majestic, Atlantic, City of Toronto* and many others. These were the luxury liners of the inland seas—some were capable of accommodating up to 1,000 passengers in style and comfort.

Barrie and Orillia were the home ports of the much smaller, but no less gracious, steamers of the Simcoe County stretch of the Trent waterway, from Cook's Bay to Port Severn and the entrance into Georgian Bay. The wood-burning, two-decker vessels carried freight and mail to lakeside villages and summer resorts, hauled rafts of logs in the spring, ran moonlight excursions with waltzes and foxtrots of military bands drifting across the silver-tinged waters, and carried thousands of children to Sunday School and fraternal lodge picnics at Strawberry Island and other favourite destinations.

The *Islay*, the *Otonabee*, the *Geneva*, all white with black
trim at the tops of their jaunty smokestacks, were names to
be remembered.

By the mid-nineties the coming of the circus each summer
was one of the major events of the year, especially for the
children. "Circus Day" was always a holiday for school children, and farm families poured into town from miles around.
Watching the elephants swing down Hurontario Street in
Collingwood was a sight that no boy or girl was soon likely to
forget.

As Fred Grant remembered in the Barrier *Examiner* in
December, 1925:

> Nearly every boy—and many of our elders, too—was a volunteer
> member of those reception committees, which used to arise at
> 4 A.M. by pre-arrangement, getting snoozes through the night for
> fear he might not wake up, and hustle three or four miles out into
> the country to meet the coming circus.
>
> To our particular gang, it was the general practice to tie a
> string around your ankle and then hang the cord out the window,
> and the first one up acted as a sort of call boy, and in turn visited
> each member and pulled the signal cord until everyone was pre-
> pared for the hike out to Fisherman's Point, the Sunnidale
> Road, or down by the iron bridge, depending on which way the
> circus was coming—some half-dressed, and wiggling into their
> clothes as they hurried along.

Some boys were always lucky enough to be offered free
passes to the afternoon performance in exchange for carrying water to the elephants, little realizing that the huge
pachyderms could drain a small lake in a matter of hours.

With the circus came lions, tigers, sword-swallowers, fire-
eaters, human pin-cushions, freaks, and some famous personalities. E. C. Drury later recalled seeing Buffalo Bill Cody
in a big tent erected on the Commons, at the end of Penetang
Street in Barrie, in 1896.

In spite of the long working hours there was plenty of
social and recreational activity. Every community had its
Orange Lodge, complete with banner, costumes and L.O.L.
number. Many had organizations pledged to do battle with

demon rum, such as the Good Templars and the Sons of Temperance. Singing was popular at corn-roasts, in church choirs, in barber shop quartets, and in harmonizing the old spiritual favourites around parlour organs and pianos on Sunday evenings.

One of the most popular singers of the period was Davy Thompson of Oro, the grandson of American slaves who had reached the County in the 1860s. Thompson, who accompanied his singing with a mouth organ or jews' harp, was a welcome addition to any social gathering. He survived until the 1930s when he was buried in the African Church at Edgar.

Amateur dramatic groups performed in schools, churches, civic buildings and community halls.

By 1895 Orillia was a hotbed of chess; in 1897 it hosted the Canadian chess championships. In Beeton there was an organized group of cyclists and croquet was also high in popularity. "This summer game struck Beeton with all the force of a hurricane," Kate Aitken wrote in her book, *Never a Day so Bright*. "W. J. Bell, our local hardware merchant, couldn't get sets in fast enough to supply the demand."

Innisfil opened its first indoor curling rink in 1891. Coldwater's first hockey team was organized in 1894, and played its games at the old rink on Bush Street. In Orillia baseball games were regularly played at Couchiching Park, where, according to the rules of the day, all but the catchers were required to play barehanded.

Lacrosse (the field variety) was very popular throughout the County, and some keen rivalries existed, as indicated by this report of a final game which appeared in the Barrie *Examiner* in 1894:

The boys were driven to the Queen's hotel after the game, and were cheered all along the route. . . . With horns blowing, kazoos screeching, brooms extended in the air, the *Enterprise* whistling down at the lake, bells tolling, it was some scene and no mistake.

There were some great intertown contests in hockey too. In the championship game of the 1895 season, Orillia and Barrie fought through fifty-five minutes of scoreless, hard-played but clean hockey. The star of the game to that point had been Frank Regan, the Orillia goalie, who had come 200 miles from the lumber camp where he was employed to "bar the door" for his team. As the game entered its final minutes Orillia was swarming all over its rivals, and seemed certain to score sooner or later. But then Dr. Sam Gallie, Barrie's cover point, lofted the puck the length of the ice. It sailed high and far, disappeared for a time among the rafters, and dropped into the net behind the astonished Regan for what must have been one of the longest goals in the history of hockey. The final score was Barrie 1, Orillia 0.

Apart from fishing and swimming close to home, an occasional family picnic, and perhaps an annual excursion by steamboat, Simcoe County residents were able to make little use of the summertime recreational opportunities which lay at every hand—partly because they didn't have the money, but more particularly because they didn't have the time. There were a few cottages along the shore of Georgian Bay, but for the most part the magnificent beaches were left to the gulls and sandpipers. Lake Simcoe and Lake Couchiching were exploited to a somewhat greater extent, but only a few Orillia and Barrie families could afford to build and maintain cottages that could be used, at most, for three or four months of the year.

Instead, the sunny beaches and shadowed bays, the breeze-kissed pines of the islands, and the sudden, white-capped storms were enjoyed mainly by well-to-do families from Buffalo, Detroit, Rochester, New York, Cleveland and Toronto.

Some vacationers erected cottages—lavish, gracious, two-story buildings with wide verandahs, ornate gingerbread under the eaves, fireplaces and cupolas with stained glass windows. Others spent their summers in "houseboats." These were built on large scows and towed by steam tugs to sheltered bays among the 30,000 Islands where they were anchored from early July until the Labour Day week-end.

But most escaped the city heat in luxury hotels, where guests were expected to dress for dinner, and guides smiled at the starched collars and ties worn by the wealthy men they took out fishing. Some of these resorts operated almost as exclusive clubs, with the same clients returning year after year and, if not properly introduced, a newcomer would find himself ignored and virtually excluded from the busy round of social activities. Typical of this period, the Georgian Bay House at Penetanguishene offered gracious living, clean air, cool breezes, lovely scenery, boating, picnics, unparalleled fishing and "a table replete with the best available"—all for from $1 to $2.50 per day. Other equally splendid resorts were operated on Lake Simcoe, particularly at Bell Ewart (often spelled Belle Ewart) and Big Bay Point.

This was the beginning of a long trend in Simcoe County, which would see summer tourism become more and more important to the district economy, and find thousands of residents living off the recreational potential of the region's lakes, rivers, coastline and forests. It was the start of a growing dependency which would eventually bring the balance between the use and the misuse of natural resources under increasing scrutiny. But in 1895 that concern could be left for the seemingly distant future.

Meanwhile, there were two far more pressing problems: health care and the ever-present danger of fires.

There were not enough doctors. Medical help was often hours, even days, away from many farm families although doctors were willing to make house calls in all kinds of weather. Of necessity, much faith continued to be placed in traditional home remedies. A few drops of coal oil on sugar was used to treat croup. Castor oil was a standby. Sulphur and molasses was used for "spring fever." Bread poultices were applied to draw out the poison from infected wounds. Chest colds were combatted by hot goose grease, onion poultices and mustard plasters.

Many relied upon patent medicines, such as Burdock Blood Bitters, which were advertised in Simcoe County newspapers as "guaranteed to cure and relieve biliousness, dyspepsia, indigestion, jaundice, erysipelas, salt rheum, heartburn, headache, dizziness, dropsy, fluttering heart, acidity of the stomach, dryness of the skin—and every species of disease arising from disordered liver, kidneys, stomach, bowels or blood"!

Tuberculosis was very common, and children's diseases such as chicken pox, scarlet fever, measles and mumps were both more prevalent and much more serious then, before the discovery of antibiotics. Influenza was a recurring scourge, and diphtheria took its toll every year. The latter, to cite one example, accounted for forty deaths in Oro township alone in 1889, claiming as many as three victims in a single family.

Every year there were several major fires in the County. Most buildings were made of wood, usually tinder-dry, and required only an over-heated stovepipe or an overturned coal-oil lamp to turn them into raging infernos. Volunteer fire brigades, such as the one founded in Midland in 1884, did their best and could always count on the full support of the citizens, but lack of water pressure and proper equipment rendered their efforts all but futile against the roaring flames.

On May 8, 1891 fire almost wiped out the town of Alliston, destroying nearly every home and business establishment. When it finally burned itself out, only the Victoria Street Methodist Church and two or three other buildings were left intact.

On October 19, 1892 it was Beeton's turn. Fire broke out about 1 A.M. in a building owned by A. N. Hipwell on the north side of Main Street. Fanned by a brisk westerly breeze, the flames raced eastward, consuming building after building, then leaped across the wide street and went to work on the south side. In response to a request for help sent by Reeve Wright, a detachment of nine men and a steam pump arrived by special train from Barrie about three hours later. But, in spite of all attempts to stop it, the fire raged out of control for some four hours, and when dawn came the entire business section, including some thirty-five buildings, had burned to the ground.

In 1895, both Elmvale and Tottenham suffered equally disastrous fires—the latter losing some eighty buildings, including the beautiful, new Methodist Church. The same village was to be hit again just three years later when its four-room schoolhouse was completely demolished.

Several other schools were lost in the same fashion during those years, including S. S. No. 9 Vespra, which went up in flames on the night of February 10, 1897.

The previous summer, on August 16, 1896, the mill of the Georgian Bay Lumber Company at Port Severn burned, putting some three hundred men out of work and turning the pleasant little community into an instant ghost town. With little other employment available, many families moved away, often taking their houses with them. Those homes that were left behind could be bought for as little as $25, including the land on which they stood.

Because of fire, almost every town and village in Simcoe County was faced with the awesome challenge of having to rebuild—some, such as Elmvale (1881, 1895 and 1907) having to start over again more than once. But always the authorities and citizens rallied together and got the job done.

And, if the "Gay Nineties" were often far from joyful, people sang or whistled or hummed as they went about their work. Songs like "On the Banks of the Wabash, Far Away," "Hello, My Baby," "You Tell Me Your Dreams, I'll Tell You Mine," "Are You the O'Reilly They Speak of So Well?" and "There'll Be a Hot Time in the Old Town Tonight" were on most people's lips—except, of course, on Sundays. So was a plaintive ballad entitled "I Picked a Lemon in the Garden of Love, Where I Thought Only Peaches Grew."

2 Huronia

On top of the majestic hill which rises above even the stately, cross-topped towers of the Martyrs' Shrine near Midland, there is an historic plaque bearing this legend:

Jerome Lalemont, 1640: "This place is situated . . . on the shore of a beautiful river, less than a mile in length and joining together two lakes, one which extends to the northwest and which might pass for a freshwater sea, the other lying to the south with a contour of hardly less than six miles."

Jesuit Relation of 1640

The view from that hill is magnificent: below, the narrow, twisting Wye River; to the left, the reconstructed palisades and buildings of Sainte-Marie among the Hurons, looking much as they must have looked in the mid-seventeenth century; to the right, the sun-flecked, blue waters of Georgian Bay, stretching away to the north and east.

If you climb to the top of the hill on a warm September day, when the trees have just begun to turn and a slight haze softens the horizon, it is easy to go back three centuries in time and to imagine a Jesuit priest or layman standing in that exact spot and watching the last canoes of the season as they depart on their hazardous, 800-mile journey to the citadel of Quebec, on the lower St. Lawrence. For a while the lone observer catches occasional glints of sunlight from the paddles. Gradually the canoes become mere pinpoints, finally disappearing altogether into the autumn haze. The man lingers a moment longer, then turns and starts down the long path to the mission-fort where he and his fellow Christians will endure the hostile cold of another winter, completely cut off from any contact with the outside world. . . .

The story of Huronia began in the year 1615 when Samuel de Champlain and Etienne Brûlé came down Georgian Bay from the French River and made contact with the Huron Indians at Thunder Bay, near the present Penetanguishene. In September of that year Champlain made what was to prove a fateful decision, not only for the future of Huronia but also for the history of Canada, when he elected to accompany a Huron war party in attacking the Iroquois south of Lake Ontario. The expedition was defeated but, more importantly, the Five Nations of the Iroquois thereby became the sworn enemies of New France.

Shortly afterwards Roman Catholic missionaries—first the Recollets, later the Jesuits—followed in Champlain's footsteps and organized missions along the shores of Georgian Bay and further south on Lake Couchiching and Lake Simcoe.

In 1639, under increasing pressure from the Iroquois, Father Jerome Lalemant decided to consolidate the Jesuit missionary efforts by building a fortified village which would provide a vital nucleus for the outposts of Christianity surrounding it. It was called Ste Marie, and the location chosen for it was on the Wye River, just inland from Georgian Bay.

Five years later Ste Marie was a flourishing, self-sustaining religious community within its sturdy log stockades. There were cabinetmakers, blacksmiths, bakers, a cemetery, a hospital, storehouses and occasional small garrisons of soldiers sent to aid in its defense.

According to the Jesuit *Relation* of 1648, a total of sixty-six priests and lay-helpers were present at Ste Marie. "This house," the chronicle stated, "is the resort for the whole country, where the Christians find a hospital in their sickness, a refuge in the height of alarms, and a hostel when they come to visit us. During the past year we have reckoned over 3,000 persons to whom we have given shelter."

Meanwhile other missions in Huronia were maintained at Ossossané on Georgian Bay, Cahiagué near Lake Simcoe, and

Sainte-Marie among the Hurons and Martyrs' Shrine, Midland

Teanostayé to the south. One of the most far-ranging, dedicated and courageous of the Ste Marie priests was Father Jean de Brébeuf, a man whose devotion seemingly knew no bounds.

Year by year the Iroquois raiding parties became bolder. As early as 1641, the long journey to Quebec became a matter of running the gauntlet, as the nations of the Iroquois waited in ambush along the entire route. In 1642 Father Isaac Jogues, returning from Quebec, was captured near Trois-Rivières and managed to escape after almost a year of torture by the Senecas. In that same raid René Goupil, surgeon and lay apostle on his way to Ste Marie, was taken prisoner and put to death, thereby becoming the first of the eight canonized martyrs of the Huron mission.

By 1647 the situation was so grave that no news reached Quebec from Huronia. The Jesuits had been forced to abandon Cahiagué (near the present village of Warminster) and the Iroquois had burned Teanostayé. Thus two of the three major Huron towns had been eliminated, and all of the southern and eastern flanks of the missionary frontier lay exposed to attack by the legions of the Five Nations.

It was not long in coming. On March 16, 1649 Jean de Brébeuf and Gabriel Lalemant (nephew of Jerome) were captured, taken to St. Ignace, and put to death by slow and terrible torture. Two days later Ossossané, the last remaining Huron stronghold, was abandoned to the Iroquois. On May 1, 1649 Father Ragueneau wrote in his diary: "Part of the Huron country, as a consequence of the losses sustained, now lies desolate. Fifteen villages have been abandoned, their inhabitants scattering where they could in the thickets and forests."

It was, to all intents and purposes, the end of the Hurons as a nation, and the end of the courageous, but ill-fated mission of the Jesuits in Huronia. For a time, thought was given to the establishment of a new Ste Marie on Manitoulin Island, which might provide greater safety from the Iroquois scourge, but in the end the Fathers agreed to remain with the remnants of their Huron flock and build a sanctuary on nearby Christian Island. Prior to their departure, the original Ste Marie was burned to the ground to keep it from falling into the hands of the Iroquois.

But only further despair, in the form of starvation and terrible outbreaks of diptheria and smallpox, awaited the survivors.

Finally, in 1650, Christian Island too was abandoned and some 300 Indians and missionaries—the feeble remnants of a once powerful and promising society—departed in a flotilla of undermanned canoes. Setting out on June 10, they reached Quebec without major incident, on July 28. "It was not without tears," Father Ragueneau wrote, "that we left a country which we loved, a country watered with the blood of our brothers."

For almost two hundred years, apart from the transitory passage of such explorers as Marquette and LaSalle and the lone trapper or trader, Huronia was restored by the white man to the still, brooding wilderness.

Then, as the nineteenth century progressed, English, Irish and Scottish settlers began to move into Simcoe County in increasing numbers, and about the same time the Jesuits returned to the shores of Georgian Bay.

The first Jesuit superior to be assigned to the once-and-future Huronia was Father Pierre Chazzelle, who arrived there in the summer of 1844. By then the charred remains of Ste Marie had been reclaimed by the wilderness, and grass, trees and raspberry bushes had closed in over the site. Much of the stonework had been removed by the pioneer farmers, who knew it only vaguely as "the old ruins" or "the old French fort." Little visible evidence remained to indicate that a flourishing religious community had survived a troubled decade there on the banks of the River Wye two centuries before.

But Father Chazzelle had a vision: the creation of a shrine at Ste Marie as sacred testimony to the martyrs who had been put to death there. "May God grant that soon the ruins of our Ste Marie be ours and profaned no more," he wrote in a letter to a friend. "Shall I ever be privileged to announce to Very Reverend Father General that Sainte-Marie of the Hurons exists, that I have said Mass there? And I still have hopes of finding St. Ignace, where Fathers Brébeuf and Lalemant were martyred."

Father Chazzelle's dream was not to be realized in his lifetime, nor for almost a century. But the interest of the Jesuits in Huronia's historic past never slackened. In 1907 the pastor at Waubaushene erected a small shrine on a hilltop which had been identified as the location of St. Ignace. Eighteen years later, in June, 1925, Father John Milway Filion, Provincial of the Jesuits of Upper Canada, celebrated Mass at an open-air altar amid the ruins of Ste Marie—the first conducted there in almost three centuries. To the surprise and delight of Father Filion, a crowd estimated at over 6,000 turned out for the occasion. His own enthusiasm buoyed by the overwhelming interest and support thus shown, Father Filion pressed for the construction of a permanent shrine.

The original site of Ste Marie was not available to the Jesuits at that time (it was in private hands), but title was obtained to extensive acreage across Highway 12, bordering the River Wye and extending to the shores of Georgian Bay. Father Filion lost little time. By later summer, 1925, swarms of workmen were engaged in building a magnificent church, a rectory and an inn on the side of an impressive hill which dominates the landscape for miles around.

The work was completed within a year, and on June 21, 1926 thousands of church dignitaries, government officials, priests, the devout and the curious milled around the complex of buildings which has come to be known as the Martyrs' Shrine.

June 29, 1930 is a date that will forever stand out in the history of Huronia. On that date in Rome, many thousands of miles from the mouth of the River Wye, Pope Pius XI canonized eight of the Jesuit martyrs of Ste Marie: Jean de Brébeuf, Isaac Jogues, Gabriel Lalemant, Charles Garnier,

Anthony Daniel, Noël Chabanel, René Goupil and John de la Lande.

In 1940 the Jesuit Order succeeded in regaining ownership of the site of Sainte-Marie among the Hurons, and a year later archaeological study of the ruins was begun under Mr. Kenneth Kidd and a team from the Royal Ontario Museum. After three summers of careful, painstaking work, the outlines of some of the buildings of historic Ste Marie were established.

By 1947, working from a plan based on the *Relations* and the results of Mr. Kidd's explorations, the reconstruction of some of the stonework foundations began. But much remained to be done. From 1948 through 1951 the work was continued under the direction of Dr. Wilfrid Jury, Curator of the Museum of Indian Archaeology at the University of Western Ontario. During this period it was established that the area of Ste Marie was much greater than had been previously believed, and the location of the outer palisades and most of the buildings was (more or less) determined.

Meanwhile, a question of greatest importance to the Jesuit Order—the exact location of the burial site of Brébeuf and Lalemant—had not yet been answered. But in 1954 Father Denis Hegarty, who had worked extensively with Wilfrid Jury during his exploration of the site, made a momentous discovery. Excavating within the lines of the old Indian church, he came upon the remains of a wooden box. The excitement of that moment is captured in Father Hegarty's article in the Report of the Canadian Catholic Historical Association, published the following year:

At the 36-inch level a nail was uncovered in a vertical position, pointed downwards. It was 3 1/2 inches long, square and handmade, similar to those found in the coffins of the graveyard. . . . By ten o'clock on Tuesday morning the heads of other nails had come to light at the same level, arranged vertically in lines roughly parallel with the sides of the marked area. . . . There could not be the slightest doubt that this was the remains of a wooden box. . . . Its inside measurements were 77, 31 and 28 inches respectively. These unusual dimensions would have fitted well with the historical tradition of Brébeuf's outstanding physique.

A lead plaque bearing Brébeauf's name and a date were also found. These finds were evidence enough to have the location officially accepted by the Jesuits as the final resting place of Jean de Brébeuf, although that of his fellow martyr, Gabriel Lalemant, has not yet been discovered.

In 1964 reconstruction of Sainte-Marie among the Hurons began under Dr. Jury. It required great scholarship, followed by thousands of hours of patient, painstaking work, but by the seventies the core of seventeenth century Huronia had been reborn. Surrounded by palisades of pointed logs, more than twenty buildings have been rebuilt on their original foundations by modern craftsmen employing the tools and technology of three hundred years ago. Here a modern visitor steps back through time, sees the blacksmith at work at his forge and timbers being squared by men with broadaxes. He wanders among the workshops, barns, longhouses, the church, and chapel, just as they all were. He sees a grindstone waiting to be used, a log half sawn through, bread ready to be baked, and a birchbark canoe drawn up on the river bank. It is easy to imagine that Brébeuf, Lalemant and the others have temporarily put down their work and will be returning from some expedition before nightfall.

Sainte-Marie among the Hurons and the nearby Martyrs' Shrine are certainly the most impressive monuments to the brief, dramatic and ill-fated episode of seventeenth century Huronia, but there are many other important ties with the past along the Georgian Bay coastline of Simcoe County. Wasaga Beach has its Museum of the Upper Lakes, which features the hull of the schooner *Nancy*, lost in the War of 1812, and tells the story of three hundred years of navigation on the Upper Great Lakes. The Collingwood Museum, housed in a former railway station, has a fine collection of artifacts and displays illustrating various phases of pioneer life in the district. Penetanguishene offers the carefully re-

stored naval and military base which kept guard over the
Upper Lakes and the Northwest, for almost half a century
after the War of 1812.

The town of Midland is particularly rich in the "old"
history of Simcoe County. Besides the Martyrs' Shrine and
Sainte-Marie among the Hurons, it offers both the Huronia
Museum in Little Lake Park and an authentic re-creation
of a Huron Indian community of the seventeenth century.
Nearby, too, a different kind of conservation is represented
in the Wye Marsh Wildlife Centre, where the natural life
of the district can be studied by means of floating marsh
boardwalks, underwater windows and observation towers.

Although its 1970s population is just over 11,000, Midland began as an organized community when it was incorporated as a village in 1878, at which time it could claim 836
inhabitants. Two years later it became a town.

There have been several distinct periods or phases in
the development of this pleasant Georgian Bay community.
Probably the dominant figure in its early years was James
Playfair, an almost larger-than-life personality who used
native intelligence, hard work and good luck to become
a wealthy business tycoon during the first quarter of the
twentieth century.

Playfair arrived with his family in Midland in 1883, three
years out from Scotland and just twenty-two years of age.
Immediately entering the flourishing lumber business, he
soon became the owner of one of the largest mills in the district. But, long before most others, Playfair could see that the
lumber boom had passed its zenith, since the best timber for
a hundred miles around had already fallen to axe and saw.
As early as 1896 he began to get into the shipping industry,
where he saw the future to lie. He bought his first ship, rebuilt her and christened her the *Saint Andrew*. At that time
an extensive grain trade was developing between Port Arthur
at the head of the Great Lakes and the lower St. Lawrence,
and in 1901 Playfair and his partner, D. L. White formed
the Midland Navigation Company. Two years later the new

shipping firm was operating the Clyde-built *Midland Queen*, and had the 366-foot *Midland King* under construction in the Collingwood yards. In 1907 the still larger (486-foot) *Midland Prince* was completed at Collingwood, and these three vessels formed the nucleus of a large fleet of Great Lakes freighters and canallers.

In 1910 Playfair was one of the founders of the Midland Drydock Company, which was later reorganized as the Midland Shipbuilding Company. By then he had become a true "merchant prince," the kingpin of a huge shipping conglomerate. When he sold almost all of his holdings to Canada Steamship Lines in 1926, the young Scottish immigrant of 1883 had become a millionaire several times over.

With his heavy, dark eyebrows and neatly trimmed moustache and beard, Playfair was a dashing figure. His home "Edgehill," above Midland harbour, was a huge, graceful structure complete with turrets—a veritable wooden castle.

Playfair was a familiar sight in Midland as he was driven around in his handsome Victoria carriage, complete with coachmen and pulled by a beautiful, matched team of horses —later replaced by an early Packard limousine.

An idiosyncrasy, recalled by some older residents of Midland, was the stern military discipline Playfair maintained on his yacht, the *Pathfinder*. Aboard, guests were awakened, called to meals, summoned to evening prayer and sent to bed by calls blown by the vessel's bugler.

In 1898 huge iron ore deposits were discovered at the celebrated Helen Mine, eight miles from Michipicoten harbour at the eastern end of Lake Superior. Midland was chosen as the site for two giant blast furnaces, which were built by the Canadian Iron Corporation on the northwest side of Midland Bay in 1899 and 1900. The entire operation was controlled by the Algoma conglomerate of companies. The iron ore was shipped from Helen Mine to Michipicoten harbour in cars of the Algoma Central Railway, carried to Midland by ships such as the *Monkshaven*, *Paliki*, *Theano* and *Leafield*, belonging to the Algoma Central Steamship Lines, and smelted with coke purchased from the Algoma Steel Corporation.

Between 1899 and 1918 the Helen Mine operation produced 2,800,000 tons of hematite ore, grading 53 per cent iron on the average. By then, however, the seemingly inexhaustible supply of raw iron was in fact reaching exhaustion, and the two blast furnaces at Midland were closed down and offered for sale, marking the end of a period of industrial prosperity for the Georgian Bay town.

But whenever one source of employment and economic stability dried up, Midland alway seemed to have a second string to its industrial bow. Thus in the 1920s the shipbuilding empire launched by James Playfair, D. S. Pratt and others began to come into its own. The *Glendova* was launched there in 1920, the *Canadian Logger* in 1921, the *Glenelg* in 1923, the *Gleniffer* in 1924, the *Gleneagles* and *A. M. German* in 1925, the *City of Hamilton, City of Montreal, Saskatoon, Weyburn* and *North Shore Supply* in 1926, and the *Lemoyne* in 1927.

The Great Depression of the 1930s closed down the Midland shipyards (along with hundreds of other businesses all across Canada), but by the 1950s the town's shipbuilding industry had bounced back to the extent that it could turn out the huge, 640-foot *Coverdale*, capable of carrying 18,000 tons of iron ore or 600,000 bushels of grain.

The storage and shipping of grain was important to the economy of Midland as far back as 1881, when the first wooden elevator was built there. But with the settlement of the Prairies the flow of wheat from "the breadbasket of the world" increased year by year. The original elevator had a capacity of a quarter of a million bushels, and the grain was man-handled by shovel. By 1928 Midland had four huge cement elevators with a capacity of twelve million bushels, while the elevator at nearby Port McNicoll could handle another six million bushels. The loading and unloading operations were almost entirely mechanized through the use of electric power. The Midland-Simcoe elevator, completed in the fall of 1927, was described by the Midland *Free Press* as "the last word in grainhouses . . . a monument to engineering skill."

The other major storage house was the Tiffin elevator, just north of the bridge over the River Wye and within sight of the Martyrs' Shrine. It was managed for many years by Mr. James Hickey, one of the most experienced elevator men on the Great Lakes. Built in 1909, it doubled in capacity to four and one-half million bushels in 1923. It had yardage space for 800 grain cars and could handle up to 160 on its loading sidings. Its modern equipment enabled cars to be loaded at the rate of one every three minutes, and during the season of 1927, when grain was being rushed to the eastern seaboard, it handled 300 cars within one 24-hour period.

One of the principal reasons that Midland has always managed to progress, through boom and bust, has been its characteristic civic pride and confidence in the town's future. In Simcoe County these convictions are by no means unique to Midland, but they had served the Georgian Bay community well. Down through the years its campaign to attract new industry and commerce has always been progressive in outlook, and sometimes unabashedly aggressive in tone. A brochure entitled "Industrial Facts about Midland, Ontario, Canada" which was printed and widely distributed in 1913 had this to say:

The same enterprise that made Midland what it is today, is turning its attention to making the Midland of the future. . . .

The Beautiful Town of Midland stands out with undisputed prominence as possessing all and every feature necessary to the success of the Wholesale trade, the Manufacturer, the General distributor, or the Investor. . . .

It's a trite saying that 'God made the country, but man made the town'—and Midland, Ontario is one of THE towns that man made; and he is still working on the job.

The promotion booklet then went on to list the numerous attractions of Midland, including "a splendid High School," a magnificent new Opera House, a $50,000 post office under construction, four good hotels, a fine public hospital, three banks, a dancing academy and numerous other attractions, and concluded with:

The Board of Trade and Town Council invite correspondence from anyone, in any part of the world, regarding industrial or other opportunities in Midland.

By 1928 the spokesmen for the town remained just as enthusiastic—and not noticeably more modest in extolling Midland's advantages and attractions. In a special supplement to the Midland *Free Press* on May 17 of that year, the town was described as having "the greatest landlocked harbour on the Great Lakes" and being "one of the greatest grain ports on the continent." In addition, Midland was held to be "the centre of the greatest vacation land in North America . . . with steamers leaving daily for the famous 30,000 Islands of Georgian Bay, the greatest fresh-water trip in the world."

King Street, Midland, 1927

In a companion piece in the same edition, the town's awareness of the importance of a good education was shown by the description, with comparable fervour, complete with photographs, of four "modern places of learning," the Midland High School, and the Regent Street, Manley Street and Central Public Schools. The School Board for the year 1928 was headed by R. S. McLaughlin, and included P. E. Angle, M. J. Bray, J. W. Bald, W. G. Cave, Dr. J. B. M. McClinton, George J. Moore, H. H. McGill, Thomas McCullough and Thomas Nottingham.

A mere two years later Midland was plunged into the lean years of "the Dirty Thirties," a decade which it survived only with considerable hardship and suffering. Then, during World War II, its shipyards again hummed with activity as they turned out corvettes and minesweepers for the Royal Canadian Navy (a subject which is dealt with at greater length in a later chapter).

The development of the St. Lawrence Seaway during the fifties, which allowed the ships of all nations to probe into the very heart of Canada, caused a decline in the importance of intermediate Great Lakes' ports like Midland. Yet, typically, the town rallied once more, and by the mid-seventies its waterfront was again a busy, sprawling perimeter of docks, railway lines, strings of freight cars, mountain-like piles of coal and gravel, shipbuilding plants, other industrial complexes, boat tours, luxury yachts, and acres of anchored dinghies and sloops—and old men and small boys fishing from the ends of piers.

A Chamber of Commerce publication in 1976 indicated that the long years of "selling Midland" to the outside world was still paying off. This two-page "Industrial List" identified 26 companies which were doing business in Midland, and which were employing over 3,800 out of a total population of just over 11,000, or more than one per average family. The plants included ranged from giants like RCA Limited (998 employees) and Decor Metal Products (844) down to small establishments such as Midland Simcoe Elevator Ltd.,

Nebs Business Forms and Webster-Smallwood, each of which provided employment for from 10 to 12 people.

In spite of this industrial expansion, however, it still remains true, as noted by the Midland *Free Press* in 1928, that, in spirit and in historical memory, "Midland is primarily a lakeport and shipbuilding town," with its roots planted firmly in the rocky, often inhospitable, south shore of Georgian Bay.

Three-quarters of the way through the twentieth century, it has also become a very important tourist centre, with legions of Canadian and American families being drawn there by such attractions as Sainte-Marie among the Hurons, the Martyrs' Shrine, and other monuments to the past located nearby.

During the long, cold months of winter, Midland's community life centres around its hockey rink, bowling alley, main street restaurants and taverns, laundromats, Legion Hall, service club activities—and whatever television may have to offer. But, from May to October each year, it is a gateway to a long-passed era that is important to Simcoe County and the Canadian heritage.

3 The Great Days of Lumbering

When the first settlers moved into Simcoe County in the early part of the nineteenth century, they encountered an almost unbroken forest, there for countless centuries before the beginning of recorded time. The huge trees stood shoulder to shoulder, their canopy blocking out the sky so that it was possible to ride for hours in cathedral-like silence on a thick carpet of pine needles. Little undergrowth marred the park-like neatness, for the forest floor was almost constantly shadowed beneath the swaying, sighing boughs, and the sun seldom penetrated there.

On the ridges, where the soil was more fertile, the trees were chiefly hardwoods: great oaks, hard maples, beech, cherry, birch, basswood and ironwood. Over the rolling sand hills, towering, virgin pines—mainly white, with some red—spread in giant stands over thousands upon thousands of acres. In the lowlands, as on the perimeters of the sprawling Minesing swamp, the dominant varieties were cedar, alder, black ash, soft maple, spruce, poplar and white birch.

In the beginning the forest was regarded as an enemy— more so even than the cold and the isolation. To the pioneers, faced with the relentless threat of hunger, the clearing of the land was the key to survival. Each tree felled, stripped, burned and destroyed meant so many additional square yards in which to plant the potatoes, corn, wheat, oats, barley and turnips that were the staples of their frontier existence.

But the land-clearing of the settlers was a preliminary skirmish compared to the campaign of destruction that was waged by profit-hungry lumbering companies.

The exploitation began in the early 1800s when special

contractors were appointed "to search the woods of Upper and Lower Canada and there to fell and cut so many good and sound trees as may answer the number and dimensions stated in the Contract." The purpose at that time was to supply the King's Royal Navy with squared timbers for construction and masts to carry sail.

The size of the trees sacrificed for these purposes is difficult to imagine a century and a half later. To qualify as a potential mast for the Royal Navy, a red or white pine had to be perfectly straight and with the first branches (and therefore the first knots) appearing not less than sixty feet above ground. The two largest sticks ever taken out of Simcoe County were a 60-foot long timber, squared to a uniform 36 inches, in Oro township, and a 118-foot mast felled in Innisfil, which required fourteen teams of horses to draw it out of the bush to the railhead.

The demands for masts dwindled after about 1820, first because a surplus had been cut and stockpiled, and later because steam began to replace sail in the Royal Navy. The trade in square timbers dried up about the same time, but

Dragging logs over the ice, Flos Township, c. 1910

experienced a boom revival after mid-century. From 1868 to 1877 a total of 119,250,000 cubic feet were removed from Ontario, a healthy share of it from Simcoe County. The "squaring" process, like so many other practices of the time, represented an awesome waste of resources, many times more good wood being left to rot than was floated in rafts down the lakes and rivers to Toronto and Montreal.

But the final decimation of the forests of Simcoe County began with the increasing demand for sawn lumber. As the cities of Canada and the United States grew, there was a building boom which lasted for several decades.

Two developments were needed to turn the felling of trees into an exploitive and highly profitable commercial venture: fast and efficient transportation, and sawmills. The first need was met by the coming of the railroads in the middle-third of the nineteenth century. The cost of laying track was often subsidized by the granting of extensive timber rights. Hence the railway barons and the lumber kings were often one and the same, or at least connected by marriage. Many a leading Simcoe County family owed its wealth and its social prominence to such alliances.

One of the first mills had been established at Holland Landing as early as 1811, and for twenty years it was the source of sawn lumber for many miles around, as well as supplying the 3-inch cedar planks that were used for road-building. In 1818, when the fort was built at Penetanguishene, a pit saw was used to make the lumber for the officers' quarters. By 1830 there were some 130 sawmills operating in Simcoe County, with every township having at least one. But these were hand-powered or water-driven operations with very limited production capacity. Two men operating a pit saw would do well to turn out four boards, 16 feet long by 16 inches wide, between dawn and dusk, and few stream-side mills could saw more than 500 boardfeet per day.

By 1850, however, steam-powered sawmills were in operation, often with the boilers set up in rows to provide maximum production. The change from the small operations of

earlier days was dramatic. A large mill at Belle Ewart produced 15 million boardfeet of sawn lumber in 1852, and in
1858 a Bradford mill was turning out an average of 150,000
boardfeet per day.

Records show that there were 25 large mills in operation
in Medonte and Matchedash townships in the early sixties,
19 in Oro, and 22 in Tiny. In 1861 total production in Simcoe County was around 200 million boardfeet, mostly white
pine, which represented one third of the total cut in all of
Ontario that year.

Here and there a lone voice expressed concern over the
wholesale slaughter of the forests, but most felt—as with the
carrier pigeon—that no man would ever see an end to the
trees.

To satisfy the insatiable hunger of the mills thousands
of men went into the bush each year to work in the lumber
camps. It was not an easy life. The typical logging camp consisted of one or more cabins, usually called "camboose shanties," made of logs trimmed on the spot. Each shanty might
be thirty or forty feet long, and there would be two tiers of
rough-cut lumber bunks along three sides. Heating and cooking facilities were provided by a huge fire-pit in the centre of
the building, where a roaring log fire blazed continuously
from late September to break-up in April. Light and ventilation came through a 6-foot square hole in the roof over the
fire-pit.

The food was made mainly from barrelled staples such as
beans, salt pork, flour and blackstrap molasses and was occasionally supplemented by potatoes, turnips and other root
crops raised on lumber company depot farms. There was
usually plenty of fresh-baked bread, and a good lumber camp
cook would make sure that there were pies made of raisins or
dried apples on the table each night. The diet was filling
enough, but deadly monotonous and lacking in the fresh ingredients necessary to ward off scurvy and similar diseases.

Working hours were from dawn to dusk, with the men
walking through the bush to the edge of the cutting in dark-

ness. One elderly Simcoe County resident remembers his father telling him that "I never saw the shanty by daylight except on Sundays. We had to be out to work before sun-up, and never came back before sun-down."

Since fires were customarily forbidden in the bush, the mid-day meal, gulped at sub-zero temperatures and eaten standing up, normally consisted of a loaf of bread in which a hole had been scooped and filled with molasses, plus a piece of half-frozen salt pork.

Certainly it was no way to get rich. "Each man had to bring his own knife and fork," a veteran of the lumber camps reported many years later, "and he had to buy his own tobacco and tea, if he wanted any . . . and top wages came to about $20 a month."

The average axeman would be lucky to come out with $40 to $50 dollars after six months' hard work, and luckier still to evade the tavern keepers and jewelry drummers along the spring break-up roads and arrive home with his hard-earned poke intact.

The railroads prospered from the great lumbering era. The shipping of sawn timber accounted for almost ninety-five per cent of the revenue of the Northern Railway, which extended its line to Orillia in the late 1860s. The Hamilton and Northwestern was built, passing through Cookstown and Thornton, with its terminus at Barrie, and with a branch line from Beeton, through Alliston, Lisle, Glencairn and Creemore to Collingwood. The North Simcoe Railway was built from Colwell Junction (between Barrie and Angus), through Minesing, Hendrie, Phelpston, Elmvale, and Wyvale to Penetanguishene in 1879. In the mid-1880s the Flos Tramway Company was organized to build a short line from Elmvale to Hillsdale to take off the pine from the Orr Lake district. And so on. Many of these lines wound up as abandoned, overgrown, barely detectable rights-of-way, while others were eventually incorporated into the Canadian National Railway system.

Many a village, too, prospered from the lumbering boom

James Playfair's Mill, Midland, 1901

and had visions of becoming a major city. Angus, for example, prospered for a decade or more as the shipping point for the millions of boardfeet of lumber taken from the adjacent plains of what was to become Camp Borden. But all too soon the great stands of pine were stripped away, leaving only acres of stumps, and the dreams of Angus died.

By the 1890s the timber trade seemed to be at its peak in Simcoe County, and few saw any reason to think that it would ever decline. Giant, sprawling enterprises like the Christie Mill in Port Severn (which burned to the ground in 1896), and the Georgian Bay Lumber Company Mill at Waubaushene were working to capacity. Lumber tycoons in all of the mill-towns of the County lived in their mansions, entertained lavishly, were elders of their churches and patrons of the arts, and sent their sons and daughters to private schools in Toronto to be educated.

But for those who cared to see it, there was abundant evidence that the heyday was all but over, the trees nearly all gone. Each winter the lumber camps had to move further and further north along Georgian Bay to find virgin timber. In the 1912 navigation season two powerful tugs, the *Charlton* and *Reginald*, were used to tow huge rafts of logs to Victoria Harbour from the far north shore of Georgian Bay, west of Little Current. Each raft was as large as some farms, contained as many as 170,000 logs, and would eventually produce up to four million boardfeet of lumber.

The towing of huge booms of logs across the eighty miles of Georgian Bay required great patience and was not without its risks, especially in the capricious days of early spring and the somber, slate-grey days of late fall. On June 13, 1918, for example, the Penetanguishene *Herald* reported, "The McGibbon Lumber Company had the misfortune to lose a fine raft of logs a few days ago. The tug . . . had the raft in tow when she got caught in a big blow. The tug hung onto the raft until she found she was being drawn into a danger zone, and then let it go." And, on September 12 of that same year: "The C. Beck Co. met with a heavy loss last Tuesday when their tug *Wahnapitae* was forced to let go of a boom of logs out near the Western Islands. With an east wind blowing, the logs will be scattered all over Georgian Bay.''

Around this period all Georgian Bay lumber companies owned tugs or other steam-driven ships. In addition to the *Wahnapitae*, the C. Beck Company had the *Chamberlain*. Also at Penetanguishene were the Firstbrook Box Company's tug, *Penetang*, the Gropp Brothers' *Topsy*, and the Breithaupt Leather Company's tug *Geraldine*, which was used to tow barges of hemlock tanbark from the Moon River area.

Collingwood, Midland, Victoria Harbour and Severn Falls also had their fleets of log-towing vessels.

The lumbering business in Simcoe County lingered on into the 1920s, but long before that there were indications that the presumably inexhaustible supply of prime timber was, in fact, close to exhaustion. As a harbinger of things to come, the giant mill at Waubaushene closed down as early as 1900 because it could no longer be sure of a supply of first-grade pine. The C. Beck Company hung on until the late 1920s before disposing of its holdings, including the *Wahnapitae*. Even after that a few managed to grub out a living from the lumber trade, including the "log-pickers" who scoured the shores of Georgian Bay and the 30,000 Islands, salvaging logs which had been washed over the booms of the great tows or otherwise gone adrift.

But the great days of lumbering in Simcoe County were long since over. The camboose shanties were left to rot in what had once been the deep bush. The buzz of saws and the bite of axes were heard no more. Many a railway spur line was closed down, abandoned to the weeds and berry bushes.

Most of the good pine was gone, along with the hard maple, oak, beech, ash and basswood. Simcoe County was denuded and the sand hills which covered much of it became dangerously vulnerable to erosion through rain and melting snows and wind. Only the future could tell whether dedicated reinvestment in the land could overcome the effects of ruthless exploitation and the rape of natural resources.

Among the many Simcoe County towns and villages involved in the great era of lumbering was the Georgian Bay community of Penetanguishene.

At the beginning of the twentieth century Penetanguishene (or "Penetang" as it is more often called) had a population of just over 2300. Its name, of Indian origin, is said to mean "Place of the White Rolling Sands." Whatever the accuracy of that translation, it is a matter of historical record that Penetanguishene Peninsula, which houses the town, was purchased from the Ojibways by Lieutenant-Governor John Graves Simcoe in 1798 for the princely sum of one hundred pounds.

Penetanguishene came into existence as a naval establishment in 1815, not long after the War of 1812 and at a time when the British Admiralty felt it necessary to maintain a show of strength on the Upper Lakes. The choice of this site was a logical one, the base being located at the southern end of a seven-mile land-locked bay. It was one of the best anchorages between Kingston and the Lakehead. Two schooners were to be maintained there, without masts or rigging, but otherwise in a state of readiness should hostilities again threaten between the United States and British North America.

By the early 1820s the dockyard and most of the whitewashed log buildings had been completed. They included barracks, officers' quarters, a hospital and the three-storied red storehouse which dominated the waterfront.

In 1828 a military attachment was assigned there to join the naval ranks, and six years later the British Admiralty decided to abandon the base. By then the two schooners, no longer seaworthy, had been cut adrift and allowed to sink in the harbour. From then on it was a purely military establishment, and over the next two decades units of many famous British Regiments served there, including the Royal Canadian Rifle Regiment, a British force especially trained to staff the frontier forts of Upper Canada.

Plans were drawn up for a great military complex on the

hill above the place where the Ontario Mental Health Centre now stands, but they were never implemented. As the years passed and no serious threat of invasion from below the border materialized, the regular units were called home and replaced by half-pay soldiers who, to supplement their pensions, were allotted land nearby. Since they were allowed to bring their families with them, they were essentially farmer-settlers who manned the military establishment on a part-time basis.

Finally, in 1856, "the fort that never fired a shot" was closed down permanently. Just over a hundred years later, in 1964, the Ontario Government announced its intention to reconstruct the British Naval and Military Establishments at Penetanguishene as an historical site and tourist attraction. Archaeological investigations had been carried out during the 1950s and early 1960s under the direction of Dr. Wilfrid Jury. Reconstruction began in 1968, and in 1971 the rebuilt fort was turned over to the Huronia Historical Parks authority for administration.

The town of Penetanguishene itself grew up around the military establishment, and its original population was composed of two distinct groups: the British half-pay officers and men, and the French-speaking Canadians who were engaged in the fur trade in winter and fished and farmed in summer.

In the 1970s the town and surrounding countryside still reflect that twin heritage. One of the most interesting buildings in Penetanguishene is the historic church with the intriguing name of St. James on-the-Lines, which was built between 1836 and 1842 to provide a place of worship for the Anglican soldiers posted to the military establishment and for their families. The broad centre aisle was so constructed as to allow the troops to march in in columns of four, and it is believed that the pews were designed and carved by individual members of the garrison—which would account for the wide variety of styles represented.

The men who were most responsible for the building of St. James on-the-Lines now lie buried in the well-kept cemetery adjacent to it: James Keating, Fort Adjutant; John Moberly, a retired Naval Captain; and Rev. George Hallen, who was its first pastor and served its congregation for thirty-six years. Also at rest there is the body of a young child who died of diphtheria. Because of the danger of contagion, pall-bearers were not forthcoming until some Roman Catholics volunteered. The epitaph on the gravestone reads:

Dear Brother, o'er your body here I weep;
One week after with you I sleep;
Four kind papists here me laid;
The Rev. George Hallen the service read.

This unusual example could well serve to illustrate the spirit of co-operation and harmony that has existed from the early days between the French- and English-speaking residents of the Penetanguishene community.

In the 1970s there is a distinctly French-Canadian feel to the town. It is there in the *habitant* look of many of the surrounding farms which might have been moved intact from the lower St. Lawrence, and in the degree to which French is spoken on the main street and in the stores and restaurants. It is there in the statue of Father Joseph LeCaron, a Récollet priest who arrived in the wake of Champlain's canoes, and it is of little matter that the figure was cast in the likeness of St. Francis of Assisi, the founder of the Franciscan Order, and used for reasons of economy.

It is there too in St. Ann's, the splendid Roman Catholic church which was begun in 1886 and officially opened in 1902. Its founder, Father Laboureau, received support and contributions, not only from France and Rome, but also from such Canadians as Sir John A. MacDonald, Sir Wilfrid Laurier, Sir Charles Tupper and Edward Blake. In the late 1930s it was substantially repaired and remodelled under the direction of Father Jean Marie Castex.

The essential character of Penetanguishene is proclaimed by the two statues of angels which stand at the outskirts beside the two main highways leading into the town. They were unveiled as part of an "Old Home Week" celebration in the summer of 1921, and they owe their existence to the efforts of Father Athol Murray and a young priest named Gerald Lahey.

Father Murray felt that something should be done to commemorate the 300-year-old history of Huronia, and also to celebrate the long-standing good relations between the French and English elements of the community. Gerald Lahey, the only son of the town's leading merchant at that time, had taken a vow of poverty on entering the Jesuit Order at the age of twenty a year or two previously. He soon became enthused over Father Murray's plan and his enthusiasm was passed on to his father, D. A. Lahey, who offered to pay for whatever monument might seem most appropriate.

The result was the twin angels, one marked "Ontario" and the other "Quebec," to symbolize and pay tribute to the spirit of harmony between the town's two founding groups. Fifty years later, in 1971, Father Lahey returned to Penetanguishene to rededicate the bronze statutes which now stand in small, well maintained parks at the southern limits of the town.

Penetanguishene was primarily a lake port, with its eyes turned towards Georgian Bay, and its economic well-being largely tied to maritime activities such as ship-building, shipping and fishing. But in the winter months, when ice locked in the bays and rivers, it was largely dependent upon the railway for survival—a dependency which was dramatically underlined in January, 1904 when the Grand Trunk tracks were snowbound and impassable for twenty-one straight days. When the first train finally broke through the snowdrifts and pulled into the station to the accompaniment of resounding cheers, food was in critically short supply and the threat of starvation was becoming a real possibility.

During the 1890s and through the first years of the new century Penetanguishene was at the centre of the lumbering boom, and the town prospered and was a hive of activity. By 1907 it had six sawmills, two box factories, a couple of planing mills, sash and door factories, a pail and tub factory, and other related industries. The docks were busy with incoming rafts of logs, and many townspeople went into the bush in winter to work in the lumber camps.

There were four major lumber mills in operation at that time: the Firstbrook Company, Beck's, McGibbon's and Gropp Bros.

The Firstbrook Box Company was one of the first industries in the Georgian Bay region, opening its doors for business in 1867, the year of Canadian Confederation. The Company had its head office in Toronto. By the end of the century its Penetanguishene operation sprawled over some seventy waterfront acres and was served by a spur line of the Grand Trunk Railway. The plant was capable of turning out some 100,000 feet of custom-sawn lumber per day, and its box-making section used some 700,000 feet of timber every month. Firstbrook had a payroll which fluctuated between 250 and 300, making it a major employer in Penetanguishene.

The Gropp Brothers' Penetanguishene Lumber and Shingle Mills came into being in 1900 and occupied some ten acres between the waterfront and the railway. They had a capacity of about 25,000 feet of lumber a day, and they supplied both rough and dressed lumber, shingles, laths and many other wood products required by the building trades in Toronto and other major cities.

The McGibbon Lumber Company was established back in 1855 by Finlay McGibbon, and by the turn of the century it was being operated by his son, Charles, while the family's other mills at Sarnia, Ontario were directed by Finlay, Jr. and John. The Penetanguishene plant employed about sixty millhands.

Charles McGibbon, a young man of great drive and intelligence, was also very active in politics. He was elected Warden of Simcoe County in 1889, when he was just twenty-two years of age, and later served three terms as Mayor of Penetanguishene.

The largest of the Penetanguishene mill operations, the C. Beck Company, went into production in 1878, and was

incorporated under the laws of the Province of Ontario two
years later, with a capital of a quarter of a million dollars.
The company had two of the best-equipped sawmills in Ontario, with a combined capacity of some 175,000 feet per day,
and a lath mill which produced a record 128,000 pieces in
a single, ten-hour day in 1910. Its saw and planing mills,
warehouses, drying sheds, yards and offices stretched for
almost a mile along the town's waterfront and provided
employment for almost 250 men.

All of these firms owned or leased the timber rights on
huge tracts of forest along the eastern and northern shores of
Georgian Bay, the North Channel, and west to Michipicoten
and beyond on Lake Superior. Each year the cutting-ground
was more remote as stand after stand of accessible timber
was stripped clean. Countless thousands of logs were floated
down Georgian Bay in great rafts, fenced in by booms, behind tugs and other towing vessels.

Of all the tugs that hauled logs into Penetanguishene,
the most famous by far was the powerful and hard-working
Wahnapitae. The popularity of the big two-master was enhanced by the fact that she was a home-town product in all
respects, an object of much local pride. The *Wahnapitae* was
built in the winter of 1904-05 by the C. Beck Company at
their waterfront yards, the oak timbers for her keel and ribs
having been sawn at the Gropp Brothers new mill in Penetanguishene. When launched she was 90 feet in length, had a
breadth of 18 feet, and a 10-foot draft.

And she sailed under an all-Penetanguishene crew. Captain Paul Dusome was her master and Bill Tuton his mate,
and she carried a complement of two engineers, two firemen,
two wheelsmen and a cook. The latter had the reputation of
"serving the best grub" to be found on any vessel engaged
in the towing business in Georgian Bay.

For almost a quarter of a century the *Wahnapitae* was engaged in coaxing huge rafts of logs—"sticks" the lumbermen
called them—across the Bay from such points as the French
River, Little Current and Thesalon. Often the booms en-

closed as many as 180,000 logs, enough to keep the Beck
Company mills in operation for a month or more. Many of
the rafts towed into Penetanguishene Bay were so massive
that they had to be split in order to get them around the narrow, sharp turn at Reformatory Point.

Pulling those huge, cumbersome, stubborn sticks was work
that required infinite patience, great stamina, a thorough
knowledge of every shoal and other danger point on the big
Bay, and an instinctive wariness for sudden shifts in the
weather—from sunshine to fog, from off-shore to on-shore
winds, from calm to lashing gale. At the stern of the *Wahnapitae*, as on every other towing vessel, was a steam deck-
winch, on the drum of which was wound the steel towing
cable. Rafts were always towed at a distance of at least two
hundred yards to keep them out of the tug's backwash. The
other end of the cable was attached to a heavy chain on a
specially selected "boom log." The connecting device
almost never failed, even under the strain of the most violent
November squall. If the situation became really dangerous,
the tug's Captain would give orders to let the cable run off
the winch and would head for shelter under full steam. When
the gale had blown itself out, the *Wahnapitae* would return to
the scene, locate the raft, pick up the towing cable and continue on its way.

In the winter of 1921-22 the *Wahnapitae* was put into
dry dock and substantially rebuilt. Twenty feet were added
to her length, and such modern devices as a steam-powered
steering gear and a wireless were added. But by then the
great days of lumbering were gone. In 1929 the C. Beck Company, faced with the exhaustion of the timber limits, sold the
Wahnapitae to the Keenan Towing Company of Owen Sound.
From 1929 until 1937 she was used to pull the barge *Don
Proctor*, loaded with logs and pulpwood, to that town. Then
she was sold again, this time to the J. J. McFadden Lumber
Co. of Blind River. In 1940 she went down the Great Lakes
and the St. Lawrence to work for Sorel Harbour Tugs, towing barges of pulpwood between Lévis and Trois-Rivières,

53

Quebec. There she was rechristened the *Dick T.*, but a year later she collided with another vessel at the entrance to De la Chaudiere Basin and was written off as a total loss. After that she lay beached and abandoned at Windsor Cove, just above Lévis, on the south shore of the St. Lawrence—a sad ending, far from home, for the Georgian Bay veteran.

The lumber barons of Penetanguishene, men like Charles Beck and Charles McGibbon, attained great wealth, social prominence and influence during the late nineteenth and early twentieth centuries. Another hard-driving businessman, who attained his success in other fields, was J. T. Payette, who took over the foundry business which had been launched by his uncle Peter in 1880 and who used it as a base upon which to build an industrial and financial empire.

J. T.'s motto was "Business and more business." The Payette foundry, built on the waterfront near the present site of the Grew Boats Ltd. warehouse, began with the production of sawmill machinery. Seizing the industrial opportunities offered by World War I, Payette expanded into marine repair, bought out the Adams Engine Works, and soon earned a reputation for being able to deliver huge custom-made pieces of machinery made from cast iron, copper and other metals (for example, a 70,000 pound double-ended punch for the Dominion Ship Building Company of Toronto).

A man of seemingly unflagging physical and mental endurance, J. T. inaugurated round-the-clock, seven-days-a-week shift work to keep up with the orders that kept pouring in—a practice virtually unheard of at that time. He also branched out into other fields, including land speculation. Foreseeing the future boom in summer homes, he was the primary force behind the development of the cottage subdivision at Crescentwood Beach.

But his greatest personal interest lay in harness racing. He owned a stable of high quality trotters and pacers, including Cream of Tartar and the famed Lucy L., which once broke the two-minute mile—a standard that is still considered elusive almost three-quarters of a century later. Payette was also the prime moving force behind the building of a half-mile track at Penetang which was generally conceded to be the best in Canada. Each Dominion Day for many years J. T. staged his own personal racing meet there, and it was regarded as one of the main annual social and sporting events in Simcoe County.

In later years his empire was struck by a series of disastrous fires; but for a quarter of a century or more the Payette name had been synonymous with success, riches, and industrial and civic power.

The deterioration and final demise of the lumbering business dealt a severe blow to Penetanguishene, as it did to other Georgian Bay ports like Midland, Victoria Harbour and Collingwood. But, because it was a gradual process, the town had time to adjust to changing conditions and to find new paths to economic and civic progress. One indicator of this was that Penetang's population grew steadily, from 2,391 in 1901, to 3,370 in 1910, 3,664 in 1920, and 4,811 in 1938.

Some of its citizens were among the first to understand the potential that was waiting to be realized by catering to summer vacationers eager to escape the heat of the big Canadian and American cities. Early in the twentieth century the steamer *Georgina*, operated by C. Beck & Company was offering three-day-a-week service from Penetanguishene to Parry Sound, calling at summer resorts along the way, and promising that campers and cottagers would be "conveyed to their destinations, together with their supplies and outfits, and left on any island they may desire . . . to be brought in again on any of the steamer's regular trips."

But, while some vacationers continued on via cruise ships such as the *Georgina* and *Waubic*, many others chose to spend their summer vacations in the immediate vicinity of Penetanguishene. These included some heads of state, wealthy industrialists from Canada and the United States, famous artists and musicians, and even the Wright brothers who inaugurated the age of aviation.

For this group one of the principal attractions was the

Penetanguishene Hotel. Built in 1889, the Penetanguishene was soon offering the finest in luxury accommodation and gracious living—acres of well cared-for, shaded lawns, an orchestra which played for lunch and dinner, excellent tennis courts and lawn-bowling lanes, its own supply of electricity, steam heat in every room and a dedication to attracting "the annual patronage of the best class of people." Unfortunately, sharing the fate which was to befall other famous Georgian Bay hotels like the Palmer house and the Georgian Bay House, the Penetanguishene burned to the ground during the years of the Great War, 1914-18.

About the same time the Penetanguishene Volunteer Fire Department was earning the reputation of being among the fastest and best trained in Simcoe County. In those years there was an annual competition between the fire-fighting units of the district towns. This had two main events. The hose race involved stringing out and coupling a stipulated number of lengths, then knocking down a target with a jet of water. The ladder-climbing contest was a race between four-man teams to see which one could get a ladder into position and have its best ladder-man reach the top rung in the shortest possible time.

Penetanguishene's volunteer department was always a strong contender in these affairs and at least once, in 1916 or 1917, captured the overall championship. Among the members were Arthur (Jumbo), Bert and George Dubeau, George Dion, Charlie Kaus, Jake Parker, Jack McLaughlin, Kurt Spearn, George Robillard, Jack O'Hearn, Alex Gendron, Antoine Charlebois and two Marchildons, Oliver and Joe. The latter surname would become famous a few decades later in an entirely different type of competition when another Marchildon earned fame as an outstanding major league baseball pitcher.

For most of this century an important factor in Penetang's history and development has been the presence there of an institution for the confinement and the treatment of the mentally ill. From the late 1850s until 1904 the barracks of the old naval and military base had been used as a reformatory for boys. It was then converted into an "Asylum for the Insane." At that time, and for several decades to come, those committed were treated as inmates, rather than as patients, and the main function of the institution was to remove them from society and to place them behind bars. "It used to be that patients were committed for vague reasons," Vern Farrow, Public Relations Officer at the Penetang Mental Health Centre, said in April, 1975. "After that they were isolated and usually soon forgotten. There was little training, and almost no attempt towards repatriation."

Over the years old buildings were renovated or replaced, and new ones added. The Oak Ridge division was built in two stages, half in 1933 and the balance in 1958. In 1967 the two apartment retraining buildings, now called Bayfield and Brébeuf, were opened. Five years later the impressive and modern seven-storey treatment building went into operation.

Of still greater significance are the revolutionary changes that have taken place in mental health care, notably after the appointment of Dr. Boyd as Supervisor in 1958. Under his administration the emphasis shifted dramatically from simple confinement to retraining, rehabilitation, far greater social involvement for patients, and a generally much more liberal and progressive attitude towards the problems of mental health. An indication of the evolution that has taken place since 1904 is that the average stay of patients has dropped from over four years in the beginning to about thirty days in the 1970s. The staff-patient ratio has also changed from an original one to six to a present-day level of almost one to one (approximately 560 staff to about 600 patients). As a result of such changes, the mental health operation at Penetanguishene is regarded by most authorities in the field as one of the best in Canada.

The great days of lumbering are long since over, but Penetanguishene remains a progressive and pleasant town, rich in memories and standing at one of the crossroads of English- and French-Canadian history.

4 Into the Modern Era

Probably less than half of those born upon this earth live to see the turning of a century. For those who do, the experience must be a unique occasion for reflection upon the past and for contemplation of the future. It is enough to go from one decade to the next, or even from one year to its successor, but a one-in-a-hundred New Year is very special. For a short while after January 1, 1900 Simcoe County residents must have found it difficult to change the ingrained habit of dating their letters, cheques and legal documents eighteen hundred and something.

But it *was* a new century and, although the continuity of history is not usually influenced by calendar dates, it does seem that a new age of ever-accelerating technological advance began with the dawn of the 1900s—a revolutionary era which would encompass the wireless, the coming of "moving pictures" and then the "talkies," the medical conquest of diabetes, tuberculosis, diphtheria and poliomyelitis, the splitting of the atom, radar, television and the driving of a golf ball across the craters of the moon.

The development that was to have the most fundamental and far-reaching effect on the future of Simcoe County was the advent of the motorcar, automobile or "horseless carriage." Its appearance foreshadowed not only the gradual disappearance of "old Dobbin," but the eventual demise of the graceful, white steamboats which serviced resorts and cottagers on Lake Simcoe and the 30,000 Islands of Georgian Bay. The day would come when travel by train was a thing of the past except for commuters to and from Toronto. In time the family car would help to break down the isolation of rural living—and to undermine the self-sufficiency of towns and villages.

Most important of all perhaps, the coming of the automobile brought the lakes, beaches and ski slopes of Simcoe County within easy driving distance of Toronto—a development which would make catering to big city recreational needs a major industry, and culminate in bumper-to-bumper traffic on Highway 400 at the beginning and the end of most weekends.

All of that, of course, lay in the future as the new century dawned. No one can be quite sure when the first "horseless carriage" appeared in Simcoe County. A claim can be made for the 1903 Oldsmobile which was delivered to Penetang on a tug-drawn lumber barge and which is now on display in the Penetanguishene museum. But, according to an item in the Barrie *Examiner*, it occurred in 1900. "The horseless carriage attracted much attention in Barrie when driven down the street by a Mr. Eaton, said to be the son of Timothy Eaton of Toronto Department Store fame." Billy Baycroft, the Beeton undertaker, was one of the first owners in that part of the County.

In any event the first makes, Whippets, Fords, Chevrolets, Oldsmobiles and Buicks, soon began to appear in ever-increasing numbers. In the early days they were subjects of great curiosity and more than a little excitement. Controls in the first models were quite primitive (some were steered by levers), and going for a ride in one was roughly equivalent to what taking a first flight would be like three or four decades later. Mufflers had not yet been invented, and the noise made by an original Model "T" as it roared and backfired along at the reckless speed of 10 m.p.h., could be heard all over the countryside. Little wonder that countless horses tried to climb fences, and even trees, to get away from the infernal racket.

But the car was here to stay. Gas pumps began to replace hitching posts and watering troughs. Garages multiplied. One of the early ones was set up by a Mr. Hunsinger of Fisher-

The Tudhope, "The Car Ahead," 1913

ville, who bought property on Beeton's Main Street and turned a former general store into a repair garage and Ford sales agency. By the advent of World War I he was offering the popular Model "T" for about $500, and selling more than fifty cars a year.

With the coming of the age of the automobile it became necessary to make extensive improvements in the roads of the County. The original surveys called for all road allowances to be one chain or 66 feet in width. In practice most roads were much narrower—at best barely wide enough for two horse-drawn vehicles to pass, and often providing only for single-lane traffic. Roads were built and maintained according to the Statute of Labour, by which County farmers were required to provide so many days' labour per year—the number varying according to the assessment of their holdings. For each two or three miles of road there was a "Pathmaster," appointed by the Township Council, whose duty it was to organize his neighbours in constructing bridges, uprooting stumps, hauling sand and gravel, grading, filling, and generally keeping up the access routes essential to social survival as well as to the procurement of supplies and the continuance of trade and commerce. In the absence of adequate equipment, no attempt was made to keep the roads open in winter: each farmer was left to his own resources in "bucking the drifts," if he wanted to get out to the nearest general store or obtain medical help.

The Statute of Labour was not abolished until 1921, but long before that the system of citizen responsibility for the roads had proven entirely inadequate. The number of cars in the County increased dramatically year by year. By the mid-1930s they were being used year-round instead of only in the summer months, and the speed of which they were capable went up year-by-year and model-by-model.

As early as 1903 the Ontario Government realized the great change that was taking place and inaugurated the County Road System which provided for provincial subsidization of municipal road improvement programs. Simcoe County was among the first to take advantage of this offer and, due to the foresight of its Council, has always enjoyed better roads than are found in most other regions of the province. The 1918 Annual Report of the Department of Roads, for instance, pointed out that "Simcoe County has the second greatest mileage of roads of all the counties in the province."

It was not until the mid-1930s that provincial highways in the County and County roads were plowed for winter use, and it was still later before an attempt was made to keep township roads open. The latter proved a formidable task, as the experiences of Innisfil township will serve to illustrate. Following the repeal of the Statute of Labour, Innisfil, like other townships in the County, appointed Road Superintendents to oversee new construction and maintenance. During the years of the Great Depression little could be done due to lack of funds. Some gravel was hauled, but many roads remained impassable during the annual spring break-up. Rates of pay were very low—18¢ per hour, or 35¢ if the man provided a team and wagon.

In 1940, when economic conditions were rapidly improving, the township purchased a truck-mounted snowplow, which performed well enough but was inadequate to meet township-wide responsibilities. During the time of World War II, and for two or three years afterwards, it was virtually impossible to buy additional equipment. In the very hard winter of 1946-47 many township roads lay buried under up to 20-foot drifts and were blocked for as long as six weeks.

Eventually, however, the situation eased as the necessary machinery became available. Before the end of another decade most Innisfil roads could be classified as "all-weather." The transformation was not, of course, without substantial cost—the Innisfil road budget increased from about $50,000 in 1949 to $348,000 in 1966. The upward spiral was inevitable, however, in view of the ever-increasing number of cars on the road after World War II, the expanding use of school buses, and the growing, year-round influx of recreation seekers from Toronto and other major metropolitan centres to the south.

What happened in Innisfil was more or less typical of what happened throughout Simcoe County, and by the 1970s a web of excellent provincial, county and township roads—prey only to the most violent of winter blizzards—criss-crossed from Tottenham to Port Severn, and from Collingwood to Orillia.

Another major area of technological advance was in the development and provision of hydro power, without which, of course, there could be no automatic washers and dryers, refrigerators, touch-button ranges, television sets, movie theatres and numerous other electronic conveniences and luxuries of the modern age. Throughout Simcoe County people had always wanted better and more efficient light than could be provided by candles and kerosene lamps. All of the other appliances were developments made possible by the search for a more efficient source of power by which to dispel the darkness.

There is a sameness about the attempts of each town and village to obtain this magic flow of current; yet to some extent every story is unique.

In Orillia the saga begins with the establishment of the Orillia Fire, Water and Light Committee in 1896, the members of which proposed the establishment of a hydraulic plant at Ragged Rapids on the Severn River. The plan involved the transmission of electric power across nineteen miles of line, an unheard of distance at that time, but the citizens of the town approved the recommendation by 399 votes to 61. Work began in the spring of 1900, with men, supplies and equipment being taken in to the construction site by canoe—a trip that involved the sometimes hazardous crossing of Sparrow Lake. More than one boat was swamped, and more than one life lost, but the building of a dam and powerhouse proceeded at a rapid pace. The substation and administrative building were built on West Street North, and on January 21, 1901 the first power reached Orillia from Ragged Rapids. The dam was christened the "Patriarche Dam," after P. H.

Patriarche, who had been its engineer.

Unfortunately, heavy flooding caused the dam to burst in the spring of 1904. Orillia citizens voted $80,000 for a new plant at Ragged Rapids, but it too failed a couple of years later. In 1913 the Dominion Department of Railways and Canals (as part of its plan to improve the Trent Waterways System) suggested that the power plant be moved one and a half miles downstream to Swift Rapids. This recommendation was approved and, despite interruptions occasioned by World War I, a new dam, with 47-foot head, was eventually completed. The increase in current was expected to meet Orillia's power requirements for some time to come. But steadily expanding subscribership and increasing industrialization soon overloaded the system, and even the subsequent addition of other plants (Minden in 1935, and Mathias in 1950) left the town with a sometimes uneasy balance between supply and demand.

In Stayner, the Reeve and Town Council entered into an agreement with Joseph Knox to supply the community with electricity from the flour mill he operated on the site later occupied by Watson Motors. The contract called for the installation of twenty-seven incandescent lights of 32 candlepower to illuminate the streets of the town.

In 1900 the first electric street lights appeared in Tottenham.

Windmills were fairly common in Oro township; they were used to grind grain, pulp turnips and pump water. In 1920, E. C. Drury installed a Delco lighting plant, powered by a gasoline engine, and some years later Vernon Caldwell and Henry Dunsmore put in a Fairbanks Morse system. However, little progress was made towards a communal electrical system until the early 1930s.

Midland obtained its first electrical energy from a private source, the Midland Electric Company, which operated a coal-fired steam generator. In 1894 and again in 1895 the Midland Electric Company applied to the Ontario Government for incorporation and was finally granted a charter to provide

Midland with light, heat and power in 1899. Four years later the Municipal Council issued debentures to buy out the private company and convert it to public ownership in order to inaugurate a community electric power system, which went into effect in August, 1903. As was typical of that period, there were strict rules governing the amount of power a subscriber was entitled to use. For example, one all-night light was permitted for every ten to twenty lights in regular usage, a concession which only applied to factories and other commercial enterprises.

Residents of Barrie saw electric lights for the first time in the early 1880s, when a circus thrilled district residents with a display of arc lamps, probably battery-powered. In the late 1880s three prominent local citizens acquired the capital to form the Barrie Electric Light Company and to install the first street lights in the town. They were James L. Burton and George Ball, both prominent lumbermen, and Samuel Lount, the County's second registrar, after whom a Barrie street is named. Power was supplied by two dams in Midhurst, and the poles came into Barrie along Bayfield Street to a set of transformers set up in an old wooden warehouse at the rear of the present Ontario Hydro building. The night the lights were turned on was a gala occasion in Barrie, and most of the hundreds of citizens who turned out were much too enthralled by the instant illumination to pay attention to the official speeches. "There was a ceremony at the town plant for only a very few minutes," Nellie Rankin Sissons, an observer, wrote in 1950, "for all attention was outside on the new lights to be admired."

Within a few months, however, there was still light but little sweetness between the company and the town, as disagreements arose over rates and other matters. The Barrie Electric Light Company offered to sell out for $80,000 but, after long and sometimes bitter negotiations, Barrie acquired its assets for $22,501 in 1898. A Board of Commissioners consisting of J. H. Bennett, as chairman, Mayor W. A. Boys and Mrs. S. Dyment, was set up to run the now publicly owned system, and met for the first time on January 13, 1902. Under its direction an efficient and highly successful program of reconstruction and expansion was carried out in 1903, and continued in a second phase three years later.

By 1910 Barrie's electrical utility was humming. Business was increasing rapidly, service was being supplied twenty-four hours a day, many additional street lights were in operation, and a contract had been let for the construction of a new office building at the corner of Simcoe and Bayfield Streets.

Penetanguishene erected its first three street lights in 1889, with power being supplied by a small dynamo driven by a water wheel on Copeland's Creek. Shortly afterwards George Copeland formed the Copeland Light Company, and service was extended to several homes and buildings, including McCrosson's Hall (also known as "the Opera House"). In 1904, when it became evident that heavier equipment would be necessary to meet the increasing demand for power, Copeland sold out to a group headed by C. Beck. The new company, which laboured under the name the "Penetang-Midland Electric Street Railway, Light and Power Company Limited" (or P.M.E.S.R.L. and P., for short) built a large steam-operated generating station on Fox Street. The Penetang-Midland Electric Street Railway never got off the drawing board (if, indeed, it ever reached that stage), but electrical services expanded rapidly during the first decade of the new century and by 1910 were available to virtually the entire community.

In 1906 the Ontario Government, aware of the need to co-ordinate the hydro-electric resources of the province in order to meet future requirements, established the Hydro-Electric Power Commission of Ontario. Under the Power Commission Act, it was to function as a self-sustaining, corporate public enterprise, and was given broad powers in order to supply electricity at cost throughout the province. Any municipal corporation could "apply to the Commission for . . . electrical power or energy . . . for lighting, heating and power purposes." Adam Beck (later to become Sir Adam Beck) was the first chairman of the Hydro-Electric Power Commission, and under his active leadership the goal of establishing a province-wide system soon began to be realized. In 1910, for example, Penetang ratepayers voted to buy out the P.M.E.S.R.L. and P. Company, and the next year the town signed a contract with Ontario Hydro. Barrie also joined the system in 1911, and on April 6, 1913 a power line was activated to bring current from the Big Chute generating station on the Severn River. Other Simcoe County communities soon followed suit.

In 1913 a generating station, the first to be designed and constructed by Ontario Hydro, came into being at Wasdell Falls on the Severn River about three miles northeast of Washago. Named after Joseph Wasdell, a Methodist minister and the original owner of the property, it remained in service until 1955. On July 1, 1914 the Commission purchased the station at the Big Chute, nine miles from the mouth of the Severn, which had been built three years earlier by the Simcoe Railway and Power Company. In the winter of 1916 the Big Chute operation, which served much of Simcoe County, including Midland, Penetang, Coldwater, Barrie, Collingwood, Elmvale and Stayner, was expanded by the addition of a fourth power unit. The 20-ton piece of equipment was hauled in by the largest team of horses ever seen in the area, and, after the seven-mile trip over a rough, snow-covered bush road, the runners of the sleigh were found to be worn down and badly cracked.

A few rural lines were built after 1912, but farm electrification did not really get underway until the passage of the Rural Hydro-Electric Distribution Act of 1921. By this legislation, the province agreed to pay up to half of the capital cost of installing primary lines designed to provide electrification for farmers. From then on the program moved ahead steadily, although not always fast enough to satisfy all rural residents, and by the 1950s service was available to virtually everyone in the County, including many cottage residents.

In many respects the coming of telephone service to Simcoe County closely paralleled the development of hydro-electric power. In both cases the pioneering was done through local initiative by far-sighted individuals, private companies, and progressively-minded municipal officials. Later on, as the scope, complexity, and capital investment involved in future expansion became apparent, the separate parts were amalgamated and standardized into giant corporations. Thus, just as Ontario Hydro took over the supply of electrical power for the whole province, so the Bell Telephone Company (later to be nick-named "Ma Bell") gradually absorbed most (though not all) of the local and regional telephone systems into its gigantic international operation.

*Utopia Conservation Area Dam, built in 1968,
and Bell's Grist Mill, built in 1904*

As early as 1885 many Simcoe County communities had local telephone service. These included Barrie, Orillia, Bradford, Beeton, Alliston and Cookstown. Within the next year lines built from Newmarket to Barrie and from Barrie to Orillia opened up long-distance communications with all of North America. By 1888 Coldwater and Tottenham had been added to this roster. For other communities the telephone was somewhat longer in coming.

Stroud, for example, had to wait until 1910, when a group of interested citizens met to discuss the possibility of establishing a telephone system. A year later, after trees had been cut, holes dug, poles installed, and wires strung through countless hours of volunteer labour, the Stroud Telephone Co. Ltd. was incorporated, with R. A. Sutherland as the first president. The original switchboard was set up in a store owned by Thomas Sproule at the intersection of the 10th Concession and Highway 11. Fred Mathers, the local blacksmith, was given a contract to run the operation and his daughters became the "Hello Girls" who took calls and pushed plugs to make connections. The company continued as a local operation for almost half a century, but eventually sold its assets to Bell of Canada in the late 1950s and early 1960s.

Similarly, the Vespra Municipal Telephone System was organized in 1912 with about a dozen original subscribers who paid nine dollars per year for the service. It, too, eventually became part of the Bell conglomerate in 1958.

The Oro Telephone Company Limited, incorporated in 1909 with an original forty-one subscribers, was purchased by Bell in the early 1960s for $45,000, plus $12,405.80 for new cable which was on hand but had not yet been installed.

In the early days telephone service was limited in a number of ways. In Oro, for example, the switchboard was only in operation during certain hours until 1939, when it was converted to an around-the-clock service. Most subscribers throughout the County shared party lines and were urged to keep their conversations to a three-minute maximum.

"Listening in" on party line conversations provided much material for gossip, and to some extent presaged the popularity of radio and television soap operas in later decades.

The new instrument provided the basis for considerable humour, as shown in an article in the Orillia *Times* of July 9, 1887:

People ask for queer things through the telephone sometimes. Think of an ordinary, everyday man in a most authoritative tone of voice . . . 'Give me A. Tait's residence.' Now the residence of Mr. Tait cost in the neighbourhood of $20,000 and a man who wants it is a hog. And it is not in the power of the young lady who presides at the central office—however sweet or good-natured she may be—to hand over this mansion on demand. Another man will be heard to make the modest request, 'Give me the Town Hall,' or 'Let me have Thomson's Shingle Mill.' But the most audacious order yet given to the operator was made by a prominent citizen who coolly and calmly called, 'Give me Mrs.— , please.' And yet the Good Book says, 'Thou shalt not covet thy neighbour's wife.' It is time to call a halt!

As the years passed "Ma Bell" swallowed up most of these local enterprises and merged them into a corporate system that was probably more efficient, though certainly less individualistic and not as warmly human.

One Simcoe County community, though, provided a pleasant exception by reversing the process. Coldwater started out with the Bell Telephone Company in 1889, the first exchange operating out of a hardware store. The number of customers grew rapidly, and in 1916 some of them, convinced that Bell's rates were too high, got together to discuss the possibility of buying out the company. This was accomplished a few months later when one hundred residents put up their properties as collateral to finance the take-over.

In the 1970s there are still eighty-four subscribers whose property could theoretically be mortgaged, should the company encounter financial difficulties. Based on the last sixty years, during which the system has been run entirely by the villagers, this would seem to be an unlikely eventuality. From the beginning a strong sense of community involvement has kept the company progressive, efficient and financially stable. Starting out with no experience and with many different skills to be mastered, the Coldwater pioneers and their descendants have kept abreast of technological changes and the enterprise is now conceded to be one of the most modern and best integrated telephone systems in Canada.

No doubt the key figure in the success of the Coldwater Municipal Telephone System was Mord Millard, who joined it when it began in 1916 and continued to be its chief technical expert into the 1970s. "The service we're offering today is as good as the service anywhere," he said in an interview in 1976. "We've kept pace with technology. There wasn't a single system that updated like we did."

Because of its sound technical and financial operation, the Coldwater Municipal Telephone System was able to expand its operation by buying out the Moonstone and North River exchanges during the 1950s, and by 1975 had 771 customers in Coldwater and Fesserton, and in Matchedash Township.

Somewhat ironically, "Ma Bell" tried to buy the Coldwater system back in 1957, but, according to Mr. Millard, "They couldn't afford to pay us what we thought it was worth." The assets of the company then were in excess of two million dollars.

But relations with Bell have been harmonious for many years. "We have learned to respect them and they have learned to respect us," Commissioner Walter Dean said in 1976. Long distance calls are handled through Bell-serviced equipment installed in the Coldwater exchange. "The really big factor," Commissioner Ruth Brown said recently, "is that this is all ours. . . . We all get along well, everybody's available at a few minutes' notice to do a job. You can't beat it."

Another example of co-operation between Bell and a local telephone company occurred in Beeton, and under somewhat unusual circumstances. Bell established the original system in 1885, installing the switchboard in the drug store operated by J. F. Darby. Then, in 1909, two private exchanges were established—one by W. J. Anderson, with lines running to

Tottenham, Penville, Alliston and Newton Robinson; the other set up by Dr. R. S. Brewster for the use of his rural customers. Two years later these two small companies joined forces to form the Beeton Telephone Company. Later, when the private company purchased a building on Main Street (which became the library at a much later date), Bell lent assistance by installing and agreeing to maintain the switchboard. Thus Bell provided service for the village and the Beeton Telephone Company took care of the surrounding rural area. For a long period N. P. McDonald acted as manager of both operations. This dual arrangement continued efficiently and harmoniously for more than four decades, until 1957 when Bell Telephone bought out the assets and equipment of the Beeton Telephone Company and took over service for the whole district.

The story of the formative period in the history of Beeton centres around one man, David Allanson Jones. Born in York County, Jones had lived for some years in the United States before returning to what was then called Clarksville in the 1860s. He was a man of seemingly limitless energy, great ambition and wide curiosity. He gained experience and knowledge in more fields, and dabbled in more business ventures, than any ten average men do in their lifetimes.

Before coming to Clarksville and while still only in his thirties, he had been a farmer in Illinois, had operated a training school for dogs and horses, and had sold books and fruit trees as a travelling salesman.

Soon after his arrival in Clarksville he opened a general store in partnership with his brother. Shortly afterward he became Postmaster, a position that he would hold for almost half a century. Before the end of the sixties he began to purchase property in and around the village, beginning with a modest purchase of some fifty acres.

As time went on he became involved in more and more enterprises: lumbering, building, gardening, and land speculation and development on an increasingly large scale. He also became a figure of substantial political influence, partly because of his dedication to the progress of the village in which he had chosen to live, and partly, no doubt, because he eventually owned most of the land upon which its future expansion would take place. An example of this influence was his success in having the main north-south axis of the village switched from Patterson Street to Centre Street, and thus a block closer to the extensive property he owned in the west end of the village.

He was one of the Canada's first real-estate developers, dividing some of his holdings into building lots (which he advertised as available at "a price to suit the purchaser"), laying out streets and planting rows of shade trees which helped to beautify the village long after his death.

But of all Jones' varied interests, the one that lasted longest and seemed to touch the deepest vein, was his preoccupation with the raising of bees and the marketing of honey. It began with the purchase of two swarms of honeybees from a neighbour in 1870. Jones soon opened a large factory which manufactured a wide variety of beekeeping supplies and equipment, as well as turning out some sashes and doors. He established apiaries in different parts of the County, and during the summer months some of these were transported to Jones Island in Georgian Bay. As time went on, he became undoubtedly one of the foremost authorities on bees and was known as the "Bee King of Canada." He made trips to such foreign countries as Palestine and Cyprus to study current practices in beekeeping and the evolution of the industry.

Jones experimented in breeding and imported queen bees from Italy. He also shipped bees to many parts of the world, a difficult undertaking in those pre-airmail days when ship or rail transport might take weeks or even months.

He was the first President of the Canadian Beekeepers' Association, which he founded almost single-handedly. He was the only exhibitor of honey at the first Industrial Exhibition in Toronto (later to become the C.N.E). He was a gracious host for dozens of Professors of Agriculture and their students who came to Beeton from all over North America and abroad to study his methods.

In his spare time, if it is possible to think of D. A. Jones as having spare time, he published, edited and wrote most of the copy for three weekly and monthly news magazines: the *Canadian Bee Journal* the first edition of which appeared on April 1, 1885; the general news *Beeton World*; and the *Canadian Poultry Journal*. In 1892 a disastrous fire burned his printing plant to the ground and sounded the death knell for both the *Canadian Bee Journal* and the *Canadian Poultry Journal*. The *Beeton World*, however, survived for several more decades.

This remarkable man, who quietly performed many charitable acts on behalf of the less fortunate, also managed to squeeze some exploring into his busy life and on several occasions made trips into the far north on behalf of the government. These took him into largely unexplored territory reaching as far into the Arctic Regions as the shore of Baffin's Bay, and involved considerable hardships and danger.

D. A. Jones died on Sunday, November 20, 1910. In his obituary in the local newspaper he was described as the "Founder of Beeton," and as a man who had worked for its progress "for nearly half a century." By then, the name of his adopted community had been changed from Clarksville (which had been given in recognition to Robert Clark, a blacksmith, who set up his forge there in 1856), to Beetown, which was later abbreviated to Beeton.

Yet it would be quite wrong, of course, to credit the development of the village to one man. Along with many other communities in Simcoe County, Beeton shared in the heady, if short-sighted, bonanza of the great lumber boom. At its height, there were no less than five sawmills working at capacity on, or close to, Main Street. Along with the abundance of prime trees, the key to this prosperity was the presence of the Grand Trunk Railway, which operated from Hamilton, through Georgetown, to Beeton, and thence to either Collingwood or Allandale. An important element in this system was Beeton's hand-operated turntable, by which engines could be switched from one line to the other.

By about 1890 Beeton could boast of no less than seventy-seven business enterprises, including seven general stores, six shoe stores, four hotels, four stationers, four carriage-builders, four dealers in dry goods, four dressmakers, four blacksmiths, and an oyster bar—not to mention a photographer, a dealer in pianos and organs, two barbers, a weekly newspaper, a millinery and a bookbinder.

In those days the prevailing mood in Beeton, as in so many other villages in Simcoe County and the rest of Ontario, was confidence in the future. The *Beeton World*, with a staff of fourteen, consistently editorialized "The boom is coming." The Grand Trunk yard was a hive of activity, with four trains arriving daily, bringing everything from mail to drummers, from Eaton's catalogue deliveries to farm machinery, from government officials to internationally known singers and other entertainers. In 1906 the Canadian Pacific Railway put through a line just west of the village. Farmers along the railway right-of-ways cut trees and fashioned them into ties, and sold them to the railway. They also sold, for $1.75 a cord, oak, maple and ash to fire the woodburning engines.

In 1910 the population of the village was 758, the same as it had been at the turn of the century. But the disappearance of the forests caused the lumber mills to shut down, and the coming of the automobile saw a steady decline in train service. A number of firms went out of business, and the number of citizens dropped to a low of 468 in 1920. It took forty years for the population to climb back over the 700 mark, but by the beginning of the 1970s it stood at slightly better than 1,000.

Beeton has had many sons and daughters who achieved fame and/or fortune, including pharmacist Gordon Tamblyn, founder of the nation-wide chain of drug stores, and G. T. Somers, who became president of the Crown Life Insurance Company in 1926 (later to be succeeded in that office by his son).

But no doubt the best-known Beeton citizen was Kate Aitken, born Katherine Scott in 1891, the daughter of a Beeton general merchant. The list of her accomplishments and interests challenges that of D. A. Jones. Before her death in 1971, Kate (as she was known to almost everyone) was a school teacher, merchant, poultry-raiser and fruit farmer, agricultural advisor, community and church worker, cooking expert, writer of books, articles and newspaper columns, housewife, and a founder of the Women's Institute in Beeton.

Married to Henry Aitken of Beeton in 1914, she also helped him to run the family mill during the early years of their life together. In the late 1930s she became Director of the Women's Division of Toronto's Canadian National Exhibition.

But, despite all these achievements, her greatest fame came later. As a commentator on radio and television she attracted an ever-widening audience as she discoursed on such varied subjects as travel, etiquette, cooking, international glamour and intrigue, famous personalities and numerous other subjects. The introduction to her regular feature program, "And now here's Mrs. A.," became a household phrase from coast to coast in Canada.

Her assignments took her to virtually every part of the world, and she was almost as much of an international globe-trotter as the *Toronto Star's* Gordon Sinclair. Yet, as was made clear by her nostalgic book about growing up in that pleasant community, her heart always remained in Beeton. It was called *Never a Day so Bright*.

5 The Sunshine Years

In 1912 Stephen Leacock, then the forty-three-year-old head of McGill University's department of Economics and Political Science, published a slim volume called *Sunshine Sketches of a Little Town*. The book, which was to gain general acceptance as *the* Canadian classic in its field, took a wry and sometimes ribald look at daily life in a purportedly fictional Ontario town called Mariposa.

In his preface Leacock wrote, "I must disclaim at once all intention of trying to do anything so ridiculously easy as writing about a real place and real people. Mariposa is not a real town. On the contrary, it is about seventy or eighty of them."

That might have been taken at face value in such places as Montreal, Toronto or London, but it didn't fool anyone in Orillia. *They* knew what town Leacock had written about and recognized many of its citizens as people they saw on the street almost every day—and, unlike readers in the rest of the world, they were not greatly amused. Many, indeed, were outraged.

To be sure, Leacock was not particulary kind to some of the characters he immortalized. "The Mariposa Knights of Pythias are, by their constitution, dedicated to temperance," he had written, "and there's Henry Mullins, the manager of the Exchange Bank, also a Knight of Pythias, with a small flask of Pogram's Special in his hip pocket as a sort of amendment to the constitution." Then there was the Mariposa Band; Mr. Diston, the school teacher (commonly known as "the one who drank"); Judge Peperleigh, whose competence and impartiality were equally open to question; and Canon

Drone, who cut short Sunday morning services so that he could go fishing, pretended to read Theocritus when he didn't know a word of Greek, and was not above fudging parish accounts to help pay his daughter's way through private school.

By intent, however, Leacock's barbs were good-natured, and not meant to inflict anything worse than surface wounds. "The very essence of humour," he wrote in 1916, "is that it must be without harm or malice." And there was no doubt about his love for Orillia and its vicinity. "To my way of thinking," he wrote in 1913, "nothing will stand comparison with the smiling beauty of the waters, shores and bays of Lake Simcoe and its sister lake, Couchiching; the sunlight flashes back in lighter colour from the sandbar on the shoals; the passing clouds of summer throw moving shadows as over a ripening field, and the mimic gales that play over the surface send curling caps of foam as white as ever broke under the bow of the Aegean galley."

Leacock's home in Orillia, "Old Brewery Bay"

Though some Orillians were slow to adopt the writer of *Sunshine Sketches*, Leacock's genuine affection for the town evolved from youthful romance, through love affair, to lifelong marriage. It began when, as a youth, he paddled up through the narrows from Lake Simcoe into Lake Couchiching and was cemented when his mother settled in Orillia in 1895. From then on, it was his summer home, and eventually his year-round home. It was there that he met Beatrix Hamilton, daughter of a prominent and wealthy Toronto family, whom he married in 1900 in the famed Little Church around the Corner in New York City.

He and his bride dreamed of the day when they could retire to Orillia. "I want to have, if I can, at least ten acres, a sort of small farm, room for a very big garden, an orchard, a wooded lot and a field of root crops," he wrote in 1907. "I shall make it very plain, but at the same time very large. . . . I am tired of cities and people. It's a case of 'Good-bye, proud world, I'm going home!'"

The next year he and Beatrix bought thirty-three acres of lakeshore property just east of the town. It took some years, but in time Leacock's mounting literary success provided the funds with which to build a house overlooking the lake. There they lived happily until Beatrix died in 1925. Four years later Leacock had a much larger house built on higher ground—a veritable mansion, with graceful pillars and arches, two furnaces, more rooms than he ever bothered to count, and no less than five bathrooms.

Leacock, who liked to drink, took delight in naming his new home "Old Brewery Bay," because the ruins of a stone brewery from an earlier day were nearby. "I have known that name . . . to make people thirsty by correspondence as far away as Nevada," he wrote in 1930. A mile or more removed from town, hidden behind the trees at the end of a winding road that bumped over railway tracks, "Old Brewery Bay" provided Leacock with the seclusion and quiet he needed. Not that he led a monastic life there; far from it. He enjoyed being called the "Baron of Brewery Bay" and he liked to entertain such interesting guests as Vilhjalmur Stefansson, the arctic explorer, and the sounds of revelry often continued far into the night. For Leacock, however, it was usually "early to bed, and early to rise"; it was his habit to get out of bed before dawn and finish the day's writing by breakfast time, so that he could get on with more serious matters such as fishing and gardening.

Leacock's later success would have been difficult to predict on the basis of his early years. He was born on December 30, 1869 in a thatched-roof cottage in the Hampshire village of Swanmore in England, the third of the eleven children of Peter and Agnes Butler Leacock. When he was six he sailed with his mother and brothers and sisters to join his father on a hundred-acre farm near Egypt, Ontario, four miles from the Lake Simcoe village of Sutton.

Life in their new home was anything but easy for the Leacock family. Unsuccessful at farming, and having failed to find a fortune during a couple of years spent in the Canadian Northwest, Stephen's father abandoned his wife and offspring in favour of a drifter's life in Nova Scotia. Somehow out of this broken-home environment, Stephen managed to gain admission to Toronto's socially prestigious Upper Canada College (where he became "head boy") and later to obtain his B.A. in modern languages at the University of Toronto.

During most of this period, from 1891 to 1899, he financed himself and his studies by teaching, a profession which he later described as "the most dreary, the most thankless, and the worst paid . . . in the world."

Eventually he borrowed enough money to take a degree in economics and political science at the University of Chicago, and in 1903 he became a Doctor of Philosophy while on the staff of McGill University. Ever irascible, but never pompous, Leacock wrote of the latter: "The meaning of this degree is that the recipient of instruction is examined for the last time in his life, and is pronounced completely full. After this, no new ideas can be imparted to him."

His brilliant career as a humorist and literary figure had been launched two years before the appearance of *Sunshine Sketches of a Little Town*, with the publication of a 125-page, 35¢ volume called *Literary Lapses*, which Leacock had printed at his own expense in 1910. Thanks to a chance reading by a British publisher, the book became an international success and was to be reprinted sixteen times within the next twenty years. It was followed by *Nonsense Novels* in 1911 and *Sunshine Sketches* a year later, and, after that, by a steady stream of books and articles, many of which were later collected into books. From his prolific pen came biographies of Jacques Cartier, Abraham Lincoln, Mark Twain and Charles Dickens; articles on economic subjects for the *Financial Post*; popular histories of Canada's far North; essays on town-planning and population; and numerous other serious pieces of writing. But humour remained his first love. "The writing of solid, instructive stuff, fortified by facts and figures, is easy enough," he wrote in the 1930s. "There is no trouble in writing a scientific treatise on the folklore of Central China, or a statistical enquiry into the declining population of Prince Edward Island. But to write something out of one's own mind, worth reading for its own sake, is an arduous contrivance only to be achieved in fortunate moments, few and far between. Personally, I would sooner have written *Alice in Wonderland* than the whole *Encylopaedia Britannica*."

By the time of his death in 1944, the "Baron of Brewery Bay" enjoyed the respect and admiration of many famous literary peers. Presented with the Mark Twain Medal in St. Louis, Missouri in 1935, Leacock had much earlier been recognized as a great humorist by such contemporaries as F. Scott Fitzgerald and Robert Benchley. The latter wrote on the flyleaf of the copy of his first book of humour that he mailed to Leacock in 1922: "To Stephen Leacock, who certainly *ought* to like most of the stuff in this book, as he wrote it himself first. Gratefully, Bob Benchley."

After *Sunshine Sketches*, Leacock never again wrote about Mariposa, and the citizens of Orillia, recovering from their

original sense of outrage, soon came to be proud of their
famous fellow townsman. Before long they, like the rest of
the world, were laughing at his hilarious description of trying
to open a bank account, entitled "My Financial Career." Nor
could they ultimately resist the charm of such pieces as "The
New Food," in which Leacock anticipated the one-pill meal
of later science fiction, and told of the terrible fate of a child,
Gustavus Adolphus, who gobbled up thirteen Christmas
dinners in a single swallow:

"Clap him on the back!" cried the distracted mother. "Give him
water."
    The idea was fatal. The water striking the pill caused it to
expand. There was a dull, rumbling sound and then, with an
awful bang, Gustavus Adolphus exploded into fragments.

Shortly after his death in 1944, a group of Orillia citizens
formed the Leacock Memorial Committee and organized an
annual banquet at which the Stephen Leacock medal was
awarded to each year's outstanding Canadian humorist. Later
this evolved into a yearly festival, dedicated to the expression
and enjoyment of all that was contemporarily Canadian and
fun-loving—rock music and folk dancing and other things
that would have set Leacock's toes to tapping and put a smile
upon his face.
    In 1956, Orillia took over Leacock's home at Old Brewery
Bay and turned it into a combined national shrine and tourist
attraction. To reach it, you turn off a main thoroughfare
just east of the town, and follow a gently twisting, gravel
road across a set of railway tracks until you come to the
stately home, tucked away behind its protective shield of
big trees, overlooking the lake. Inside, everything has been
restored with such loving care and attention to detail that
a visitor might expect Leacock to come through one of the
screen doors at any moment, fishing rod in hand. It is all as
he might have left it—from fresh-cut flowers on the dining
room table, to the bucket he hung under the leak in the roof
that he never got around to fixing, to the original, hand-
written manuscript of *Sunshine Sketches of a Little Town*.

Actually, the notion that Orillia was a special "sunshine" kind of town predated Leacock. Some years before him, a group of influential and community-minded men, including J. B. Tudhope, Arthur Thompson, Erastus Long, J. B. Henderson and Joe Donnelly, had formed a committee to foster and promote what became known as "the Orillia Spirit." Dedicated to the proposition that their town was just about the best place in the world in which to live, these leading citizens were determined to make it even better and to build a sense of civic pride in its attractive buildings, clean streets, decent people and enthusiasm for progress.

The idea caught on, and out of it came a great many "firsts" for Orillia. It was the first town in Ontario to have a Canadian Club and it rivalled the Toronto clubs for lavish furnishings and atmosphere of affluence. The power plant built on the Severn River, eighteen miles away, supplied Orillia with the first municipally-owned, long-distance electrical system in Ontario—one which supplied the cheapest electricity in Canada for some forty years after it was opened in 1902. Later, the Orillia Public Library was the first outside of the big cities to employ professional librarians. In 1912, it was the first place in Canada to adopt Daylight Saving Time—an idea that didn't work out satisfactorily then, but which was implemented on a nation-wide basis during the Great War of 1914-18.

The "Orillia Spirit" is also there in the magnificent Champlain monument, erected in Couchiching Park, and unveiled on July 1, 1925. Beautifully crafted in bronze by sculptor Vernon March, it is dominated by the imposing figure of Champlain, the first European to pass through the Couchiching Narrows, near which it stands. Below are two clusters of figures—one to represent the coming of the Jesuits to Huronia, the other depicting the fur-trading *coureurs de bois*, who soon followed in Champlain's footsteps. It would be impossible to estimate the number of people, local citizens and visitors alike, who have stood in awe before this monument during the half-century since its unveiling. Built with financial assistance from the federal and provincial governments and from the Simcoe County Council, it was made possible also by the large and small contributions of individual Orillians, and particularly by the vision and not-to-be-denied determination of one local man, C. H. Hale, who was a prime mover in the project from start to finish.

One aspect of "the Orillia Spirit" actively supported by the local Board of Trade was a continuing campaign to attract new industry to the town in order to increase employment and add to its general prosperity. Orillia, like most other communities in Simcoe County, profited from the coming of the railroads and the great lumber boom. The Couchiching Mill, operated by Oliva and Company, was one of the largest in the district, employing as many as 120 men and cutting close to three million feet of lumber in its peak years.

Later other industries developed in Orillia, encouraged partly by the low cost of electrical power, and also by tax exemptions granted through local by-laws passed in the late 1890s and early 1900s. In some instances, too, the Simcoe County Council granted loans to industry—$50,000 to the Tudhope Carriage Co. in 1909, for example. The Tudhope Co. and the Wm. Ramsay Co., both of which grew out of small Orillia wagon-making and blacksmith shops, were two of the largest carriage factories in Canada. Other industries, including foundries, planing mills, machinery manufacturers, a furniture factory, and a canoe company joined the lengthening list of Orillia employers. By about 1910 the town enjoyed the reputation of being "the principal industrial centre between Toronto and North Bay."

During the war years from 1914 to 1918, industry hummed in the town, as many plants switched to the production of munitions, particularly shells and the wooden crates in which they were shipped. Many women were added to the work force at this time. Overtime and shift work were common. Some factories were working on an around-the-clock basis and several production records were set—which, in the patriotic fervor of the times, made Orillians very proud. A new generating plant was built on the Severn River, at Swift Rapids, in 1917 to augment wartime power requirements.

With the Armistice in 1918, civilian production was gradually restored and Orillia again courted new industries.

From the beginning, however, there was another school of thought in Orillia, one which ran counter to the drive for more industrialization. Many citizens wanted the town to remain a quiet, charming and orderly place in which to live, and a pleasant, peaceful Mecca for summer visitors, fishermen, cottage-owners and resort hotel guests—in short, a "sunshine" town. They were concerned with the potential dangers of too rapid population growth, too indiscriminate industrial expansion, too much "progress" too soon.

The view of Orillia as a pastoral community in harmony with and complementing the natural beauty of the countryside surrounding it goes far back, as witnessed by this paragraph from the Orillia *Packet* of September 5, 1870:

. . . handsome residences surrounded by beautiful trees, churches with lofty steeples, glittering poplars . . . this lovely scenery afforded by the town itself, laid out as it is with trees shading the streets, and rearing themselves towards the sky . . . then, against the summer grounds, lay the splendid lakes.

Beginning in the 1890s, and continuing far into the twentieth century, an active campaign, supported by newspaper editors, citizens' committees and civic by-laws, urged local residents to maintain their properties by cleaning up, painting up, getting rid of weeds, and in general doing everything they could to beautify their community.

In 1901 a Social Improvement Committee was established, shortly to be followed by a Local Improvement Committee; these two were combined a few years later to form a Civic Betterment Committee. All three were designed to maintain what was termed "the rightful character" of the town, and many campaigns were conducted to promote clean streets, trim lawns, colorful flowerbeds and well-cared-for homes and business establishments. Everything unsightly was to be removed, repaired, hidden behind shrubbery or painted over.

Even during the Great Depression of the 1930s, the Civic Betterment Committee maintained its efforts on behalf of a neater, cleaner, more beautiful Orillia.

Closely related to all of this, was the emergence of the town as the hub of a flourishing summer vacation paradise, with an abundance of clear, sparkling water, unsurpassed fishing, clean air, boating, swimming, and numerous points and islands where the summer breezes sighed through the boughs of towering pines. As time passed, more and more residents would profit from the short, but lucrative annual influx of pleasure seekers.

One development which greatly increased the importance of the summer vacation industry was the completion of the Trent Waterway System which, via a network of dams, canals, liftlocks, marine railways and other engineering triumphs, eventually opened up pleasure-craft navigation all the way from Trenton, on Lake Ontario, to the Port Severn entrance into Georgian Bay. First proposed as early as 1827, the system was almost a century in reaching final realization.

Beginning in 1833, a few crude locks were constructed at various points along the necklace of lakes and rivers to permit passage between connecting bodies of water. By 1872 some 171 miles of "through navigation" had been opened up, but only in a fragmented chain consisting of six unconnected reaches: Healey Falls to Peterborough, Buckhorn to Fenelon Falls, Fenelon Falls to Coboconk, Sturgeon Lake to Port Perry, and Lake Simcoe to Lake Couchiching.

By 1907, all of these links had been joined and another thirty-odd miles added, but it remained an internal system, without outlet to the Great Lakes at either end. The Lake Ontario terminus was achieved with the opening of the Trenton to Rice Lake section, but the Severn division, from Lake Couchiching to Georgian Bay had to wait until after the Great War of 1914-18. Then, in 1919 and the early months of 1920, with the completion of the Couchiching lock near Washago, and the finishing of the marine railways at the Big Chute and Swift rapids on the Severn, the long dreamed-of waterway became a reality.

The main challenge in completing the system was the problem of raising vessels over the height of land which cuts diagonally across southern Ontario, from which all waters flow either south-easterly to Lake Ontario, or north-westerly into Georgian Bay and the Upper Great Lakes. It was finally achieved through the construction of liftlocks at Peterborough in 1904, and at Kirkfield in 1907. These massive structures, which operated on the hydraulic principle, were regarded as scientific marvels at the time, comparable, some said, to other "Wonders of the World" such as Egypt's Pyramids and the Great Wall of China.

The first system-length passage was completed by the motor launch *Irene*, which left Trenton on July 3, 1920 and arrived at Port Severn nine days later. From then on the steady stream of passenger craft added considerably to Orillia's summer vacation industry. Year-by-year they came in ever-increasing numbers and in changing modes of transport —from the steam launches of the early days, with the men wearing stiff collars and ties and the women in summer bonnets, to family house boats, with the laundry hung out on lines to dry, to half-million dollar yachts, with stereo systems, well-stocked bars, and bikini-clad worshippers of the sun.

The number of cottages also grew steadily until Lake Couchiching, Lake Simcoe and Sparrow Lake were almost entirely encircled, and most of the accessible islands at the mouth of the Severn and out into Georgian Bay were occupied—mainly by well-to-do summer visitors from Toronto and the northern United States. Summer regattas were popular, with each district having its local champion to compete against the paddlers who came from dozens of near and far points. A familiar sight was a motor-launch towing a string of canoes through the Couchiching Narrows on the way to the next competition.

Prior to the age of the automobile, most cottagers came and went by train, making dock-side connections with such

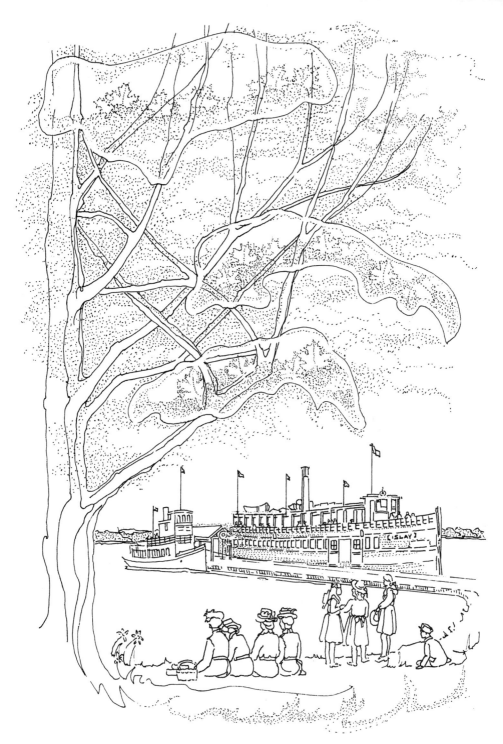

Picnic and excursion on the Islay, *from Orillia, 1910*

steamers as the *Islay, Geneva* and *Otonabee* (which were
proto-types of Leacock's *Mariposa Belle*). On weekends the
islands were ablaze with Japanese lanterns as wives and children waited to greet husbands and fathers, returning from
another busy week in the stifling heat of the cities. There
were picnics, and berry picking expeditions, and corn roasts,
and daily trips to buy milk and other supplies and to pick
up newspapers and the mail. And on Saturday nights the
waltzes and fox-trots played by local orchestras drifted out
across the still, moonlit waters from many a pavilion.

The fishing, in those early days, was excellent, as is evident from the thousands of photographs that survive in family snapshot albums, newspaper files and old summer resort
brochures. In them we see countless huge muskies being held
up by men, women and children, their broad trails dangling
on the ground; heavy stringers of bass, pickerel and perch;
and rows of giant northern pike stretched out, side-by-side,
on the grass in front of hotel verandahs. There were famous
guides to take the visiting anglers out to where the fish were
—men like Frank Geroux, Simon Bonneville, Jerry Casca-
gnette and Paul Bressette, who knew every shoal and patch
of weeds, and were often booked-up a year in advance by
their steady clients. The "shore dinners" they provided
—fresh pickerel fillets, crisped to a golden brown over crack-
ling open fires; sizzling strips of bacon; bubbling pots of
pork and beans; thick slices of fresh, home-baked bread;
generous wedges of blueberry or apple pie; limitless mugs
of steaming coffee and strong tea—were open-air feasts
to be relished in the shade of towering pines, and to be
remembered on many a cold winter night.

The influx of summer visitors, together with the manipu-
lation of water levels for navigational purposes and to supply
electrical power, inevitably caused some changes in the wild
life of the district. Wolverines, which were once plentiful in
the Port Severn area, gradually disappeared, commemorated
only by Wolverine Beach near Honey Harbour. So did the
last, scattered herds of woodland elk, and most, though not

all, of the Mississauga rattlesnakes. The mighty sturgeon, once the prime target of a substantial fishing fleet, and the main product of Booth's processing plant at Victoria Harbour, became rare. But the deer increased in numbers, the beaver population recovered to the point where it would eventually become a nuisance in some areas, and the fishing, while not as good as in the pioneer period of summer-vacationing, stood up well throughout the years and continued to produce record catches into the 1970s.

There were several fine summer hotels in the resort areas of Simcoe County, such as Bayview House, owned by Mrs. Bessie Hurl, and Camp Rawley, owned by Mabel Rawson and her husband, D. A. Gauley. The description of the early days of Camp Rawley, which opened in July, 1922, on the Severn, is given by the late Mabel Rawson in her booklet, "Port Severn, Crossroads Community." It illustrates both the high quality of accommodation characteristically provided, and the pride and pleasure most resort operators customarily took in providing it:

Our dreams started to materialize in the form of a lodge. Building material was brought across Georgian Bay from Midland, some 15 miles by horse and sleigh . . . during the winter of 1921-22.

The original structure was about 70 feet by 30 feet, exclusive of verandahs . . . There were 28 guest rooms, a large and airy dining room, and a rotunda with a big stone fireplace. . . .

Since there were no deliveries of milk, we bought T.B.-tested cows. . . . We also added pigs . . . along with hens for eggs. . . .

Electricity was supplied by a Fairbanks Morse battery system . . . which also pumped water from the Severn into a gravity storage tank to supply the kitchen and bathrooms. . . .

A sparkling spring nearby, bubbling out of the rock, supplied our drinking water, which was tested periodically by Dr. Frank Porter of Waubaushene, the local Medical Officer of Health. . . .

All jellies, jams, fruit and pickles were made in the kitchen, as were our bread and rolls. . . . Soap was made from excess fat by the chef and used for laundering, all of which was done on the property. Flat irons, heated on the stove, were used for ironing.

Our pavilion accommodated many people for dances and other forms of recreation. We had a good five-piece orchestra . . . (which) also played music at dinnertime. There was a bridge party each week, as well as a boat trip to the Big Chute, to Minnicognashene, or to some other point on the Bay. . . .

Winter ice was cut from the river for our refrigerator . . . and stored in sawdust in the ice-house. . . . Fish were packed in ice in boxes to be taken home, strapped to the running boards of guests' cars.

Mrs. Rawson, who died in February, 1976, fervently stated her love for the natural environment which had been so much a part of her long, productive and happy life, when she wrote: "Those of us who visit or live in this land are shareholders in a trust in which all of North America has a significant stake. May we be worthy of it!"

And, by the mid-1970s, there was abundant reason to be concerned with the preservation of the natural heritage, not only in Simcoe County, but throughout Ontario. Each year the pressure on the lakes and rivers had grown: the taking of fish, the dredging of marshy bays to make room for more cottages, the cutting of water-side trees, the intrusion of ever more powerful motor boats and the simple reality of constantly increasing numbers of city-dwellers seeking temporary escape in the steadily dwindling square miles of vacation country. But while growth had been steady (apart from a slow-down during the Great Depression), it became almost frantic after World War II. In the three decades since 1945, highways were improved dramatically, and there were ever more, and faster, cars on the road. Torontonians and residents of other sprawling metropolitan centres felt a growing need to "get out into the country," and the spreading affluence and shrinking work-week provided the means and the time to indulge it.

Bumper-to-bumper weekend traffic was a phenomenon that began in the 1950s. More and more motels opened up in Simcoe County, especially around such popular centres as Wasaga Beach. Marinas multiplied. So did drive-in hamburger stands, take-out chicken franchises, outdoor movie theatres, pizzerias and driving ranges for golfers: anything to accommodate, entertain—and exploit—weekend and summer visitors.

With the ever increasing demand for cottages, real estate developers bought up miles of lake-front property and divided it into postage stamp lots, with the result that long stretches of over-crowded shoreline looked like suburban streets—complete, in many cases, with power lawn mowers. In the late 1960s, the report of a study authorized by the federal Minister of Transport and the Ontario Minister of Tourism and Information pointed out that no less than 800 cottage subdivisions along the Trent-Severn Waterway were currently registered, with another 40 awaiting government approval.

During the same years, the number of passenger craft passing up and down the Trent-Severn System (along which the lock at Couchiching was one of the busiest) increased dramatically with each passing summer. According to government figures, the total skyrocketed from about 72,000 in 1960 to over 160,000 in 1970.

What all of this meant, of course, was that the vacation and tourist industry, long seen by many as a preferable alternative to increased industrialization, proved in the long run to pose an even greater threat to the quiet, peaceful, "sunshine" town atmosphere of Orillia than the building of more factories. It was a problem facing many other communities in Simcoe County, and throughout southern and central Ontario, but nowhere was it more evident than in Leacock's "Little Town."

The challenge of the mid-1970s is to achieve and maintain a balance between contending, and often directly opposed, forces: progress and conservation; a dedication to the preservation of things past and a recognition of the realities of the present and future; a human tendency to exploit the natural resources of the surrounding countryside and a growing awareness of the vital need to protect the environment.

Orillia has done a commendable job in meeting the challenge. More industries have set up shop in the town (which became a city in 1969). The population has grown steadily, from 5,050 in 1895 to 22,344 in 1975—with more than half of that increase occurring in the last 20 years. The cottage frontier has moved further north now, through the Muskokas to the French River, Parry Sound, the Sudbury region and beyond, but Orillia continues to be the main supply base for great numbers of summer vacationers.

Orillia is also well known for its school for the mentally retarded. It was begun by Dr. Alexander Beaton in 1878. Dr. Beaton's philosophy and methods were very progressive for his time. His school's avowed purpose was to train each resident to the limit of his or her ability. The school was soon overcrowded, and in 1885 a tract of some 150 acres on Lake Simcoe was purchased. Here, two residences and an administration centre were built, and the new institution opened its doors in 1890. By 1902, it was caring for no fewer than 654 residents.

As one reflection of Dr. Beaton's belief in training rather than mere custodial care, a highly successful farm was operated by his charges. Consisting of some fifty-five acres of farm and garden land, plus an equal acreage for pasture, the operation produced almost all of the vegetables and fruit, most of the milk, and some of the meat served in the residency dining rooms.

Beaton's uncompromisingly high standards, and his impatience with public ignorance as to the nature of mental retardation, often brought him into conflict with administrators, politicians and members of the general public. But by the time of his retirement in 1910, at the age of seventy-two, he had earned international recognition as a pioneer in special education and as a reigning authority in the care of the mentally retarded, and he had been the twice-elected president of what was to become the American Association of Mental Deficiency.

Despite some periodic declines in the quality of care and

teaching provided, and a chronic problem with overcrowd-
ing, the hospital-school generally kept pace with the steadily
more enlightened training and treatment methods that were
developed around the world. More buildings were added: in
1915, 1926, 1933, and 1945. At the same time, the number
of residents continued to grow: from 1,300 in 1926 to 2,460
in 1949.

Among Dr. Beaton's successors as Superintendent, Dr.
Bernard T. McGhie, who served from 1927 to 1930, was
probably the most progressive. It was his belief and policy
that the institution had a moral and professional responsibility to help all residents to develop the abilities they had, and
to learn all that they were capable of learning. This outlook
was pursued by Dr. S. J. W. Horne, who succeeded McGhie
in 1931.

The Orillia hospital-school, along with all other such provincial institutions, was taken over by the Mental Retardation Services Branch of the Ontario Department of Health in
July, 1965.

During the lumbering boom Orillia had been a brawling,
rowdy town, a renowned drinking centre, with as many as
twenty-nine saloons and bars. A strong temperance movement
gradually rooted these out, however, and Orillia became one
of the driest communities in Ontario. It wasn't until the late
1960s that the "wets" finally won out over the "drys," making it possible to get a drink at cocktail lounges, taverns and
licensed dining rooms along the main street and elsewhere.

Orillia today has its quota of sprawling shopping centres,
high-rise apartment buildings, and drive-in hamburger and
southern fried chicken franchises, but there are still many
residential streets, shaded in summer by tall trees, where
gracious brick houses of the late-Victorian period are surrounded by trim lawns and well-cared-for flower gardens.
And, in the mid-1970s, old men and young boys walk down
to the waterfront, with their fishing rods and minnow-
buckets and cans of worms, to try for perch, pickerel and
bass, just as they have done for a century and a half or more.

6 The Great War, 1914-18

As winter gradually relinquished its hold on the land in the spring of 1914, residents of Simcoe County thought of many familiar things associated with the changing of the seasons: digging in vegetable gardens, spring cleaning, making or buying a new bonnet for Easter Sunday, when the suckers would start running up the streams and rivers, fences that needed to be mended, or getting out baseball gloves for the year's first game of catch.

Nothing could have been further from their minds than that they would shortly become intimately involved in the most terrible war the world had ever known. To be sure, there had been mutterings in their weekly newspapers about "the growing international tension in Europe," and for years Imperial Germany had been building up its naval power to challenge Great Britain's supremacy of the seas; but these were matters that would be dealt with by the "Mother Country" on behalf of the British Empire, and that needn't trouble ordinary Canadians.

Thus, little attention was paid to the assassination of the Archduke Ferdinand, heir to the throne of Austria-Hungary, at an obscure Balkan city called Sarajevo in May, 1914. This incident seemed far away, and to have little to do with daily life in Alliston or Victoria Harbour or Washago. Yet, less than three months later, it led to the German invasion of Belgium, Luxembourg and France. An ultimatum protesting the violation of Belgian neutrality was ignored by Berlin, and upon its expiration at midnight, August 4, 1914, Great Britain was at war with Germany.

So too, as a member of the British Empire, was Canada.

During the first days of the War, crowds gathered in front of newspaper offices throughout Simcoe County to read the bulletins that were posted as wires came in from overseas. The news was received with a mixture of astonishment, solemnity and excitement, as people wondered what it would mean for themselves, their families, their communities and their country.

Along with other Canadians, County residents had had almost no experience with war and shared no real military tradition. There had been voluntary militia units in Collingwood, Barrie, Midland and Orillia since as early as the 1850s, their training consisting of weekly marching drills and annual trips to summer camps. A few district men had gone to the Niagara frontier to help fight off the Fenian Raid in 1866; some went west in the 1870s and 1880s to assist in the quelling of the first and second Riel Rebellions; and a dozen or so had taken part in the South African War against the Boers at the turn of the century. But there were no more than a handful of professional soldiers in Simcoe County in 1914. One of them, Orillia's Samuel Benfield Steele, had seen action in the Fenian Raid, participated in both Riel Rebellions, and commanded Lord Strathcona's Horse in the South African War; he would become commanding officer of the famed Second Canadian Division in France and be knighted for his services in 1917.

The citizens of Simcoe County could neither know, nor understand Sir Samuel's world; yet, when war broke out, their sense of patriotism was unrestrained, and their commitment to the British cause was unquestioning and unconditional. On the Wednesday evening, twenty-four hours after the declaration of war, the Orillia militia, led by the Collegiate Institute bugle band, paraded along muddy Mississaga Street in their red coats and white helmets, to the cheers of hundreds of local supporters. There were similar rallies in Barrie, Collingwood, Midland, Penetang and Alliston. Every newspaper in the County gave editorial endorsement to full participation in the war—so did the Simcoe County Council at its next monthly meeting and so did the ministers from their pulpits, regardless of creed. Young men, anxious to enlist, poured into hastily set up recruiting centres in the towns and major villages.

There was an air of adventure, of camaraderie, of good-humoured excitement. Everyone anticipated that the war would be won within a few months, and that the boys would be home, polishing their medals, by Christmas. The great fear of most recruits was that it would be all over before they were posted overseas and had a chance to "take part in the fun." They should not have feared—there would be plenty of time.

The Simcoe regiment had been organized in 1866, and towards the end of the century became known as the 35th Regiment Simcoe Foresters, with the motto *Spectemur agendo*, "By our deeds, let us be known." On August 20, 1914 scarcely more than two weeks after the outbreak of hostilities, advance volunteers from this unit were on their way east. Their departure was described by the Barrie *Examiner* on August 22:

The citizens turned out en masse Thursday morning to witness the departure of the 35th regiment contingent of the Overseas Expeditionary Forces for Valcartier, Quebec, where the whole Canadian contingent is being mobilized. . . . The Citizen's Band turned out in full force Thursday morning, and escorted the volunteers to the depot, playing the regimental march and other patriotic airs. Short addresses were made at the depot by Mayor Cowan of Barrie and Mayor Goffatt of Orillia, while rousing cheers were given for the gallant volunteers. Although there were many sad partings, and the eyes of many in the crowd were tear-dimmed, the volunteers appeared to be a happy lot, and answered the call to arms with cheerfulness. They are a sturdy lot, and are sure to do honour to their Empire, their King and the grand old 35th Regiment, Simcoe Foresters.

The contingent was under the command of Major Preece of Orillia, and included men from Barrie, Midland, Orillia and Collingwood—a very high percentage of whom would never see their hometowns again. At Valcartier they became part of the First Canadian Division, went overseas, and after further training on the Salisbury plains, were in position on the Western Front by the end of February, 1915.

Scarcely two months later, on April 23, the Germans used poison gas for the first time in the history of warfare at the Second Battle of Ypres. Other sectors of the front fell back, but the Canadians, choking and half-blinded, held fast in the face of heavy enemy fire. It was an heroic action which helped to prevent a disastrous Allied defeat, but the cost in lives was dreadful. By the end of the battle, the First Canadian Division had suffered 5,403 casualties: 3,241 killed or missing in action, and 2,162 wounded.

As news of the terrible struggle reached Simcoe County and was read in the bulletins posted in newspaper office windows, the horror of what lay ahead was realized for the first time. On Thursday, April 29, the Orillia *Packet* published both a letter from Captain John Donald Glover, whose parents lived in the town, and the news that he had been killed in action at Ypres. In its next edition, it announced that his brother Norman had also given his life. Many other telegrams beginning with the terrible words, "We regret to inform you . . . ," were delivered to homes throughout the County.

The first reaction was one of shock; the second was a firm determination to send as many more men overseas as might prove necessary to finish the job that had been so gallantly started. All over the County recruiting efforts were stepped up. In July, 1915, for example, a recruiting team visited Beeton. A large crowd attended the subsequent rally, the Beeton band played patriotic music, speeches were made, and six local men enlisted.

Advertisements appeared in local newspapers: "Your King and Country Need *You!*" In his sermon on Sunday, August 10, 1915, Orillia's Archdeacon Cody reflected the feelings of most of his fellow clergymen, when he said, "Every man and every dollar sent helps to hasten a just and permanent peace. It is not a time for men to say 'Why should I go?,' but rather

to ask themselves, 'Why have I not gone? . . . The future
of Canada is at stake, as well as the future of the British
Empire.''

That same week a giant recruiting rally took place in Orillia when more than 4,000 people assembled in Couchiching
Park to listen to bands and speeches. When it was over, some
$8,000 had been subscribed by local citizens for the purchase
of machine guns and ambulances, and, according to the Orillia *Packet*, thirty-three young men had come forward to
enlist.

Shortly afterwards, the idea of recruiting and forming a
County Battalion was born. The first official move in this
direction was a meeting called by A. T. Potter, Warden of
the County, in Barrie on October 5, 1915. The plan won the
immediate endorsement of the Orillia Recruiting Committee
and similar organizations in Barrie, Collingwood, Midland
and elsewhere, and soon captured the imagination of the general public, who supported it enthusiastically.

Results were dramatic. By the first of November, 150
men had enlisted, and recruits kept pouring in from all over
the County. As Christmas drew near, the number had swelled
to over 400. "One more charge, gentlemen, and the day is
ours!" the Orillia *Packet* proclaimed triumphantly in its first
edition of 1916. Before the end of January the First Simcoes,
the 157th Battalion, was up to full strength. The event was
celebrated at a giant rally in the Orillia armouries, highlighted
by the playing of the regimental march, "Cock o' the North,"
and the announcement that recruiting for a second Battalion, the 177th, would begin immediately.

The enthusiasm of the new recruits was more than a little
dampened by the fact that no uniforms were available, forc-
ing them to drill in civilian clothes for some weeks, identifi-
able as soldiers only by the armbands they wore. Nor, at
first, were there any rifles, the recruits having to be content
with locally-produced wooden dummies.

The officers of the 157th were keen and dedicated, but
almost totally lacking in wartime experience. The Adjutant,

for instance, was Captain Frederick Norman Grandy, a schoolteacher who had had charge of the Barrie Collegiate Institute's cadet corps; he was to die on the Western Front. An exception was Sergeant-Major James Johnstone of Orillia, a career soldier who had fought with distinction in the South African War as a member of the famed Black Watch. At the outbreak of hostilities, Johnstone was the Chief of Police in Collingwood, but he enlisted for service with the Simcoes and became one of the key figures in their success overseas.

Despite the lack of uniforms and rifles, military life was far from unpleasant for the new recruits of the 157th Battalion. To help the recruiting effort, they frequently marched to smaller centres in the County, where they were inevitably served a good hot dinner by the women of some local church auxiliary or similar organization, and were frequently entertained by a concert or invited to a dance. On Sunday mornings they paraded to church services, led by the 157th band—the objects of admiring glances from all sides. In the towns in which they were stationed, Barrie, Orillia, Midland and Collingwood, there was an endless round of banquets and other social affairs in their honour.

It had been expected that they would go to Niagara to complete their training, but conditions there were hopelessly overcrowded. As far back as 1904 the Department of Militia had considered purchasing land in Essa and Tosorontio townships for the purpose of establishing a new military base, but no action had been taken. By the sping of 1916, however, the situation had become acute, and in May the Minister of Militia, Sir Sam Hughes, toured the Simcoe County site.

A few days later, the government announced that a huge training camp, to be called "Camp Borden," would be established there, some fifteen miles west of Barrie. To accommodate it, an area of almost 17,000 acres, locally known as "the Plains," had been purchased. The sandy soil of the area had once been shaded by giant pines, but these had all been cut by the J. B. Smith Company of Angus, with only thousands of stumps remaining to mark their earlier existence.

Plans called for the new camp to open in July on that year, less than two months after the announcement. It was a formidable challenge; to meet it, imposing logistical requirements, including the following, would have to be satisfied:

— a network of concrete and asphalt roads, covering almost six miles in all;
— enough street lights to service a large town;
— a water supply of almost two million gallons a day;
— 15 miles of wrought-iron mains;
— 1500 taps, 300 showers;
— an up-to-date sewage system, meeting all sanitary requirements, for some 40,000 men (more than the combined populations of Barrie, Orillia, Midland and Collingwood);
— a bakery, capable of supplying 25,000 loaves of bread each day.

Incredibly, with the help of the Barrie and Collingwood Companies of the 157th Battalion, it was all accomplished on time. Early in June, the Simcoes became the first military formation to move into the extraordinary "tent city" that had risen on the dusty plains of Camp Borden. By Saturday, July 8, there were almost 40,000 men under canvas in that sprawling, dust-choked staging area.

The great opening parade and march was held on Tuesday, July 11, with some 30,000 troops, led by dozens of bands, taking part. Hour after hour, the brigades and battalions marched past, while stirring martial airs echoed across the Plains. The temperature was in the high eighties, and many a recruit fainted in the burning sun and parched air. Still, it was an impressive sight, well calculated to feed patriotic fires.

Heat, sand and dust continued to plague the troops throughout that first summer. Yet, with the rolling plains stretching away to the majesty of the distant Blue Mountains, it was a magnificent setting, and few who were there will

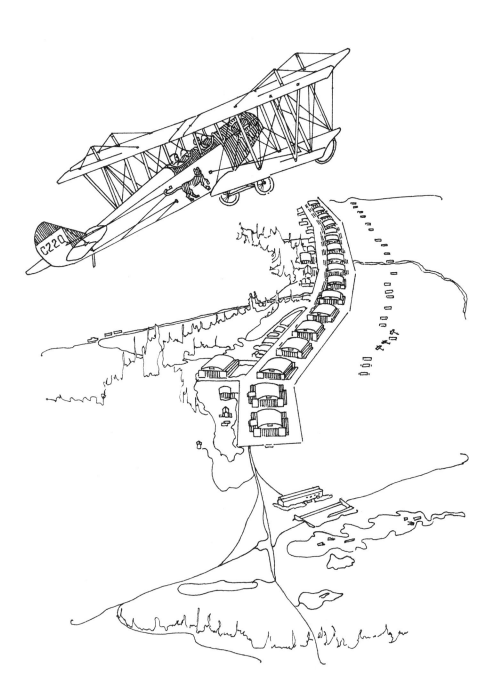

Curtiss JN4 (Can.). "Canuck," above Camp Borden, 1918

ever forget the emotion-stirring ritual that was enacted with the setting of each day's sun. As the daylight faded, bands throughout the camp would play their regimental anthems, one after another. Following that, the gripping notes of the "Last Post" would be heard, first sounded by the Headquarter's bugler, then taken up by other battalion soloists, so that they swelled and at last faded away on the clear, starlit night air. A description of one such enactment was written by J. L. Gilmour, and appeared in the Orillia *Packet* in October, 1916:

As darkness gathered, the different regimental bands stood ready to move, each accompanied by torch-bearers. At the proper signal, when the time appointed arrived, these bands moved out into place, the torches shining out against the darkness, and the band itself playing in each case its own regimental march. As each new band approached the assembly-ground, the bands already in position took up the march of the newcomer. The result of this was to gradually increase the volume of sound, so that when the last of the 28 bands marched forward, the effect was very marked.

It seemed to me that especially impressive were two—'O, Canada' and 'We'll Never Let the Old Flag Fall,' and it was quite easy to understand the emotion that swept over the throng.

In the second part of the programme, the playing by the 28 bands of 'Keep the Home Fires Burning' brought out the love of home in these men, whose faces turned towards the East, and towards the day of battle. . . .

But perhaps the most impressive of all the programme was the rendering of 'Abide with Me.' At this time the evening glow had died out of the West, and the deep-blue sky above our heads, dotted with bright stars, was the stately proof of our open-air cathedral.

Throughout the remainder of that summer, training was stepped up, as the troops prepared to go overseas. The 157th Battalion was part of the 2nd Infantry Brigade, under the command of Colonel John A. Currie. In the Brigade were two Simcoe Battalions, the Muskoka Battalion, and a battalion from Toronto. The musketry officer was Major Vincent Massey, who would become the Governor General of Canada many years later.

In 1917, Camp Borden was expanded and redesigned to in-
corporate a training school for Great Britain's Royal Flying
Corps (at that time Canada had not yet established her own
air force, although many Canadians were flying with the RFC
—including such international aces as Billy Bishop, William
Barker, and Roy Brown).

After the decision to build the airfield was made in late
January, 1917, the enormous task of turning plans into reality proceeded with amazing speed. By February 4, the
branch line from Angus to Borden, which had been shut
down for the winter, was reopened, and some 400 men from
the surrounding district were at work clearing the stumps—
in temperatures which often reached -20° F. That task force
soon swelled to some 1,800 men and more than 100 teams
of horses, as work proceeded on a 24-hour basis, with night
shifts operating under powerful arc lights.

Within four short months 850 acres of land had been
cleared of stumps, levelled and seeded with grass; 57 buildings had been erected, including 15 hangars; a railway siding
had been completed, as had 4.7 miles of asphalt roads; sewage and electrical systems were in full operation; and wire
and telephone communications linked the new camp with
Toronto, Ottawa and Royal Flying Headquarters in London.
In late March, well ahead of schedule, the first five squad-
rons had arrived from Britain, and about the same time the
first Canadian cadets reported for training. Although the
camp was not officially opened until June, the first flights
from Borden began on March 30 in Curtiss JN-4 aircraft
brought in by train and assembled in the hangars.

The first class of 40 cadets received their wings in June,
1917, and by the end of October of that year 1,081 Royal
Flying Corps pilots had graduated and proceeded overseas.
By the end of the war, that number had increased to 1,884.

With the birth of the Royal Canadian Air Force in 1920,
Camp Borden became its chief training centre, and is still regarded as "the home of the Service" by most who learned to
fly there during the next decade. By 1930, however, most of

the buildings were beginning to deteriorate, and many of the functions and responsibilities were transferred to the huge new R.C.A.F. station at Trenton, Ontario.

Later, when World War II came, Borden regained prominence as the Canadian centre for intermediate training, while Trenton was responsible for advanced instruction. In 1940, Borden began training pilots and other air crew personnel for the British Commonwealth Air Training Plan, and graduated thousands of airmen from all parts of the Commonwealth before hostilities came to an end in 1945. During this period, it was designated as "No. 1 Service Flying Training School" and saw 2,728 pilots receive their wings. In 1946, Borden was reorganized to become "No. 2 Technical Training School," the R.C.A.F.'s major centre for producing the highly skilled ground crew technicians who keep the planes flying in "the wild, blue yonder."

But, back in 1916, the first troops were ready to leave Camp Borden in the fall. On October 1 the teachers of Simcoe County presented the 157th Battalion with its colours, an occasion described in the Barrie *Examiner* as follows:

Long before noon the crowds began to assemble, and by two o'clock the largest crowd which has yet assembled before the departure of any overseas battalion surged through the lines. . . .

The Battalion was the centre of the immense crowd of visitors. . . . It was an impressive scene, with the khaki sons of Simcoe silhouetted against the background of shrubs and trees to the west, and the sea of faces forming the other three sides of the square. . . .

The ceremony commenced with the band marching in slow time to the tune of 'Coming through the Rye,' then returning to the spirited strains of 'The Girl I Left Behind Me.' The drums were then stacked, and the brilliant colours placed against them.

Three days later, the 157th went on a week's embarkation leave. It was a time of gaiety and sadness, of laughter and tears, of excitement and sober realization. There were social gatherings and countless patriotic speeches in almost every town and village in Simcoe County. Barrie, the county town, threw a great banquet to mark the occasion; the Orillia and Coldwater contingents were similarly honoured and entertained in Stephen Leacock's town.

On October 9, it was time for the men to report back for duty. The day was warm and sunny, and the autumn trees were afire with brilliant reds, golds and yellows. The departure of the Orillia detachment was described in the *Packet*:

At the Park a huge crowd gathered, running into several thousands. But, as there was plenty of room, there was comparatively little crowding. A dozen or more extra lights had been strung along the side of the track and as it was moonlight, the scene was brightly lighted. The interval of fifteen or twenty minutes was employed in saying final 'good-byes,' and promptly at 8:30 the train pulled out. There was little cheering; people were not in the humour for that, but many calls of 'good-bye,' and the largest contingent Orillia has yet sent was off.

Four days later, on October 13, the 157th left Borden on board two special trains, and the following Thursday, October 19, the troops sailed from Halifax on the *Cameronia*.

Bitter news awaited them on their arrival in England. The men of Simcoe County had built up a strong sense of pride in their Battalion, and hoped and believed that they would go to the Western Front as a unit. But it was not to be. Almost immediately, 150 men were drafted to the 1st Battalion in France, and by early December the remainder were scattered among other Battalions, including the 19th, the 116th and the 125th.

The terrible blood bath of the Somme was just coming to an end, and reinforcements were desperately needed at the front. Yet the ruthless manner in which the proud Simcoe Battalion was broken up was a severe blow to the morale of the men overseas, and later had a serious negative effect on further recruiting efforts in the County.

Throughout the war, the troops overseas received unstinting support from the home front. Hundreds of women went to work in the munition plants, learned how to operate machines, and put in long hours to help meet production requirements. Because these jobs demanded greater mobility, the hobbling, ankle-length skirts that had been popular before the war disappeared, and hem lines crept steadily upwards until they almost reached the knee.

Other groups of women knit countless pairs of wool socks and mitts to be sent to the boys at the front.

There was a patriotic rally almost every week in some Simcoe County town or village, each with its quota of military music and stirring speakers. There was a constant round of social events and entertainments to raise money for machine guns, band instruments, and comforts for the men overseas: concerts, dances, fowl suppers, bake sales, sporting events, quilting bees, and so on.

In Beeton, for instance, a Red Cross unit was established early in 1915, to be joined by a branch of the Canadian Patriotic League a few months later. Between them, an all-out effort to support the fighting troops was continued until after the final victory. Garden parties, some attended by up to one thousand guests, were hosted by such leading citizens as the Howard Wallwins and Mrs. D. A. Jones. Raffles and sales of homemade jams and jellies brought in more funds. So did the proceeds of "Red Cross Sale Days," conducted by local merchants. As one result of all these activities, hundreds of surgical kits and thousands of home-rolled bandages were shipped from Beeton to the Western Front.

As the war dragged on, and natural and human resources were strained to the limit, there was a general belt-tightening on the home front. Many stores were closed on Saturdays and Mondays to conserve fuel. A "Victory Garden" campaign was launched, by which residents of towns and villages were encouraged to grow their own food. Hundreds of backyards in Barrie, Orillia, Midland, Collingwood and other communities were dug up and planted with potatoes, beans, carrots, peas and beets; so was the track for harness racing in Orillia.

In the rural areas, farmers brought every last acre into production, including scrub land which would not normally have been worth plowing. With so many rural sons in uniform, there was a severe shortage of farm help which caused a major problem in harvesting the crops. Wives and daughters, retired farmers, high school students from the towns, and others worked long hours in the fields, but there was still a crying need for more experienced hands at harvest time. As the hard-pressed farmers said, they could not be expected "to fight and farm at the same time"; yet they did their best, using whatever makeshift help was available, and somehow brought in record yields throughout the war.

Meanwhile, the men of the Simcoes were enduring conditions along the Western Front which can be described, but never really understood, except by those who were actually there. Due largely to the stupidity and monstrous incompetence of both Allied and German High Command strategists, millions of soldiers died or were maimed, blinded and turned into human vegetables in the taking, defense, and retaking of "strategic objectives" within a totally destroyed area not many times larger than Simcoe County. Again and again, thousands were killed in contesting possession of a few hundred square-yards of waist-deep mud, in which ambulance-bearers could only gain traction by stepping on the bodies of those who had fallen earlier.

In March, 1919, David Lloyd George, the British Prime Minister, tried with all his eloquence to capture what it had been like for those who had survived the unspeakable horrors of the Western Front. He told the British Parliament:

It was not valour they displayed; it was not even heroism; it was something so new and terrible; so undreamed of, that man has created no new word for it. I try to find some word to define it, to suggest it; I can't. The nearest word I can get is 'endurance.'

They were in peril of death, and worse than death, day after day, night after night; and they endured. They were exposed to all the nerve-shattering rage of artillery, artillery which rived the soil like an earthquake, which hurled the bodies of the dead into the air, and flung the bodies of the living into a deeper sepulchre; and they endured.

They went into the darkness to storm the trenches of the enemy, to destroy machine-gun nests, to break a line of fire, the very thunders of which deafened the men; and they endured. . .

They lived in mud, and worse than mud; they lived in unutterable filth, breathing an air that choked the lungs with disgust; their young bodies attacked by vermin, their feet sinking into squalor, their hands touching at every turn things which one dare not speak about. . . .

There they lived, always in the presence of death. . . . and they endured.

But not even he could capture the hell that it was: rats, the wet, the eternal mud, the stench of the rotting corpses of friends, the deprivation and loneliness, the desperate weariness, the fear. The men of the Simcoe Battalions came to know all of this, and to know it all too well. In company with thousands of other Canadians, they fought and died in battle after battle, the Somme, Vimy Ridge, Hill 70, Passchendaele, Cambrai, Arras, Amiens, Canal du Nord, Arleux, Fresnoy, the Mons.

Meanwhile, back home the weekly newspapers of Simcoe County reported details of the lengthening lists of local sons killed in action, missing, captured and wounded. In its five issues of May, 1917, for example, the Orillia *Packet* identified twenty-six district men who had given their lives on the Western Front, plus another twenty-five who were in military hospitals with serious wounds. The same papers also carried stories of many heroic actions performed, and battle honours won by men of the County.

The last great German offensive was turned back in the late summer of 1918, and through the shortening days of that fall the Allied armies drove towards the heartland of Germany, advancing yard-by-yard at first, then mile-by-mile, as the enemy lines crumbled. The Canadian soldiers, including the men from Simcoe, had long since established a reputation as being among the best assault troops on the Western Front, and they were in the vanguard of the assault that was to bring final victory.

A crushed Germany finally accepted the surrender terms offered to her, and the Armistice was signed in General Foch's private railway car on a siding near Amiens in the

early morning of November 11, 1918. The guns fell silent
and the terrible war came to an end at the 11th hour of the
11th day of the 11th month of that year.

The long-awaited news reached Simcoe County in mid-
afternoon of that historic day and touched off joyous celebrations in towns, villages and hamlets. The dreadful ordeal was
over at last.

All across the County church bells peeled out as the early
twilight of that grey November day settled over the countryside.

In Beeton, a public holiday was declared, stores were
closed, flags and decorations appeared everywhere, and a
giant torchlight parade, led by a military band, passed along
Centre Street and then up Main. Scores of bonfires were
lit, and the cheering continued on well into the following
morning.

In Barrie, Mayor Sprott also proclaimed a holiday for the
following day. It was a gala occasion long to be remembered.
Excited, relieved people filled the streets early, with young
people starting impromptu parades, using whatever they
could lay their hands on to make noise. At 9:30 A.M. there
was a mass meeting at the Opera House where people of
every class and creed assembled to give expression to their
joy and thanksgiving. In the afternoon a procession, nearly
two miles long, with every vehicle decorated with flags and
bunting, wended its way from the Town Hall, around the
town and back to the Market Square, where the band led the
people in singing patriotic songs, such as "Rule, Brittania,"
"Red, White and Blue," "The Maple Leaf," and "O,
Canada." The celebrations continued far into the night.

If joy was not completely unrestrained, it was because of a
terrible epidemic that had been sweeping around the world,
including Canada, and was causing thousands of deaths each
day. Popularly known as the "Spanish 'Flu," it was a particularly deadly type of influenza which made its first appearance in Simcoe County some five or six weeks before the

signing of the Armistice.

In retrospect, the County was somewhat fortunate in that, while the epidemic struck with terrible impact, it ran its course in a comparatively short number of weeks. The awesome scourge of the Spanish 'Flu can be followed via the pages of the Collingwood *Enterprise*. The first mention of an emergency situation appeared in the October 17, 1918 edition of that weekly newspaper in the form of an ad placed by the Collingwood Board of Health. Under the headline "Wanted —Volunteers!" it read in part:

The Provincial Board of Health, with the authority of the Government of Ontario, has organized an Ontario Emergency Volunteer Health Auxiliary for the purpose of training and supplying nursing help to be utilized whenever needed in combating the Influenza outbreak. . . . The Volunteer Nurses will wear the officially authorized badge 'Ontario S.O.S.' (Sisters of the Service). . . . If they are not needed, so much the better; if they are needed, we hope to have them ready.

A week later, October 24, the *Enterprise* stated that seventy cases of 'flu had been reported in Collingwood. The G. and M. hospital was crowded to capacity, with extra beds set up in the corridors, and the Y.M.C.A. was being used to accommodate overflow patients. There was a critical shortage of everything, including doctors, several of whom had themselves fallen victim to the disease.

In that same edition, Bell Telephone placed this notice: "The operating staff has been seriously depleted by the present epidemic. At the same time, so many people are ill at home that the telephone has been used continuously. PLEASE USE YOUR TELEPHONE ONLY WHEN ABSOLUTELY NECESSARY!"

By October 31, the Nottawasaga Board of Health had passed a resolution closing all schools in the township, and prohibiting church services, concerts, sporting events and all other public gatherings.

Collingwood, like most other communities in Simcoe County, was like a town under siege. More and more cases were reported every day. The All Saints' Parish House was turned into another emergency hospital. Stores were closed. It was barely possible to keep up vital services and supplies; for almost a week the town was without fresh bread, as several bakers were stricken.

People tried every possible measure to ward off the disease—wearing surgical masks, disinfecting their homes with widely advertised commercial products like Johnson's "Kreoline," brewing evil-smelling, home-remedy concoctions with such ingredients as kerosene, pine-tar, skunk oil, sulphur, mustard and garlic.

But nothing seemed to work. Of course, many victims survived the ordeal. The *Enterprise* of October 31 carried this short notice: "Russell B. Weatherup, having recently recovered from an attack of Influenza, has thoroughly fumigated his barber shop, and is re-opened for business."

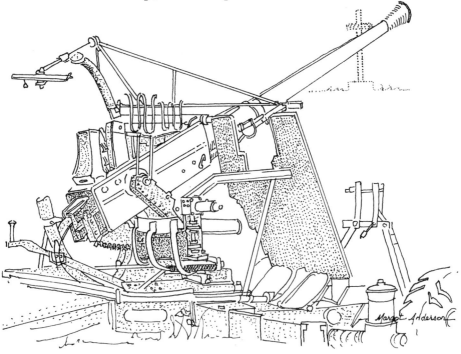

"In Memory of Those of Our Village Who Gave Their Lives" (*Victoria Harbour*)

But many other victims, especially the elderly, did not recover. Each week the *Enterprise* listed those who had died, the peak coming in the first week of November when eleven local deaths were listed.

Then, as suddenly and mysteriously as it had appeared, the Spanish 'Flu departed the scene. There were no additional deaths in Collingwood after November 7, and by the middle of the month no new cases were being reported. On November 14, the Nottawasaga Medical Health Officer removed all of the emergency restrictions, public meetings were again permitted, and churches, schools and theatres reopened their doors. The public library reopened a week later.

On November 23 the *Enterprise* ran a full-page spread, headed, "COLLINGWOOD IN FULL SWING—The 'Flu Has Passed. . . . Everything Now Going On As Usual."

In the rest of Simcoe County, too, the worst was over, although in some other parts of Ontario the epidemic continued well into the winter.

During the first six months of 1919, the soldiers and sailors, nursing sisters and airmen who had served with the Royal Flying Corps came home. There were tearful and joyful reunions with loved ones at railway stations in communities, large and small, throughout the County. Bands played, presentations were made, parades moved proudly along main streets, and countless speeches were delivered in tribute to the dedication and courage of the returning warriors.

Yet, there was a terrible sadness for the many, many fine young men who would never come back. A great victory had indeed been won, but at a dreadful, outrageous price.

Every town, every village, every rural district in Simcoe County was the poorer. There were so many dead: 59 out of the 393 who had enlisted from Orillia; 79 from Barrie; 41 from Innisfil township; 23 from Vespra; 28 from Oro; 107 from Collingwood; 31 from Penetanguishene; on and on.

But numbers on a printed page do not really begin to tell

the story. The best way now to get a feeling for the awful sacrifices that were made in the name of King, Empire and country, is to take a day and drive around the County, searching out the war memorials and plaques in each community, and getting out of your car to read the engraved names. The cumulative effect makes you begin to understand.

There is, for instance, a memorial in a small, well-maintained park on the edge of Victoria Harbour—a limestone cross, erected on a base of red granite stones, cemented together. An anti-aircraft gun, a relic of World War II, is positioned to one side. As you stand there, you look over the houses of the village to the waters of Georgian Bay. There are fifteen names on the bronze plaque dedicated to those who gave their lives in the Great War, listed alphabetically from BOURRIE, Napoleon to the WALDIE brothers, W. Scott and C. Percival.

And, reading those names, you get at least a sense of what it must have meant to this little community of some 1,400 residents and 300-odd homes to lose those 15 young men. So many familiar faces missing, so many beds that would never be slept in again. Did a son leave that red brick house just down the road, to die at Arras . . . or Courcelette . . . or Vimy Ridge? Were the responsibilities of raising a young family left to a war-widow who lived in the place with the sagging roof a bit further on?

Perhaps one home in twenty experienced intimate family loss, while the whole village shared in the sorrow and grief of neighbours and friends. Multiply the anguish of that one community many times, and you begin to have some understanding of what it cost Simcoe County to do its part in achieving the final victory.

7 The Postwar Years

For Simcoe County, as for the rest of Canada, the end of the war did not immediately bring prosperity and good times. Instead, a quite serious depression hung over the land until the mid-1920s. It was primarily caused by a shortage of consumer goods, which led to world-wide inflation.

With the signing of the Armistice in November, 1918, the demand for munitions and armaments suddenly dried up, and plants that had converted to wartime production were forced to shut down, throwing hundreds of employees out of work. The return of the servicemen compounded the problem, and many a veteran was embittered to discover that the country he had given so much to defend was unable to provide a job for him. The situation would gradually correct itself, but at the time it was a hard pill to swallow.

One pleasant diversion in the twenties was provided by the highly popular variety group of singers, dancers and comedians known as the "Dumbells." Organized overseas while members of the Third Division, they had enjoyed great success in entertaining Canadian troops during the later stages of the war. The Dumbells had a strong Orillia flavour, featuring four members of the Plunkett family from that town. Captain Morley Plunkett, who had gone to France as a Y.M.C.A. officer, was the troop's organizational boss, and three other Plunketts, Merton, Fred and Al, were among its star performers. Other members, not from Simcoe County, included Ross Hamilton, Pat Rafferty, and the inimitable Red Newman. During 1917 and 1918 the Dumbells had received considerable moral and financial support from the people of Orillia, particularly through teas, concerts and similar entertainments organized by Mrs. George Clarke, Mrs. Samuel Kerr, and other leading Orillia citizens.

After the Armistice, the Dumbells decided to stay together, and for another decade or more they played to capacity houses in theatres throughout Ontario, and beyond. There has probably never been a more popular group of Canadian entertainers. Wherever they went—Belleville, Kingston, Peterborough, Owen Sound, North Bay, Sudbury, London, Windsor—they drew large audiences and made people laugh. No one fortunate enough to have heard them will ever forget their rendition of "Oh, It's a Lovely War," a song that retained almost as much emotional impact at their final performance in the 1930s as it had enjoyed when they first sang it, close to the front lines, in 1917.

And, despite the generally depressed economic climate, progress was, of course, made in Simcoe County during the years following the Great War. To cite a few random examples:

— the Coldwater Continuation School opened in 1923;

— that same year, in recognition of the growing motor traffic, a 25 m.p.h. speed limit was established throughout the County;

— Innisfil Park, approved by a vote among ratepayers in 1922, was opened and proved even more popular than had been predicted;

— the Stayner Horticultural Society held its first meeting in 1923;

— the Elmvale waterworks opened in 1925.

The first aerial survey photo ever taken in Simcoe County was shot in the Angus area on July 16, 1927. Filmed from an altitude of 10,000 feet, it was one of a series made by the National Air Photo Library.

By then, of course, most County residents no longer considered flying a mad cap occupation. Bush pilots, almost all veterans of the Royal Flying Corps, were providing more or less regular service from such places as Orillia, Penetanguishene, Midland and Collingwood to prospectors' camps and mining operations in northern Ontario. During the war, training planes from Camp Borden had become as familiar a sight in the skies as Model 'T' Fords were on district roads. County residents remembered that the student pilots had made an inordinate number of "forced landings" in Orillia, Barrie, Elmvale, Midland, Stayner, Beeton and other communities and attributed the phenomenon more to amorous successes than to mechanical failures.

The first recorded flight in Simcoe County dates back to the summer of 1913. In June of that year, as the result of negotiations between the Beeton Celebration Committee and the Curtiss Aeroplane Company of New York. a famous pioneer aviator named Roger Niles arrived in Beeton to carry out a series of exhibition flights.

When his Curtiss aircraft arrived on a railway flatcar, half the town went down to the siding to see it. A fragile creation of bamboo, silk and wires, the biplane measured forty feet from hardwood propeller to tail-skid, and the same distance from wing tip to wing tip. It was powered by a 75 horse power motor, mounted behind the cockpit. Many local residents expressed doubts that the thing would ever get off the ground, but others (perhaps secure in the knowledge that Niles had no room for passengers) said that they would like nothing more than to be taken for a ride.

On the great day, June 3, 1913, people flocked into Beeton from near and far to witness the spectacle, hundreds arriving by special trains from various points. It was a gala occasion, a small town's version of the Roman Circus. Special constables had been appointed to control the crowd. Bands from Alliston, Ivy, Cookstown, Tottenham and other points played constantly. Hawkers sold souvenirs; families enjoyed picnic lunches wherever they could find space to spread out a table cloth or blanket; young men and women flirted; boys and girls played games, scraped their knees and threw stones.

Finally, just after 3 o'clock, the biplane was wheeled out onto the race track in the Fair Grounds, being pushed by dozens of willing hands. About ten minutes later, while four men held the plane down, its propeller was spun and its engine roared into life. Next, it was racing along the track, gaining speed, trailing a cloud of dust behind it—and then, wonder of wonders, the wheels had left the ground, and it was slowly climbing into the sky.

Niles gave the crowd its money's worth, banking, side-slipping, pulling out of dives at tree level. The climax of the show came when the Curtiss biplane easily out-distanced a racing car driven around the track oval by R. W. Brett of Shelburne.

A reporter for the *Beeton World* accurately caught the fascination and awe of the spectators, when he wrote that "the aviator climbed to 1500 feet, in the upper strata of the atmosphere!"

A month later, it was Barrie's turn to thrill to the wonder of the new flying machines. The Dominion Day holiday at the beginning of July was celebrated with particular enthusiasm that year, because it marked Barrie's Diamond Jubilee —sixty years as a town. All weekend visitors poured in, in-

Bryson's Bread Delivery, Barrie, 1927

cluding several hundred who arrived on board the steamers *Islay*, *Otonabee* and *Monarch*, which ran special excursions.

A crowd estimated at 25,000 watched the Saturday morning parade. There were outdoor concerts, featuring bands from St. Catharines, Toronto, Ivy, Port Credit and Bracebridge, and dances, motorcycle races and a baseball tournament, in which the Alliston nine triumphed over teams from Orillia, Barrie and Midland. There were pickpockets too, six of whom were arrested before the weekend was over.

But the premier attraction was the appearance of a nineteen-year-old aviator named Cecil Peoli, the "intrepid birdman" who would "make his daring, dizzy ascent into the realm of the clouds in the famous 'Red Devil' biplane, powered by an 80 h.p. Hall-Scott motor."

The success of the young pilot in capturing the hearts of his thousands of onlookers is described in the pages of the Barrie *Northern Advance* on July 3, 1913:

On Monday afternoon Monsieur Peoli, in the most unassuming manner, took off his coat and, donning an oilskin jacket, stepped into the seat, after starting the propeller. Facing a strong wind, he steered westerly, then, circling back, he sailed over the town, reaching an altitude of 2,000 feet . . . flying through the air at the rate of 75 miles an hour!

On Tuesday, he established a record for height, reaching an altitude of 5,000 feet. Higher and higher, he climbed, until the machine became a mere speck in the clouds.

In the 1920s new ground was being broken in other fields. One businessman was a young grocer named Theodore Pringle Loblaw. T. P. Loblaw was born in Essa township, near Alliston, in the 1870s, the son of Elizabeth (Stevenson) and James Loblaw. As a boy, he attended local schools, swam, played games, hunted and fished, but, while still in his teens, he went to Toronto to pursue a career in merchandising. Loblaw worked for the T. Eaton Company for a short time, then, at the age of seventeen, he became a clerk at the W. G. Cork grocery store—one of the largest in downtown Toronto. Shortly afterwards, he formed a partnership with

J. Milton Cork, the son of the owner, but before long he sold
out his interest in the business.

In 1910 he inaugurated a chain store operation which
eventually became the nucleus of the present Dominion Store
system. In 1919, he again sold out, this time to become the
Manager of the United Farmers' Co-operative of Ontario.
E. C. Drury in his book, *Farmer Premier: The Memoirs of
E. C. Drury*, recorded his impressions of Loblaw some years
later:

On the evening when the matter of a new manager was under
consideration, I went with my friend, W. L. Smith, to call on
him in his modest home in the west end of Toronto. I was
greatly impressed with him, a clean-cut, energetic young fellow.
. . . Born and brought up on a farm near Alliston in my own
County, he understood farm life and farmers, and was strongly
sympathetic towards them.

I asked him what he would do if he were appointed manager, and he outlined his plans. He would establish a central
warehouse in Toronto, and retail distributing stores throughout
the Province, all to be managed from a central office. He had the
idea, too, that household necessities could be handled by self-
service, a plan which was new to me.

I liked the man, and I liked his plan, and when the matter of
his appointment came up at the next meeting of the Directors, I
voted for it, and he was elected.

Loblaw's idea of a chain of cash-and-carry, self-serve stores,
operated from a central office and warehouse for maximum
efficiency in keeping prices down and profits up, had origi-
nated in the United States but was as yet untried in Canada.
In 1921 Loblaw, with his former partner, J. Milton Cork,
and C. B. Shields, a prominent Toronto grocer, set up a
limited company to put the new system into operation.

Their first store, managed by Cork, was a popular and
financial success; so was their second and their third. By
1928, in the short span of nine years, the operation had expanded to sixty-five stores in Ontario, with annual sales of
almost $14 million. Another forty subsidiary stores were
doing good business in New York, Illinois and Pennsylvania.
From then on, of course, the Loblaw grocery empire con-

tinued to expand until it became one of the world's largest
food store operations.

T. P. Loblaw, who died in 1933, did not forget his origins;
he became a generous benefactor of his home town. In the
late 1920s he underwrote the cost of paving Alliston's streets.
Then, in co-operation with Fred K. Morrow, another distinguished Alliston alumnus, who had won renown in the
financial field and had been awarded the Order of the British
Empire, Loblaw gave his complete support to the erection
and equipment of the town's excellent Stevenson Memorial
Hospital.

From pioneer days in Simcoe County the availability of
proper medical treatment and care had been a constant problem. During the nineteenth century and into the twentieth,
many rural families faced the uncomfortable reality that the
nearest doctor might be a half-day's horseback ride away.
When a child came down with a fever, an elderly person suffered a stroke, a man was gored by a bull, or a pregnancy
terminated in serious delivery complications, it would be
twenty-four hours or longer before the doctor arrived in his
buggy or cutter.

The problem was one of isolation: a sparse population,
with inadequate communications, and maddeningly slow
means of transportation. No one blamed the doctors, most of
whom would make house calls under the most inopportune
and hazardous of circumstances, through summer thunder-
storms, winter blizzards, or spring floods. In fact, almost
every Simcoe County community reveres the memory of at
least one physician or surgeon who served above and beyond
the call of duty. In Beeton, for example, the names of Dr.
James Watson, Dr. W. C. Law, Dr. R. S. Cheffy, Dr. K. F.
Rodgers and Dr. Frederick Spearing are likely to be long
remembered.

It was fitting, therefore, that three sons of Simcoe County
should attain world renown and lasting places in the history
of medicine. One of these was Dr. (later Sir) William Osler,

a member of one of Ontario's most distinguished families. The Oslers, children of Featherstone and Ellen Osler, rose to prominence in several different fields: medicine, law, finance, politics. Featherstone Osler had come from England in 1837 as a young Anglican prelate to minister to a parish centred around Bond Head, Simcoe County, Upper Canada. His charge consisted of the townships of Tecumseth and West Gwillimbury, each consisting of some 120 sparsely populated miles.

Between 1838 and 1851, several children were born to the Oslers, among them Featherstone, Jr., Britton Bath, Edmund Boyd, and William.

William, who became the doctor of the family, was originally scheduled to be named Walter Farquar. But on the date of his birth, July 12, 1849, his father proudly took him out onto the verandah just as the local Orangemen were parading past in their annual tribute to "King Billy," William of Orange. Several of the marchers, seeing the newly born baby, shouted out, "William! William!" and so he was subsequently christened.

In March of 1857, after almost twenty years at Bond Head, the Oslers moved to the Hamilton district, where the father had been appointed Anglican rector for Ancaster and Dundas.

About this time, the young Featherston finished school in Barrie and stayed there to article in law. Subsequently he moved to Toronto where he established a successful law practice, was appointed to judgeship in the Ontario Court of Appeals, and (in 1888) turned down a seat on the Supreme Court of Canada. His reason for the latter decision is interesting today. "My knowledge of the French language and institutions is altogether too limited," he said, "to warrant me accepting a position in what is, or ought to be, the great Court of the Dominion." He later served on the board of the University of Toronto, declined the chancellorship of Trinity College, and finished his long and distinguished career as president of the Toronto General Trusts Corporation. He died in 1924.

Another son, Britton Bath (but known to almost everyone as B.B.) also went into law and became a nationally famous crown attorney. B. B. was the successful prosecutor at many a sensational murder trial in the 1890s. Recalling that period, Hector Charlesworth, the former editor of Toronto's *Saturday Night*, wrote in 1925, "The man who really dominated the Canadian (legal) scene . . . was the late Britton Bath Osler, Q.C., by many recognized as the most brilliant of the four eminent sons of Canon Featherstone Osler. Before his death he was internationally recognized as the peer of any pleader in the world."

At the peak of his success, B. B. bought 330 acres in the Blue Mountains six miles southwest of Collingwood, built a beautiful stone and wood home, and hired a special train to bring his guests to its opening. For some years he spent considerable energy in developing "Kiontario," as the rural estate was called, planting gardens and fruit trees, starting a private deer herd, and building a series of dams to control the stream that ran through the property. But his wife Carrie died in 1895 and, although he returned there a few more times, his heart was no longer in the place he had built primarily for her. Eventually, in the 1940s, all but the stonework was destroyed by fire, and the weeds and raspberry bushes gradually grew over all that remained of Collingwood's "Osler Castle."

A third son, Edmund Boyd, became a highly successful and prominent financier. He became president of the Ontario and Quebec Railway. Later, when the O. & Q. was incorporated into the Canadian Pacific, Edmund Boyd gained a seat on the parent company's board of directors and held it for forty years. About 1890 he and his associates formed the Toronto Ferry Company, the paddle-wheelers of which earned substantial profits from transporting Toronto citizens to the Lake Ontario Islands that form the outer arm of Toronto harbour.

Somewhat reluctantly, Edmund Boyd eventually entered

politics, winning the West Toronto seat in the House of Commons for the Conservatives in 1896 and keeping it for twenty-one years. He remained an essentially modest man. Among other things, he turned down the leadership of the Conservative party, a cabinet post in the Borden Government in 1911, and a chance to succeed Lord Strathcona as Canadian High Commissioner in London. Finally, in 1912, he agreed to accept a knighthood, and became Sir Edmund Boyd Osler.

The fourth son was William Osler. Willie, as he was popularly known, was not exactly an ideal student during his school years and was expelled from Dundas Grammar School, either for letting loose a gaggle of geese in the class room, or for unfastening all the desks and hiding them in the attic (both of which offenses he had unquestionably committed). He was subsequently declared *persona non grata* at the Barrie Grammar School for similar escapades.

Eventually, however, Willie graduated from the University of Toronto and later from the McGill medical school in Montreal. That was followed by a couple of years post-graduate work in Great Britain and in Europe, after which he accepted a post with the medical faculty at McGill.

From that point on, he became one of the great teaching doctors of all time—in Canada, or anywhere else. After ten brilliant years at McGill, he became successively Chairman of the medical faculty at the University of Pennsylvania, Head of Medicine at Johns Hopkins University in Baltimore, and finally Regius Professor of Medicine at England's Oxford University in 1905.

Wherever he went he preached a simple, though revolutionary creed: that student doctors should learn not merely or primarily from text books, but from first-hand observations. He spent almost half of his first year's salary buying microscopes, so that his students could see what the medical texts of the day merely described. He contravened standard practice by bringing his students into immediate, bedside contact with the patients they were required to study. "His concern," as broadcaster Lister Sinclair later noted, "was with treating the patient, rather than the disease."

His first great textbook, *The Principles and Practices of Medicine*, was published in 1891 and ran through numerous editions.

The next year he married Grace Revere Gross, the great-granddaughter of the famous Paul Revere. They had only one child, Edward Revere Osler.

During his years at Oxford after 1905, William reached the peak of his brilliant career. A man of seemingly limitless energy, he continued to lecture and write about all phases of medicine, and was listened to around the world. His statement that ninety percent of the current drugs were useless received special attention. Throughout his life the pressures of his heavy workload were alleviated by his lively sense of humour. Once, for instance, when surrounded by inquisitive reporters, he told them that they had made a mistake in identity. "I am Egerton Yorick Davis of Caughnawaga," he said. "But I have been told that Dr. Osler and I look alike."

In 1917, he and Grace lost their only son, when Edward Revere Osler was killed in the battle of Ypres. Sir William (who had accepted a baronetcy in 1911, after having turned one down in 1905) never recovered from his son's death, and died, a victim of pneumonia, in 1919—carefully charting the course of the disease that killed him. "He belongs to medical students of all time," Wilder Penfield, his close friend, reflected, "as Lincoln belongs to the common man everywhere."

Frederick G. Banting, a generation after Sir William, was also to gain worldwide recognition in the field of medicine. Always called Fred by family and friends, Frederick was born on the Third Line of Essa township, the youngest son of William and Margaret Banting, in the early 1890s. He attended school in Alliston and then took a Bachelor of Arts degree at Toronto's Victoria College. His parents, who had hoped that he would enter the ministry, nevertheless supported his own dream of becoming a doctor. The young Banting entered Medical School in 1912, and then served overseas with the Canadian Medical Corps in the Great War of 1914-18.

After the Armistice he threw himself into a program of medical research at the University of Toronto, the dedicated purpose of which was to find a successful way of treating the dread disease diabetes, which was killing thousands of young and old around the world each year. Collaborating with Dr. Charles H. Best and Dr. John J. R. MacLeod, Banting was working in completely inadequate surroundings and with virtually no financial support.

Later, in *Farmer Premier: The Memoirs of E. C. Drury,* Drury described how he became a disciple of Banting and Best:

One early spring morning in 1920 or 1921, two young men came to see me. Their names were Banting and Best. They were graduate doctors, and they were working on what they hoped would be a remedy for Diabetes.

They were not receiving the support they needed, and they were stuck for funds. They had a workroom at the top of the Practical Science Building, and they invited me over to see what they were doing.

Two or three mornings later I went. It was a very warm morning. There were several dogs in cages, and a pile of sweetbreads on a sort of a counter, and a meat-grinder, and a big glass funnel fitted with filter paper. The place smelled horrible. They explained to me at some length that the sweetbreads were the pancreatic glands of young calves, which produced a substance called insulin, which controls the use of sugar by the body. . . . They still had a long way to go before the discovery could be used on human beings.

I went back to the Parliament Buildings, much impressed. The up-shot of it all was that we placed an item of $20,000 into the Estimates, and on this Banting and Best were able to perfect their world-famous discovery.

The real breakthrough had come a few months earlier, in the middle of a November night, when Frederick Banting, too involved in his research to sleep, had sat up in bed and written these historic seventeen words on a pad of paper: "Ligate pancreatic ducts of dogs. Wait six to eight weeks for degeneration. Remove the residue, and extract."

Thus the magic formula for a substance called "insulin" was committed to paper. Within a few months the discovery made by Banting, Best and Macleod was helping thousands of diabetics around the world to lead full, active and almost completely normal lives (in the 1970s, a half-century later, Bobby Clarke, a diabetic, was able to become an N.H.L. All Star with the Philadelphia Flyers).

Honours were heaped on the discoverers, particularly on Dr. Banting. In 1923, he and Dr. Macleod were jointly awarded the Nobel Prize for Medicine and Physiology. The research conducted by Dr. Banting and his colleagues was heralded as the most important since the work of Dr. Louis Pasteur. In 1934 Banting was knighted and became Sir Frederick. Two research buildings were erected on Toronto's College Street, not far from the University of Toronto's Medical Faculty, one named for Dr. Banting, and the other for Dr. Best.

Banting was killed in 1941 when a plane carrying him to Great Britain on an important military-medical assignment crashed in the Newfoundland wilderness. Many years prior to his death, Banting had been acclaimed as "the Discoverer of Insulin," at a banquet in Alliston's Dominion Hotel. In 1949 his home town consecrated his memory by naming its high school Banting Memorial and placing a suitable cairn and plaque on its front lawn.

Another outstanding leader in the field of medicine was Dr. W. Edward Gallie of Barrie. Dr. Gallie, who grew up on St. Mary Street near the skating rink and attended school in the old West Ward and the Barrie Collegiate Institute, achieved world fame as a surgeon.

He was Surgeon-in-Chief of the Hospital for Sick Children in Toronto from 1920 until 1929, when he became Surgeon-in-Chief of Toronto General Hospital and Dean of the Medical School of the University of Toronto.

Gallie, a man of profound empathy and compassion, believed that surgery was more than a type of carpentry or mechanics and that there was a third presence—nature—

top—Christian Reformed Church, built in 1935
center—Ansnorveld, Holland Marsh settlement, 1934
bottom—Holland Marsh

besides the doctor and the patient. He believed that in addition to having skill, the doctor must work with nature to induce healing. After experimenting with sewing up ruptures with live tissue in a criss-cross stitching, he developed the method of using living sutures for certain operations.

Another surgeon said of him in 1932: "Ed Gallie is not what you would call a super-surgeon in the operating room. . . . You will find many more flashy operators, but they are not necessarily great surgeons. Gallie is great in his ability to do constructive thinking along new lines. . . . he stands, as he has stood for years, on a kind of peak of his own."

Dr. Gallie's work was widely recognized as a revolutionary advance in the field of surgery. In 1923 he was appointed Hunterian Professor of Surgery and was asked to deliver the Moynahan Lecture to the Royal College of Surgeons in England. In 1947 he was awarded one of the highest honours a doctor can receive, the Gold Medal of the Royal Society of Surgeons—a medal which is awarded so rarely that he was the twentieth ever to receive it.

Another major development of the 1920s was the draining and reclamation of the area known as Holland Marsh. Holland Landing, at the mouth of the Holland River and at the foot of Cook's Bay, the southernmost protrusion of Lake Simcoe, had long been important historically as a terminus of the water-and-portage route from Toronto (York) to the whole of the Canadian northwest. But the flat, river bottom lands along the river had been written off as having virtually no economic importance. As early as 1825, surveyor John Galt had described the Holland as "a mere ditch, swarming with bullfrogs and snakes." Until well into the twentieth century, the area provided only one marginally useful crop—hay for mattresses. And, even to harvest that the horses pulling the mowers had to wear snowshoe-like footgear to keep from floundering in the black, some said bottomless, ooze.

But one man of vision saw a vastly different future for the Holland flats. He was William Henry Day, formerly a

Professor of Physics at the Ontario Agricultural College in Guelph. Day believed that, with proper drainage, the Holland Marsh could become one of the most prolific market-gardening areas in Canada, perhaps in the world.

For a long time he was virtually alone in that belief. In the period around 1909 to 1912 he had tried to drum up interest in his pet project, had taken surveys, and had prepared data as to the potential yield, but his dream attracted almost no support from either the provincial authorities or local residents. Almost everyone thought that "Day's dream" was an exercise in futility.

But Day went ahead, largely on his own. He dug drainage ditches and saw the swamp bottom turn into rich, black loam and harvested his first lush and bountiful crop of vegetables in the fall of 1920.

After that almost everyone became a believer. The drainage system was expanded until 7,500 acres of the flattest, richest, most productive soil in Canada were yielding incredible harvests of onions, carrots, lettuce, cabbages and other garden vegetables.

Unfortunately, Day, who had devoted all of his energy and meagre resources to developing the project, shared hardly at all in the profits, and died a poor and considerably disillusioned man. Yet he lived long enough to relish the importance of the work he had accomplished, as witnessed in a Barrie *Examiner* report of a speech he made to the Barrie Lions' Club in November, 1934: "If it were not for Bradford this year," he said, "Canada would be importing celery one month from today. . . . I say, without fear of successful contradiction, that the Holland Marsh scheme is the biggest thing north of Toronto, except, perhaps, for the mining developments of Sudbury, Cochrane, New Liskeard and beyond."

Today, the Holland Marsh operation is unique in Canada, and may well be, as some have claimed, "the largest market garden in the world." To visit the area in the late summer or early fall is to step into a different world. As flat and as devoid of trees as the Saskatchewan prairie, Holland Marsh has its own particular charm—the mosaic grid of the fields; the endless, perfectly straight rows of vegetables, stretching away to the horizon; the Dutch village of Ansnorveldt; the innumerable stacks of wooden crates, waiting to receive the produce that will soon be harvested. There is, above all, an incredible neatness and tidiness to the vista, prompted in part by the determination not to waste so much as a single square yard of the productive soil. It is like the most meticulously cared for vegetable plot one has every seen, multiplied thousands of times over.

And yet, one terrible night in 1954, Holland Marsh was the scene of indescribable chaos, of filth and debris and destruction.

Friday, October 15 of that year was a grey, sullen day in Simcoe County, as most of Southern Ontario came under the influence of a hurricane named Hazel which swept up from the American Midwest. Most of the force had gone out of the wind by the time it crossed the U.S. border, but it brought with it extreme low pressures and ominous, low-hanging, dark clouds.

The rain started before dawn that morning, continued all day, and showed no signs of letting up as the early twilight gathered. Later, people would comment that they had never seen such a heavy, sustained downpour as they witnessed that day. At the time, however, no one felt any reason for concern.

But, hour after hour, the rain continued. Unnoticed, back in the hills, ditches that had been dry since the previous spring gradually filled up. Trickles of water joined to form rivulets, which found their way into creeks, which poured into streams, which added their volume to rapidly swelling rivers. And, as darkness fell, untold billions of gallons of water were racing towards outlets that could not possibly accommodate them. In their path, among other places doomed to disaster and destruction, stood the flat, vulnerable delta area of Holland Marsh.

131

In Barrie, there was an anniversary dance that night at the Canadian Legion hall, which was well attended despite the rain. About one A.M. just as the dance was breaking up, the first word reached Barrie of the terrible flood that had swept down upon the market-gardening community. It came in the form of a frantic telephone call from Bradford, describing the catastrophe that was building up with each passing minute, and asking for every possible type of emergency assistance.

There were to be many heroes in the terrible hours that followed, among them, Squadron Leader Jack Oates, commanding officer of Barrie's 102nd Squadron of Air Cadets, and Captain Ron Pile of the Grey and Simcoe Foresters. Oates and Pile, who had just been leaving the Legion dance when the news came in from Bradford, caught a ride in a truck that was heading into the disaster area.

What they saw along the way, and especially when they arrived on the scene, simply defied belief. Abandonded cars were strewn all along Highway 400, and in many places the recently completed super route to the north was caving in and was in imminent danger of being swept away by the rampaging flood waters.

Houses floated by; so did barns, sheds, trailers, hundreds of crates of vegetables, uprooted trees, livestock—both alive and dead, boards, logs, and every conceivable kind of debris. At one point, Oates and Pile saw a house drifting by, with at least fifteen people sitting on its roof or clinging to its sides. Oates waded in and swam out to it, and managed to fasten a rope to the house, but it could not be pulled in against the raging current. Meanwhile Captain Pile had managed to find a boat, and the two men made repeated trips to the house until all the occupants, including several children and infants, were brought safely ashore.

By then Holland Marsh was a huge lake of muddy, swirling water, in many places twenty to thirty feet deep. Every home in the marsh was flooded; hundreds waited for rescue on rooftops, shivering in the chill rain, numb from exposure, shocked by the terrible catastrophe that had engulfed them. All through the night many local men, such as Alf Harris, worked without pause, bringing one boatload after another of stranded people to safety.

Bradford became a beleaguered refugee centre as hundreds of rescued men, women and children poured in, some by car or truck, other straggling along the roads like members of a retreating army. The people of the town rallied with all their energy and resources: throwing open their homes to the homeless, serving hot tea and sandwiches, rounding up blankets, arranging for transportation, and setting up cots for the children. One who was greatly praised for his organizational work was P. H. Fisher, the manager of the Bradford Royal Bank branch.

When dawn finally came, the full extent of the disaster was apparent for the first time. Scotty Taylor, the News Editor of the Barrie *Examiner*, described the desolation of the scene in a story he filed that day:

Today there is an almost terrifying stillness here, broken only by the sound made as the choppy water, which covers something like 8,000 acres of this famous vegetable-growing area, slaps idly against the destroyed buildings which litter this section of Simcoe County . . . a slapping sound which is an instant, yet mute testimony to the realization which crowds out a person's other reactions to this panorama of devastation . . . that man, with all the advantages and material safeguards of our present-day way of life, is futile against the unleashed forces of nature.

Hydro lines were barely above water. Highway 400 was under five to ten feet of water, and swept completely away in some sections. Air Force and Ontario Hydro helicopters hovered over the area, rescuing dozens from high ground. In Ansnorveldt, the steeple of the Dutch Reform Church was the only visible evidence that there was a village beneath the surface of the dirty, brown water. The loss was estimated at many millions of dollars. A half a million bags of onions and as many of carrots were gone; ironically, they were all crated, and would have been shipped out to market within the next forty-eight hours.

133

Many other parts of Simcoe County were also hard hit by Hurricane Hazel. Coldwater was under four feet of water. In Orillia, dozens of launches and other boats were sunk at their docks. Four miles east of Beeton, five people lost their lives when their cars were swept away by raging torrents. In Essa township a total of sixteen bridges were washed out, and the CNR reported that 150 of its bridges had been damaged or destroyed throughout the County.

Miraculously, not a single life was lost in the Holland Marsh flood. Within a few days the flood waters began to recede, helped considerably by the arrival of several huge pumps, some from Ontario Hydro and three from the Steep Rock Mine at Atikokan, which were capable of pumping 23,000 gallons per minute. Gradually the buildings, and then the contours of the land, began to re-emerge. It was sickeningly apparent that the task of restoring what nature had so contemptuously destroyed would be an enormous one. Many homes had been overturned, swept away, or destroyed. Those that were still standing were coated, inside and out, with slime and silt. The once tailored, parlor-clean fields were littered with every conceivable kind of flotsam.

But the work was begun almost immediately, with the help of private donations and funds granted by the County, Provincial and Federal Governments. And, by the following summer, through the dedication and determination of many people, the endless, neat, geometrically perfect rows of onions, celery, carrots and other vegetables were again growing in Holland Marsh.

8 The New Forests

By 1900 it was becoming apparent that the great lumbering boom had passed its zenith and was clearly on the wane. True, the saw mills were still operating at near capacity; but most of the timber being processed came from as far away as the North Channel of upper Georgian Bay, or even from the shores of Lake Superior. The harsh reality was that there was little left in Simcoe County that was worth cutting.

For a half a century it had seemed that the supply of trees was inexhaustible; the axes and the crosscut saws had swept all before them, with no thought of conservation, of the preservation of an industry, or of tomorrow.

E. C. Drury, one of the great pioneers in reforestation, summed it up well in a speech he made in 1937:

And then the lumbermen came. Unlike the early settler, who was a builder, the lumberman was an exploiter, pure and simple . . . destroying the Angus Plains, the Vespra area, the Orr Lake district. . . . He took off the cream of the timber and left a slash to be burned over, and reburned . . . until the surface soil was destroyed . . . and nothing but a barren plain remained.

I can remember the night sky red with such fires—at Midhurst and Anten Mills and Orr Lake.

Only gradually did the full extent of the terrible legacy left by the exploitation become evident—thousands of acres of stumps, graveyards where there had once stood tall trees; erosion and drifting soil; dried-up streams, ponds and springs. In 1908 Dr. E. J. Zavitz referred to Simcoe County, particularly the Orr Lake district, as "a waste area."

A few far-sighted and dedicated men, led by E. C. Drury (later to become Premier of Ontario), and Dr. Zavitz (often referred to as "the father of reforestation"), set about the business of righting the wrong that had been committed. The answer lay in reforestation, but it would be no easy task, no victory quickly won. While a good axeman could fell a towering pine in a few minutes, it would take upwards of half a century to replace it. "The immediate benefits of reforestation are small indeed, compared to the future benefits," Drury told the Ontario legislature in 1919, after he became Premier. "If, therefore, you are concerned only with yourself, and the immediate present, I advise you to have nothing to do with it. . . . But, if you have concern for future generations, if you have desire to hand this country of ours down to them as good as we found it, or a little better, then you will wish to support it to the utmost of your power."

In 1902, Drury was president of the Ontario Experimental Union, a group composed of several hundred graduates of the Ontario Agricultural College at Guelph under the general guidance of Dr. Zavitz. Among other agricultural matters, they were concerned with achieving a proper balance between cultivated land and forests. A committee was formed to investigate the existing situation, with Drury as chairman, and including Nelson Montieth, later to become Minister of Agriculture in the Whitney Government, and Dr. J. B. Farrow, head of Department of Forestry at the University of Toronto.

In 1903 the committee sent a resolution pointing out the need for the development of a reforestation policy and program to Hon. John Dryden, Minister of Agriculture in the Ross Government, then in power. The presentation bore some fruit, and a year later the first Provincial Forester was appointed.

In 1905 the first tree nursery was begun at Guelph, a program of lectures was launched by Dr. Zavitz, and advice on forestry was provided to landowners. Under the Whitney Government a Forestry Station was established in Norfolk County, some local areas were planted, and a few demonstration plots developed.

Legislation passed in 1911 provided for municipalities

to acquire land for reforestation purposes, and attempts
were made to encourage greater participation at a local level
through education. However well-intended, the program
moved along at a somewhat slow pace, and was brought to a
virtual standstill by the demands of the Great War.

In 1919 E. C. Drury became Premier of Ontario and,
with the help of his old colleague, Dr. Zavitz, pressed for a
much more active and comprehensive approach to the challenge of restoring the forests. His key recommendation was
that the province would share the costs of reforestation projects undertaken by county and municipal governments.

Addressing the Ontario Parliament, in support of the
legislation he needed to carry out his program, Drury spoke
movingly of a Simcoe County spring he had known as a
boy—a beautiful, shaded place, where ferns grew, and the
clean water gurgled over moss-covered stones; and of how,
when he returned many years later, after the rape of the
lumbermen, it was to find only a barren, dried-up hillside,
the magic spring of his memory buried under drifting sand.
"No work can be done," he concluded, "which will accrue to
the greater advantage of municipality, province and country."

Appropriately enough, the first county to take advantage
of the financial support offered by the provincial government
was Simcoe County. In 1920, 1000 acres of waste land were
purchased in Vespra Township. One of the major elements in
the Drury Government's plan was the management of "agreement forests," established on lands purchased by local authorities and then turned over to the provincial Department
of Lands and Forests, which agreed to control, protect and
develop them for forestry purposes, as provided for in the
Reforestation Act of 1921.

The first tree planted in Simcoe County under this program was set in the ground on the afternoon of Monday,
May 8, 1922. The scene was recaptured in a booklet published in connection with the County of Simcoe Forest and
Field Day in August, 1937:

In the shade of a small grove of murmuring pines near the sixth concession on the Vespra-Flos townline, Anten Mills, the inaugural ceremony and formal opening of the Simcoe County reforestation plantation took place.

On a little knoll near the grove, J. J. D. Banting, County Warden, nestled an infant pine. . . . That event is destined to mark an historic event in the annals of Simcoe County.

"I hope to see each township start on this enterprise," Warden Banting said, "and I hope the school children will cooperate. If they do, they will see the advantages before they reach the age of their present Warden. . . . This project will become an asset for all interests."

The Simcoe County reforestation program broadened in scope and became more precisely defined as the years went by; but from early in its history it could be said to have had these goals:

— to restore idle, marginal and waste lands to productive use;

— to prevent soil erosion, and conserve water resources;

— to manage the forests scientifically, in order to produce the best quality and quantity of growth;

— to provide demonstration areas for the education of the public in general, and school children in particular;

— to give advice and support to private landowners in their reforestation efforts;

— to make the new forests available for public recreation, such as hiking, family picnics, camping, swimming, hunting and fishing.

Over the years, the results of this program became more and more noticeable. By 1963 a "History of Lake Simcoe Forest District," prepared by the Department of Lands and Forests, was able to report that many of the properties placed under agreement, which had been open, sandy lands with blow sand conditions and erosion problems, had become healthy pine plantations producing good returns.

The same document pointed out that the Department was supplying extensive services to "private landowners seeking advice in managing woodlots, tree-planting, protection of

138

plantations from insects, etc. . . . . the extension programme has continued to grown and broaden."

In a 1971 article for "Your Forests," W. S. McNeice, Management Forester for the Lake Simcoe district, pointed out that the Department had helped to plant an average of about three-quarters of a million trees on private lands each year. "The Department, as manager of these lands, has a policy of allowing public use," McNeice added. "Several of the properties are heavily fished. Horseback riding and hiking are popular on others. Snowmobiling is common on all of the larger tracts. . . . The County forest lands . . . have obvious recreational and watershed protection value, in addition to their potential to produce forest products."

The harvest potential of the new forest increased steadily as the years passed and helped to offset the costs of the reforestation program. In 1948 the first thinnings for pulpwood were carried out at Hendrie and Orr Lake, and at Angus and the Wildman Forest in 1957. By June of 1966, the Alliston *Herald* was able to report a booming business in this type of yield:

Piles of pale, gold pulpwood alongside roads in Simcoe County may come as a surprise to those who think of pulpwood operations being only in the north, and in remote regions. And yet, only a few weeks ago, there were long rows of 4-foot pulp logs lying, glistening in the sun, on County Road 21, just a little east of Baxter.

The forests are providing employment, improving land values, and becoming an ever-growing asset. In 1965, about 6,000 cords of pulpwood were cut from Simcoe County forests.

In March, 1968 the Barrie *Examiner* estimated that an all-time high of 7,000 cords had been cut that season and predicted that the total production would climb even higher in the future.

Other plantings, old and comparatively new, were harvested for hydro and telephone poles, stove and fireplace wood, Christmas trees and prime lumber. One aspect of the forestry industry that did not come back to any great extent was the springtime production of maple syrup and maple sugar. In the middle of the nineteenth century, Simcoe County residents boiled the sap down to about 162,000 pounds of sugar each year; a hundred years later, in 1959, the yield for all of Ontario was only about 142,000 pounds.

It is astonishing to realize that in the first forty years of the program, from 1922 to 1962, well over 28 million trees were planted on agreement forests in Simcoe County. And the total area under management, which had reached 12,000 acres by 1955, continues to increase:

Year	Total Acres Under Management
1955	12,000
1963	17,050
1966	18,000
1971	21,000
1974	22,335

Raising enough trees to support such a massive planting campaign is, of course, a major undertaking, and one which requires very special technical knowledge and skills. The men who launched the program in 1922 were, in every sense of the word, pioneers. There was, at that time, only a very limited backlog of information available, and it was almost a matter of starting from scratch. Hence, the methods and techniques required had to be developed through trial-and-error, intuition, ingenuity and inventiveness.

One of the prerequisites was to establish a facility where the large number of seeds required for the program could be extracted. For some years Mr. George Latimer of Angus had been collecting red pine cones for the Department of Lands and Forests, and in 1922 Mr. A. H. Richardson, who was in charge of reforestation for the Ontario Government, visited Angus and arranged to use a Camp Borden building for storing cones. A year later, Mr. Richardson's department purchased eight acres near Angus; this was the beginning of the Ontario Tree Seed Plant. Over the years additional property was purchased, to bring the total plant area to some twenty-eight acres by 1961.

The choice of Angus as the site of this vital operation was both appropriate and ironic. It had been a boom town during the lumbering era, thriving on the great stands of red and white pine around it, and at one time having seventeen sawmills, a population of over 2,000, and a bustling main street with stores, hotels, livery stables and a theatre. But by the turn of the century, boom had turned to bust, and in 1901 there was not even a general store in the village. Some had tried to farm the land around it, but the sandy, drifting soil that had been ravaged by the lumbermen would not sustain agriculture.

The revival of the community was brought about by two developments: the establishment of nearby Camp Borden during the Great War, and the Ontario Tree Seed Plant. To the latter, the only seed-extracting plant operated by the provincial government, came pine cones collected from all over Ontario. Before long the seed was being forwarded to eleven government nurseries, capable of producing 50 million or more seedlings each year.

As time went on, new methods evolved and changes were made, but they all owed their heritage to the men who had led the way into largely unknown territory during the early years of reforestation in Simcoe County.

In 1959 the extractory building at Angus was destroyed by fire. By 1963 a new extractory, designed to take advantage of all the knowledge and experience gained during the preceding forty years, was completed. When it opened, it had the capacity to handle 24,000 bushels of cones each year, providing for an annual supply of over 100 million seeds.

A year before the Angus plant was established, the Midhurst Forest Station came into being. Opened in 1922, it is situated on Highway 26, some six miles northwest of Barrie. The primary function of this Station, operated by the Department of Lands and Forests, is to raise seedlings, about 15 million of which are produced annually for both government and private reforestation throughout Ontario. Most of the seeds used by the Midhurst Station are extracted by the plant at Angus.

The Midhurst operation also includes a Forest Tree Nursery Research Centre and a hatchery which produces brook trout for restocking Ontario waters. Its Springwater Provincial Park provides day-use recreational facilities for the public, both winter and summer, and offers an interesting, educational display of living birds and animals.

The older planting areas, thinned and pruned, are used as demonstration lots to show school groups and other visitors how light, sandy soils can be rehabilitated through careful management to produce trees for quality lumber, pulpwood, poles and firewood.

A pamphlet issued by the Department of Lands and Forests describes the Midhurst nursery operation:

In the late fall each year, the specially prepared compartments are sown with forest tree seeds. The seedbeds, four feet wide, are formed, levelled and rolled with a special roller that makes uniform ridges along the length of the beds. A mechanical seeding machine broadcasts the seeds on the beds at a rate to correspond with the desired seedling stocking. A drag-type implement then scrapes the ridges to cover the seeds with a light layer of soil. Finally, the beds are covered with straw to protect the seeds through the winter and early spring.

In the spring, when the seeds begin to grow, and when danger of heavy frost is past, the straw mulch is carefully removed. Wooden lath shades are erected over some of the beds to protect the tiny seedlings from strong sunlight during their first summer. The amount of shading is varied to suit the different species of trees. . . .

Transplanting is done every spring and fall by means of two large transplanting machines. Each machine, manned by six workers, plants six rows of trees simultaneously, and will set out 100,000 trees a day. . . .

To meet the annual shipping target of 15 million trees, the nursery maintains approximately 70 million seedlings and transplants in various stages of development.

Originally, most operations at Midhurst were performed by

hand, but over the years machines—some of them built to
the specifications of the Station staff—have been introduced
into the major operations, such as sowing, transplanting, lift-
ing and shipping. By 1963, for example, machines operated
by twelve men could sow more seeds per day than a hundred
men could have set out per day in the early years of reforestation.

Throughout the years the program has received the enthusiastic support of the general public—not just from landowners, but also from schools, service clubs and other groups
and individuals. In 1949, for example, the Midland Kiwanis
Club (whose members had planted over 20,000 trees on its
45-acre reforestation plot) sent a brief to the Ontario Government, urging "the enactment of legislation setting minimum size standards for tree-cutting."

Thousands of Simcoe County children have also been involved in reforestation, especially during Canada's Centennial
Year of 1967. For instance, in April of that year, the Barrie
Examiner reported that 340 Base Borden Public School children planted 1800 new trees at Canada's largest military
training base. The seedlings, one foot high, were provided
by the Department of Lands and Forests through its Angus
representative, W. McNeice.

During that same month, 12,000 trees were planted by
Oro school children on a special forestry lot near the 7th Line
Road and Simcoe County Road 11. "We considered this a
most appropriate way of commemorating Centennial Year,"
Simcoe County Warden George A. MacKay said on that occasion. "The children will be able to follow the growth and
development of these trees for years and will recall that they
helped to plant them on Canada's 100th birthday year."

Quite a number of dedicated, visionary and resourceful
men have been in the forefront of establishing and maintaining the reforestation program in Simcoe County, such as
Arthur H. Richardson, W. S. ("Wally") McNeice, George
Barr of Medonte, Sid Cox and Joe Lea, County Foresters
and many others. But, if one name should be singled out for

special recognition, it would have to be that of E. C. Drury. He was a hard-working patron of reforestation long before the first concrete steps were taken in the early 1920s; he fought for "the new forests" with all his energy during his term as Premier of Ontario; and he continued to be a dedicated exponent of "the noble scheme" until the day he died. Above all, perhaps, he used his moving and persuasive powers as an orator in dozens of speeches to further the cause in which he so passionately believed.

Later, in his autobiography *Farmer Premier*, he noted that

Hendrie Forest, first County forest in Ontario, planted with jack pine in 1924

Simcoe County had elected to name one of its agreement forests after him, and he made this comment: "I would rather have this for a monument than a statute in Queen's Park or on University Avenue."

Drury was one of several Simcoe County native sons who rose to political prominence. Among them were: the Hon. Leslie Frost, of Orillia, the 16th Premier of Ontario (1949-61); the Hon. Earl Rowe, of Newton Robinson, who was Lieutenant-Governor of the province from 1961 to 1968; and Sir William Mulock, of Bond Head, who was Postmaster General of Canada from 1896 to 1905, the first Minister of Labour (1900), and Chief Justice of Ontario (1923).

"E. C.," as Drury was known to almost everyone, was born at Crown Hill in 1878, and subsequently educated at Barrie Collegiate and the Ontario Agricultural College at Guelph. His father, the Hon. Charles Drury, was the first Minister of Agriculture in Ontario.

Drury was a man of enormous and varied talents, and he seemed to have a particular knack for chalking up "firsts." In 1909 he became the first secretary of the Canadian Council of Agriculture; in 1914, the first president of the United Farmers of Ontario; in 1919, as the Premier of Ontario, the first head of a "farmers' government" in Canada (actually a coalition of farmer and labour members).

Drury remained active in politics until 1931, when his wife, Ella, died suddenly. After that, he returned to the farm where he was born near Crown Hill, and subsequently served as Sheriff, County Court Clerk and local Registrar of the Supreme Court for the County of Simcoe.

He was also an accomplished writer, which is not surprising in the light of his numerous eloquent speeches over the years. In addition to the autobiographical *Farmer Premier*, he wrote a book in 1932 called *Forts of Folly*, a critique of Canadian tariff policies, and, later, the well-known *All for a Beaver Hat*. The latter was originally intended to be a history of Simcoe County from the earliest times to the present, but

—typical of his enthusiasm—Drury was so fascinated by the world of the Jesuits, Hurons, Iroquois and fur-traders that he failed to get out of the 17th century.

Yet, for all his other interests, reforestation remained his greatest cause, and it is for his long and dedicated efforts on its behalf that he will be best remembered.

On Friday, June 16, 1972, Simcoe County marked the 50th anniversary of its reforestation program with the dedication of a stone cairn, constructed in E. C. Drury's memory, a tour of several historic and modern forestry sites, and a well-attended banquet.

The tour, which covered some forty miles, often left the highways to penetrate deep into the wooded areas, and included such points of interest as Springwater Provincial Park, Midhurst Forest Station, Willow Creek, Hendrie, the Freele tract, the Crawford tract, and, as a highlight, the Hon. E. C. Drury Forest. The guests who travelled in four buses, visited forest developments in three townships, Vespra, Oro and Medonte.

Incorporated into the tour was the unveiling of the E. C. Drury cairn. A handsone monument, constructed of granite rocks, it is located on County Road 11 in Oro, not far from the Edgar Radar Station which was in operation for some years after World War II. Appropriately, the cairn stands only a few miles northeast of the original Drury homestead at Crown Hill.

The monument was unveiled by Drury's son, Harold, and Reeve Allan McLean of Oro Township. The address was given by Allan Ironside, a director of the Simcoe County Historical Society and a highly regarded writer on a variety of historical subjects. Mr. Ironside, a resident of Washago, described E. C. Drury as "one of Simcoe County's most remarkable men," and nominated him as the area's "most outstanding citizen." He pointed out that the former Premier of Ontario had made many important contributions to the development of his province, in such divergent fields as farm organization, social welfare, education, civil service reform, highway development, rural electrification and, above all, reforestation.

He noted that Drury's grandfather, one of the first pioneers of the County, had settled on the old Penetang Road in 1819. His father, Charles Drury, had represented his riding in the provincial government from 1882 to 1890. Both father and grandfather had been Reeves of their township, and had served on the County Council.

"In 1921, a thousand acres of sandy area near Midhurst were planted," said Ironside. "This is known as the Hendrie Forest. Simcoe County, with the dream of Dr. Zavitz and the stimulus of Ernest C. Drury, became the showcase county of Ontario in reforestation."

Mr. Ironside described the former Premier as "a farmer, a tireless worker for farm organization, an author, a politician (in the better sense), an historian, and one who, as he put it in *Farmer Premier*, strove to 'walk humbly with his God'." He concluded his moving address with these words: "It is not only for what he did, but for what he was, that I nominate him as Simcoe County's greatest citizen. Few, if any men could claim to be so much a part of Simcoe County as could Ernest Drury."

An evening banquet was attended by some 200 officials and interested citizens. William Thurston, Supervisor of the Timber Management branch of the Department of Natural Resources (which had replaced the Department of Lands and Forests), gave the main address. He retold the history of the reforestation program and cited many encouraging facts: that [in 1972] forests owned by the County and under agreement with the Ministry of Natural Resources total 22,180 acres and are located in sixteen townships; these forests have over 18 million trees; since 1948 more than 60,000 cords of pulpwood have been produced by them; private landowners have planted over 40 million trees; there are 251 agreements between the Ministry and private landowners which provide assistance in tree planting and stand improvement on 11,800 acres of land.

Whisky Creek, flowing into Lake Simcoe at Minet's Point

Mr. Thurston saw this trend as continuing into the future with increased acreage in agreement forests and expanded use for recreation, wildlife protection, crop improvement and pollution control. He concluded, "My crystal ball says that the future for agreement forests continues, and that it is brighter because they will give you more pleasure, more use, and more benefits."

The committee responsible for the success of the 50th anniversary celebration included Chairman Morris Darby, Reeve of Tiny Township. Simcoe County Warden Lloyd Pridham, and Deputy Reeves Horace Vasey (Medonte), Calvin Ireland (Tosorontio), Donald MacDonald (Flos) and William Gowanlock (Orillia Township). County Clerk Gordon Watson served as secretary for the committee, and Wally McNeice represented the Department of Natural Resources.

And so, a half-century after it began, the long, patient struggle to reforest the ravaged land has come a long way. Trees are once again being cut, this time on a selective and minimum-size basis, to conserve and perpetuate the forest industry. Driving through the County, one passes stand after stand of stately pines. To walk on the thick carpet of pine needles between the rows of mature trees—as neat and perfect as the vegetable plots of Holland Marsh—is to enter an almost unreal world of utter peace and shaded, cool tranquility.

The original, practical goals of reforestation, to stop soil erosion, preserve or restore water tables, and bring marginal land into forest production, have substantially been achieved. And there are many very real fringe benefits. People now hike, and picnic, and ski, listen to the silence, and study nature where once there was only desolation, and sand drifting around the stumps of slaughtered, century-old pines.

The task is not over nor will it ever be. But, meanwhile, it is nice to think that, somewhere in the hills around Crown Hill, the magical, boyhood spring of E. C. Drury may once again be bubbling and gurgling over shaded moss-covered rocks.

9 Sports

In 1928 at Amsterdam, Canada enjoyed its greatest-ever
Olympic success. There, a shy, unheralded, almost delicate-
looking Vancouver sprinter named Percy Williams astonished
and electrified the sporting world by winning both the 100-
metre and 200-metre events. Alberta's graceful and beautiful
Ethel Catherwood won the gold medal in the women's high
jump. Many other young Canadian men and women turned
in outstanding performances, including Penetang's appeal-
ing, fresh-faced Jean Thompson, who finished fourth in the
women's 800-metre final. In the women's 4 × 100-metre
relay Ethel Smith, Jane Bell, Myrtle Cook and Barrie's
Fanny ("Bobbie") Rosenfeld—who had already won a silver
medal in the 100-metre dash—sped to victory.

Bobbie Rosenfeld's success at Amsterdam came as no
surprise to the people of her home town. She had come to
Canada in 1904, the infant daughter of Russian parents who
elected to settle in Barrie. As she grew up, it soon became
apparent that she was an extraordinary athlete, one who ex-
celled at every sport she tried—and she tried most of them.

In hockey (which remained her first love), she held her
own against the boys on Barrie's natural-ice, outdoor rinks.
In track and field she was outstanding in the long jump and
discus, as well as being one of the world's best sprinters.
She later played on Eastern Canadian championship basketball teams, was an outstanding softball player, and won the
Toronto women's tennis championship.

Some of the track and field records she established survived for more than a quarter of a century. Her prowess is
the more amazing in that she was in her late teens before she

turned her attention to this sport, and then only by accident. In the summer of 1921 Bobbie was in Beaverton to participate in a Sports Day as a member of a Barrie girls' softball team. There was also a small track meet, and Bobbie agreed to enter the 100-yard dash—in which she proceeded to defeat Rosa Grosse, the Canadian champion in this event.

This feat attracted considerable outside attention, and shortly afterwards Bobbie moved to Toronto to join the Toronto Ladies' Athletic Club, where she could get good coaching and high calibre competition. From there the path led straight to the Amsterdam Olympics.

Slight of build, but wiry and very quick, she knew only one way to compete, and that was all-out. Always aggressive, she was not belligerent by nature and she enjoyed great popularity wherever she went. Within a year after her success at Amsterdam Bobbie was stricken with arthritis, and although she competed successfully for several more seasons, the disease would be with her, growing progressively worse, for the rest of her life.

After she retired from active competition, Bobbie turned to journalism and wrote a highly regarded daily column called "Sports Reel" for the Toronto *Globe and Mail* for many years.

In 1967, Canada's Centennial Year, a testimonial dinner was held in her honour in Barrie. That same year she was elected to the Sports Hall of Fame and named as the top Canadian female athlete of the twentieth century. Bobbie died in 1969.

Simcoe County has produced so many exceptional athletes —at the local, provincial, national and world levels—that a whole book could be devoted to their exploits and triumphs.

There were, for instance, the five grandsons of Jacob Gill, one of the County's original pioneers. Among them, "Jake" Gaudaur became champion oarsman of the world; George G. Gray was among the top two or three shot-putters on earth; his brothers, John and Joe Gray, established many Canadian records in track and field; and Harry Gill was recognized as the best all-round athlete in North America. A contemporary, Walter Knox of Orillia, gained recognition as the champion all-round athlete of the world in the first years of the twentieth century.

Coldwater's George Gray was undoubtedly one of the greatest shotputters who ever lived, a claim that he established with his very first throw in his very first meet. That was in Toronto in 1885 when, as "an unknown from the backwoods," he defeated an outstanding international field, which included the reigning world's champion.

Gray, who worked in his father's drygoods store, had had no technical training, having developed his talent by competing against other young Coldwater athletes. The year following his sensational Toronto debut, however, he was invited to join the prestigious New York Athletic Club, known in track and field circles as "the home of champions."

And a champion Gray certainly was. By the time he retired many years later, he had won no fewer than 188 medals. He set a world's record with a toss of 43.11 feet in 1887, which stood until 1902. Then, on August 1, 1909, when he was forty-four years old, he had a phenomenal throw of 48 feet, 3 inches—a performance that would seldom be equalled over the next half century.

Many experts believe that Walter Knox may have been the best all-round athlete that Canada ever produced. Knox, who was a native of Listowel but was raised in Orillia, competed for more than three decades. In a single afternoon in 1907 he won no less than five Canadan championships: the 100-metre dash, the long jump, pole vault, shotput and hammer throw. In 1909 he tied the world's record for the 100-metre dash with a time of 9.6 seconds. In 1914 he won the world's all-round title in London, England, taking six out of eight events from the British champion, F. R. Cramb. He was then thirty-six years of age. Knox also coached the Canadian Olympic teams at Stockholm in 1912 and at Antwerp in 1920.

Wherever the action was—in London, Paris, New York,

San Francisco, Berlin, or the rich mining towns of northern Ontario—Walter Knox would be there. He was usually sponsored and often ran under assumed names. He knew all of the angles and took particular delight in playing the dumb yokel to set up side-bets at long odds. Then, to his own delight and the consternation of the local gamblers, he would leave the hometown hot-shot runner far behind—laughing all the while.

A charming, ahead-of-his-time free spirit, Knox won the incredible total of 359 events during his long career, and no one will ever know how many impromptu matched races against local heroes. He was, quite simply, one of the very best track and field competitors in the history of the sport.

Harry Gill was another Simcoe County product who starred in track and field around the turn of the century. After winning a drawerful of medals and trophies, including several Canadian championships, he became the all-round North American track and field title holder in 1900 after a series of competitions in New York City. Later he coached the track team at the University of Iowa, afterwards switching to Illinois, where his teams won eleven Big Ten conference championships. One of the athletes he coached there was Avery Brundage, who was to become the president of the International Olympic Committee, and the often controversial champion of "amateurism" in athletics.

Collingwood's Jack Portland, who starred in many sports, was another great Simcoe County track and field athlete, winning two national championships in the high jump, and representing Canada at the 1932 Olympics at Los Angeles in that event.

From the same town came Alex MacMurchy, a fine distance runner who won many national and international events in the late thirties and was scheduled to compete in the 1940 Olympic Games. But World War II sidelined the Olympics until 1948, and an industrial accident eventually brought an end to MacMurchy's promising career.

Other outstanding track and field athletes were Irene

top—Walter Knox;
centre—Jake Gaudaur;
bottom—Bobbie Rosenfeld

Storey, a fine sprinter from Barrie who ran for Canada at the 1934 British Empire Games, and the incomparable Mamie Shrum who was raised on a Uhthoff farm and who gained national and international fame as a champion in the shotput and discus.

Miss Shrum was discovered early in the summer of 1930, when Harry Warren, a local butcher, saw her hefting bags of grain as if they were down-filled pillows. Impressed by the seventeen-year-old girl's hefty, 183-pound body and great strength, Warren talked about Mamie to his friend, Great Lakes Captain Jack McGinnis, who in turn passed the word along to Walter Knox.

Knox went out to the Shrum farm to visit her, and became Mamie's coach. Soon to become known as "the Milk-maid Shotputter" (because, in addition to her other farm chores, she milked nine cows each morning and evening), Mamie Shrum won the Ontario championship just seven weeks after she first held an eight-pound shotput ball in her hands. From there she went on to become the Canadian title holder, after which she was feted and welcomed home at a rally in Orillia's Couchiching Beach Park, which was attended by more than one thousand.

"Orillia and Simcoe County have reason to be proud of their contribution to the list of great athletes of the world," Walter Knox told the assembly. Of the guest of honour, he said, "Never in my association with athletics have I ever seen a parallel to this. . . . I predict that she has the greatest future of any woman athlete in Canada." Mamie went on to many more triumphs and was named as Orillia's top female athlete by the *Packet and Times* in 1969.

Undoubtedly one of the best oarsmen of all time was Jacob Gill "Jake" Gaudaur of Orillia. Jake's mother, Jennet Gill had married Francis Gaudaur, whose Métis father, Antoine Gaudaur, had been Orillia's first settler in the early nineteenth century.

The Gaudaur home was on the narrows between Lake Simcoe and Lake Couchiching, and Jake won several rowing championships on local waters before moving on to challenge the best scullers in the world. His brilliant career was punctuated by a series of classic races against the fabled Ned Hanlan of Toronto. The two men were strikingly different in personality. Hanlan was the somewhat swaggering, publicity-conscious showman; Gaudaur was the withdrawn, modest, publicity-shy athlete who believed in letting his oars do the talking for him.

In 1887, Gaudaur won the North American championship and a prize of $5,000 by beating Hanlan in an exciting duel on Lake Calumet near Chicago. Although his career took him to many faraway places, Jake liked to compete before his Orillia and Simcoe County fans whenever he could. On one such occasion he teamed with his brother Frank to win a two-mile race over McCann and Elliott of Toronto on Lake Couchiching, an event that was held so late in the fall that many spectators arrived by sleigh, and the lake froze over the following day.

In 1892 a crowd estimated at 10,000 crowded the Orillia waterfront to watch Gaudaur and Ed Hosmer of Boston take on Hanlan and William O'Connor for the world's double sculls championship. People had come from all parts of the County, many by special trains and steamboat excursions. The three-mile course ran from the foot of Mississauga Street, around buoys off Lehman's Point, and back. To the delight of the roaring crowd, Gaudaur and Hosmer won by about a boat-length in an exciting finish.

From about 1890 until his retirement in 1901, at the age of forty-three, Gaudaur was all but invincible. In 1893, rowing against a magnificent field which included the world's champion, James Stanbury of Australia, and Hanlan, he set a new world's record for the three miles on the Colorado River in Austin, Texas. Three years later, on the famed Henley course in England, he won the world's championship. Upon his return he received a triumphant welcome in Toronto. Then it was on to Orillia, where he arrived on board the steamer *Islay*, decorated for the occasion with pennants and bunting, and accompanied by six other passenger steamers, to be greeted by one of the largest crowds in the history of Simcoe County.

After his racing career was over, Jake continued to live in Orillia, doing a lot of fishing with his friend Stephen Leacock, until his death in 1937. "Jake was a magnicent figure of a man," Leacock wrote of him in "Too Much College." "He stood nicely over six feet . . . was broad in the shoulders, straight as a lathe, and till the time when he died, just short of eighty, he could pick up the twenty-five pound anchor of his motorboat, and throw it around like a tack-hammer."

There were several other fine scullers in the Lake Simcoe-Lake Couchiching area in the 1890s and early 1900s: George Whiten, Charles Annis, J. H. Wilson, Colin Ralston, Robert Curran, Arthur Cameron and John Gray, to name some of the most prominent.

In Simcoe County, as in most other parts of Canada, hockey has always been a highly popular sport. Since the turn of the century, almost every community has had a hockey rink of some kind, and most have had town or village teams playing in organized leagues. Each era has produced its star players, many of whom went on to professional careers in various cities all over North America.

In the early days, from about 1905 to 1915, three names were especially prominent on the sports pages of County newspapers: Steve Vair, Gordon Meeking and Frank Foyston. The latter, a member of a hockey family, learned to play the game in Minesing, where he grew up. The local Princess rink was a far cry from the latter-day Maple Leaf Gardens, its playing surface being more-or-less lit by a couple of dozen lanterns, and the water used to make ice having to be hauled in a tank from a well some two miles distant. Foyston graduated to the famed Dyment Colts of Barrie, later played for a Toronto team in the Allan Cup finals, and starred for many years as a professional in Toronto, Detroit and Seattle.

Then, as now, rough play was sometimes a problem. The

famed Collingwood Shipbuilders had come into existence in the mid-1890s and had proceeded to win two Northern Ontario Hockey League championships. Collingwood's chief hockey rival was Midland, and that already bitter rivalry boiled over during a game between the two teams in the winter of 1902-03.

Play had been rough from the opening face-off, and midway in the game Collingwood's Nick Labatt and Midland's Ed English became involved in a violent stick-swinging duel. English, a great centre for Midland, struck Labatt over the head with a violent blow, and the Collingwood player fell to the ice, unconscious. Neither of the two men was ever to play hockey again. Labatt finally recovered, after lingering between life and death for several days, but his playing career was behind him. English was tried in the courts, fined heavily and permanently barred from organized hockey.

The incident started a hockey feud between the two towns that lasted for more than sixty years. Two weeks after the trial Collingwood's Dougald Darroch, then President of the Ontario Hockey Association, was stoned by a Midland mob while on a business visit to that town. So great was the bitterness caused by the Labatt-English affair that Midland grocers refused to stock biscuits manufactured by the Telfer Bros. of Collingwood.

The hostility of Midland fans was not soothed to any great extent when the Shipbuilders persuaded three of Midland's best players, Webb Beatty, Captain Angus McLellan and Frank Cook, to move to Collingwood for the 1909-10 season, especially when the Shipbuilders proceeded to win the Ontario championship with considerable ease.

The Shipbuilders were a powerful team during those years, but their brightest star by far was Ernest "Rabbi" Fryer, who was later described by Lou Marsh, the editor of the *Toronto Star*, as the greatest amateur hockey player he had ever seen. Fryer captained the Collingwood team to Ontario Intermediate 'A' titles in 1913, 1918, 1919 and 1920. There are many stories about his brilliant play, but one of his best remembered feats was that of ragging the puck for the final two minutes of the 1913 championship game against London, enabling the Shipbuilders to cling to a 3-2 lead.

Fryer continued to star for almost three decades, playing his final game in Midland when he was forty-eight years old—an earlier day Gordie Howe. When he skated off the ice for the final time, the archrival Midland fans showed their sportsmanship by giving him a rousing ovation.

Down through the years other Simcoe County towns and villages had their hockey stars, too. Orillia fans thrilled to the exploits of such players as Ken McNab, the colourful Lovering Jupp, centre George Ross, fast-skating Fred Smith of the Orillia Juniors in the late thirties, and goalie Herb Stevens. Waubaushene's Tye Arbour was outstanding for many years. Lawrence Devine and Sonny Manning gave Coldwater fans plenty to cheer about. Penetang turned out such fine players as the McNamara brothers, George, Harold and Howard, all three of whom played with the Toronto Ontarios when they won the Stanley Cup in 1914; Bert and Con Corbeau, who were also members of Stanley Cup championship teams; and the slight, fast-skating Andrew Bellehumeur.

Until 1933 all rinks in Simcoe County were natural-ice rinks. On January 7, 1933 some 4000 spectators were on hand to witness the official opening of the new Midland arena, the only rink between Toronto and Winnipeg to have artificial ice, and legitimately described by Mayor J. B. Roebuck as "one of the finest in Canada."

To list all of the players who graduated from Simcoe County teams to the professional ranks would require at least several pages. One team alone, the Memorial Cup-winning Barrie Flyers of 1950-51 sent at least five members on to star in the National Hockey League. One player who deserves special mention is Barrie's "Red" Storey. Like so many other great Simcoe County athletes, "the Old Redhead" was an all-round performer, excelling in baseball, softball, lacrosse, basketball and football as well as in hockey. He later became an N.H.L. referee, and still later a part-time commentator on

"Hockey Night in Canada" telecasts.

But his finest hour, or rather quarter-hour, came in the 1938 Grey Cup game. In Toronto's jam-packed Varsity Stadium that chilly, late fall Saturday afternoon, the Winnipeg Blue Bombers were clinging to a 7-6 lead over the Argonauts at three-quarter time. As the final quarter began, Storey was sent in to take the place of an injured player. During the next fifteen minutes of play, "Red" was simply uncontainable. He made several long runs and scored no fewer than three touchdowns, as the 25,000 fans went wild. The final score was Argonauts 30, Blue Bombers 7. The *Toronto Telegram* subsequently described Storey's performance as "one of the greatest, most explosive, one-man displays in the history of football."

Although football was never as widely played there as in Toronto and the other larger Ontario cities, Simcoe County has produced some other fine players. One of the best was Jake Gaudaur, Jr., son of the great Orillia sculler, who captained the Hamilton Tiger Cats for several seasons, and went on to become the Commissioner of the Canadian Football League. In an earlier era, there was Collingwood's "Huck" Welch, a magnificent kicker, who starred in the Ontario Rugby Football Union for fifteen years and is now a member of the Sports Hall of Fame.

Early in the present century, baseball was a big sport in Essa township, with Ivy, Cookstown, Utopia and Elm Grove all having strong teams. An interesting sidelight to the baseball of those days was the number of brother combinations that appeared in the line-ups, especially as pitcher and catcher battery mates. Utopia, for instance, had the Bell brothers, with Ralph pitching and Harold behind the plate, while, over in Ivy, Herman Jennett often took the mound, with his brother Elwood doing the catching.

Cookstown always fielded a strong nine, especially when "Dewey" Hopper was pitching to Otto "Pat" Arnold. Elm Grove, too, won its share of games, with Edgar "Baldy" Whiteside and Harry Dundas forming a strong battery.

About 1906, a young pitcher named Bill Banting, one of five members of that family in the line-up of the Ivy team, became the sensation of the Essa league. Legend has it that the youthful Banting had developed a drop-ball that dipped as much as *two feet* on its way to the batter. (The same "legend" makes no comment upon the fact that it must have been equally impossible to catch.)

Baseball was also popular in Beeton, with players like Earl Barrett, Jack Dale, "Bing" Speck, "Metz" Hill, D. W. Watson and many others providing thrills on the diamond down through the years.

In Collingwood baseball was played as early as 1870, but the first team to join the Ontario Baseball Association was organized in 1889. They were dubbed the "Blue Mountain Heroes," and their captain was Hiram Bush, the grandfather of Eddie Bush of later hockey fame. As was the custom in those days, Hiram played barehanded behind the plate, positioning himself ten yards or so back, and acting more as a backstop than as a catcher in the modern sense.

The Collingwood team, which was shortly rechristened the "Shipbuilders," enjoyed many fine seasons as the years rolled by, but the best by far came in the summer of 1935, when it won the Ontario Intermediate championship. That club had such fine players as Ron Randall, Bob Lamb, "Nip" Spooner, Jack Dobson, Bob Crosby, "Shorty" Johnston, "Buck" Oliver, Paddy Young, Brit Burns, Reg Westbrooke, Lyle Wright and Jack Owen; but its backbone was the great battery of rookie pitcher Deverde "Smokey" Smith and veteran catcher "Huck" Caesar. Young Smith, who had a blazing fastball, finished that championship season with an amazing record of 23 wins and just 4 losses.

A year or two later Smith was lured to Orillia, where he pitched well for several more seasons. The history of baseball in that town dates back to the 1870s, and a team called the "Merry Nine Alerts." "Smokey" Smith became the latest in a long line of fine pitchers who had taken the mound for the Orillia team. In the early days there had been Archie Burton and William Teskey, whose son, Howard later became probably the best hurler ever developed in the Orillia area; in the twenties there was Leighton "Hap" Emms; in the thirties, the brilliant Allan "Cotty" Tribble.

In more recent years the Orillia Majors swept to two Ontario Amateur Baseball Association provincial championships, bringing home the cup in 1964 and again in 1969.

One of the few Simcoe County baseball players to make the major professional leagues was Phil "the Babe" Marchildon of Penetang. Marchildon was discovered by a scout for Connie Mack's Philadelphia Athletics and joined that American League club for the season of 1942. "Peerless Phil," as he was later to be dubbed in a feature article in MacLean's Magazine, proceeded to win 17 games as a twenty-nine-year-old rookie.

But the war was on, and Marchildon turned his back on major league baseball to join the Royal Canadian Air Force as a gunner. On his twenty-seventh mission, he was shot down over Germany.

After the War, in 1946, despite the fact that he was thirty-three years old, he returned to Philadelphia to win 13 games for them. 1947 was his last full season in the major leagues. But "the Babe" went out in a blaze of glory, winning 19 games that year while losing only 9, to rank among the top pitchers in the American League.

Softball, a game that came into its own in the 1920s, has also been popular in most Simcoe County communities large and small, and popular with female as well as male athletes. Collingwood, for example, has had a flourishing industrial league since the early 1930s, and was particularly strong during the early years of World War II, when it had such teams as Dickson's Aces, the Pros, Clyde Aircraft, Nottawa, Trinity Livewires and Collingwood Shipyards. Much the same story is true of Midland, Barrie and Orillia.

Like many other small communities, Beeton has had softball teams since the mid-1920s, with the girls' teams enjoying particular success, perhaps because the local men's nine was once defeated by a travelling girls' team called the "Boston Bloomers," which had a slogan that went: "The Boston Belles in Bloomers Bright Can Bat the Ball Right Out of Sight!"

The first lacrosse played in Simcoe County was field lacrosse, a sport directly adapted from the Indian game called *bagataway*, which was once a favourite among the Hurons and, especially, the Iroquois. It was highly popular throughout the County around the turn of the century, but nowhere more so than in Bradford. The Holland River community had a fine field, which was famous among followers of the sport, and a half-holiday was proclaimed in Bradford whenever a game was played there. It also had some fine teams, including the 1905 Intermediate Champions of Ontario.

Box lacrosse, a game with fewer (6) players, and tailored to an enclosed, and much smaller, playing surface (about the size of a hockey rink) came into its own in the 1930s, and Orillia has always been its Simcoe County home. The Orillia teams have captured more Ontario and Canadian championships than any other city or town in Canada. Probably the most brilliant period in the saga of Orillia lacrosse began in 1934, the first year that the local team bore the proud name of the "Terriers." In August of that summer Orillia won the Mann Cup, emblematic of Canadian Senior lacrosse supremacy, by trouncing British Columbia's New Westminster Salmonbellies in three straight games. The next year the Terriers successfully defended their championship by defeating the Richmond, B. C. club, three games to one. In 1936, Orillia again took the championship, this time winning three out of four games from the Vancouver North Shore Indians.

Orillia has produced so many great lacrosse players down through the years that only a very intrepid observer would presume to name an all-time, all-star Terrier team. However, few would dispute the fact that the following players (all from the 1930s) would have to be given serious consideration in compiling such a mythical line-up: Ed Downey; "Bucko'

McDonald, the magical stick-handler; Piper Bain, the hard-rock defenseman; Merv McKenzie, who would have become a magnificent football player, had not lacrosse been his first love; and two great goalkeepers, Ambrose Hinds and Bill McArthur.

It seems probable that curling was first introduced into the County around 1865 by two Orillia brothers named Jackson. In those early years it was played on the frozen surface of Lake Couchiching, with no protection from the midwinter winds that swept across the wide open spaces.

The Orillia Curling Club was formed in 1873 and, after trying several other locations, finally built the Elgin Street rink, of which the curlers were very proud. In February, 1886, teams from Orillia, Collingwood, Waubaushene and Churchill were engaged in a bonspiel to decide which would represent the County in the Ontario Tankard. The deciding game found Orillia pitted against Collingwood, and a capacity crowd of over 200 was on hand to see it.

As the teams got ready to play the first end, a snow storm was threatening to bury the town. It was a heavy, wet snow, and a few spectators left early, afraid that the roof might collapse under the accumulating weight. It didn't—that evening —and most of the fans stayed to watch Orillia win an exciting match in the final end. But about 9:30 the next morning the whole building came crashing down, heavy wooden beams and tons of snow descending on the area where players and spectators had been just twelve hours earlier. A new rink was built on St. Andrews Street and it served the curlers until the present club was erected in 1964.

Orillia rinks have enjoyed considerable success through the years, among them those skipped by Stan Sarjeant in 1957 and Tom Caldwell in 1961, both of which won Ontario championships and went on to the Brier. Others won the Tankard in 1933, 1950 and 1956.

In Barrie curling began on the ice of Kempenfelt Bay back in 1877. In 1907 a rink skipped by H. J. Grassett and George Hogg won the first Ontario Tankard by defeating

Preston in the final at Toronto's Granite Club. Another Barrie rink repeated the feat in 1927, and there were to be many other victories in later years.

In Collingwood, some of the pioneers of curling were John Wright, W. T. Toner, Charlie Stephens, W. A. Copeland, Donald Knight, Hal Telfer and George Watson, who was the first President of the Collingwood Curling Club. Collingwood rinks won the Ontario Tankard in 1913 and again in 1920. The skips of those two successful teams were W. E. Vernon and Norman Rule in 1913, and H. G. Wymes and W. B. Fryer in 1920.

Curling was first introduced to Midland in the early 1880s, and that town too has sent its share of rinks into Tankard competition.

In the early days of horse racing, most County tracks were surfaced with tan bark, which was later replaced with clay. As previously mentioned, among the best tracks in Canada was the one built at Penetang by J. T. Payette in the 1890s. There were other fine racing ovals in Barrie, Orillia, Midland and Collingwood, and most County fair grounds had dirt tracks that were used for one or two days of racing each fall.

In those years horse racing was not entirely restricted to the summer months. In the winter, horsemen often laid out courses on the ice of Collingwood's Little Harbour and Barrie's Kempenfelt Bay, where some of the most colourful races of all took place—with the bright silks of the drivers flashing in the winter sun, the breath of the horses making puffs of white in the cold air, and the spectators sitting on logs around the roaring fires on the ice.

Collingwood has always been a centre for horse racing, and that town has seen some good stables and outstanding trotters and pacers. To name just a few: Thomas Collins and his Dolly C; R. W. O'Brien and his Lady Collingwood; Alex Blue and his mare Minnie Blue, Thomas Neville with Texas Rocker and Collingwood Rooker; P. J. Stone with Tony Brino and Collingwood Boy; and W. Densbury and Bee's

Wing. Nate Sproule, one of the best known of all Colling-
wood horsemen, had such outstanding horses as Long Sandy,
Arlie Hal, Joe S. and Bertie Brind. In the 1950s, Clarence
Lockhart raced such fine standardbreds as Single Chips,
Chinook Can and Bomb A. Then there was W. P. McLean
and his Bunny Gratton—the list could go on and on.

However, one of the most notable horsemen was W. Earl
Rowe of Newton Robinson. In July, 1953 at Toronto's Thorn-
cliffe Park, Rowe drove a pair of mares, Celia's Counsel and
Volo Van, to a new world's record time of 2:07.2. He was
then in his fortieth year of racing, having previously driven
his great, Canadian-bred trotter Van Riddell in the famed
Hambletonian Classic in the United States. His Roweland

Downhill and cross-country skiing

Stables had been producing excellent horses since 1913. Finally, in 1963, he gave up a professional driving career that had spanned a half century when he became the Hon. Earl Rowe and the fourteenth Lieutenant-Governor of Ontario.

Simcoe County has also produced some fine boxers. In 1932 Waubaushene's Horace "Lefty" Gwynne, a short and somewhat stocky bantamweight, was chosen as a member of the boxing team to represent Canada at the Los Angeles Olympics, where he won the gold medal.

Cal Rooney of Barrie was a fine amateur boxer in the years just prior to World War II, and Don Wallace of Stroud won some good bouts in the 1950s. Then, in the late 1960s, Orillia's Walter Henry gained prominence by winning several championships.

James J. Parker was the only Simcoe County boxer to hit the big time as a professional, winning several important bouts before he lost out in a bid to take the world's heavyweight championship away from Archie Moore in the early 1950s.

Skiing has always had its adherents in Simcoe County, but this sport really came into its own in the years after World War II. A growing number of enthusiasts flocked to the chalets and skiing lodges during the next three decades.

Thanks primarily to the efforts of one man, Pete Pettersen, a fine, 113 ft.-high ski jump was built just west of Midland, and opened officially on January 29, 1956. Several important national and international competitions were held there during the next few years, but interest flagged after Pettersen was killed in a car accident, and the jump was torn down in 1966.

Basketball has been essentially a high school sport in Simcoe County. Golf has had its full share of devotees since the early years of this century, and has produced some fine amateur players. Among them was Jack Portland of Collingwood, who was as proficient at getting from tee to green as he was at playing a half-dozen other games. Soccer, cricket, paddling, sailing, wrestling, speed skating and several other sports have all had their adherents in various parts of the County.

The 1960s saw the emergence of one game, sport, contest, or whatever it should properly be called, that was unique to villages with the name of Stroud. The "Great Stroud Annual Brick and Rolling Pin Competition" came into being in 1960 when the U.S. community of Stroud, Oklahoma and the English town of Stroud discovered that they had something in common besides the name they shared—each had a brick factory. A competition was arranged to see who could throw a brick farther, an American Strouder or an English Strouder.

A year later an invitation was extended to other Strouds around the world to take part, and Stroud, Ontario and Stroud, Australia accepted the challenge. Through correspondence, a Stroud International Brick-Throwing Committee was formed, with Robert G. Simpkin of the Ontario Stroud as international secretary. A date for the first competition was agreed upon, arrangements were made to communicate the results from each Stroud to all other Strouds (competitors making their throws on their home turf), and a few basic rules were formulated. Since the whole idea of the competition was to provide good fun and foster good will, the rules were considerably less complicated than those governing other sports. Essentially what they established was that a competitor could not win unless he actually threw a brick. The Stroud, Oklahoma organization undertook to supply the bricks (each weighing exactly five pounds) to all competing teams.

In 1962, the Australian Stroud suggested a rolling pin throwing competition for women, and the idea was enthusiastically endorsed by all three other Strouds. The rolling pins came from Australia, were made of a native wood called Mulga, and weighed two pounds apiece.

In 1965, Canada's Stroud enjoyed its finest hour, sweeping both the brick and rolling pin competitions, and winning the overall World's Championship—the "world" in this case consisting of the four Strouds. Jack Hunter captured the brick-throwing with a toss of 114 feet, 5 inches; and Donna Watson captured the women's division by throwing a rolling pin 112 feet, 9 inches.

In Simcoe County's Stroud the whole community has become involved in the annual event, with a large crowd of supporters turning out each year. Many volunteer officials are on hand to measure the throws; local sponsors offer to provide uniforms, jackets, crests and trophies; and a good-natured, happy, holiday-like mood prevails at all times. It is true amateur sport at its very best.

In any community successful sport programs are based, not only on the talents and triumphs of the athletes, but also on the tireless efforts of men and women who work behind the scenes, taking care of the time-consuming and often tedious matters of organization and administration: people who sit on committees, draw up schedules, find ways of raising money for equipment and transportation; coaches who give up evenings and weekends to work with young players; referees and umpires, who often pay their own expenses, and shrug off the abuse they frequently receive; local sponsors who donate sweaters; mothers who wash and mend team uniforms; and fathers who drive sons to 6 A.M. hockey games on way-below-zero Saturday mornings.

Most of those who work for amateur sports do so in relative obscurity, far from the glamour, publicity and excitement that goes with winning provincial, national or international championships. Their contribution is to church leagues, rural leagues, industrial leagues, Minor Atom kids who can barely stand up on their skates, basketball leagues in which the scores look like baseball scores—leagues in which the emphasis is on having fun and doing the best you can. Simcoe County has had hundreds, no doubt thousands, of such dedicated, unsung heroes and heriones—to all of whom, this chapter is respectfully dedicated.

10 The Dirty Thirties

The last half of the 1920s were good years for Simcoe County, as they were for most of the rest of the country. After the postwar slump, new industries opened up in Barrie, Midland, Collingwood, Orillia, Penetang and elsewhere. There were plenty of jobs to go around, and most breadwinners brought home decent, if not overly generous, paychecks. People could afford a few luxuries: a car, perhaps, or one of the new-fangled radios that kept you sitting up late at night, twisting the dials in hope that you might tune in some distant station like WGN, Chicago, through the earphones, or a vacuum cleaner, or a new piece of farm machinery.

It was nice to know that there would be a roast sizzling in the oven, come Sunday afternoon, and that you could afford to let the kids go to the movies once in a while. By then most Simcoe County towns and some of the villages had motion picture theatres—most often named the "Capitol," the "Regent" or the "Roxy"—where the figures on the screen not only moved but talked as well.

Farm crops were generally good during this period, and market prices were at least a good deal better than they had been.

For most Simcoe County people it was a time of confidence, of belief in the future. Things were pretty good, and there was every reason to expect that they would get better. It was a time of easy credit—when people were encouraged to "buy now, pay later."

It was also a time of progress. Throughout the County, communities went ahead with improvement projects. In Coldwater, for example, the Continuation School was built in

170

1923, and the decision to pave the streets was made in 1928. In Elmvale, waterworks were installed in 1925, and paving of the main street began in 1929. The Oro Town Hall, built in 1868, was extensively remodelled in 1929. In Beeton, the Brennan Paving Company of Hamilton was engaged to pave Main and Centre Streets in 1927.

It was a time of prosperity.

There was very little, in Simcoe County, of the wild, crazy, try-anything-once, bathtub gin, don't-go-home-until-morning, "flapper" mood that swept across the United States and was reflected to some extent in the larger Canadian cities —no coonskin coats, few open roadsters, few women who smoked cigarettes in public. To be sure, each town and village had its community drunk and its "bootlegger," where thirsts could be relieved by an illegal cold beer or two. A certain amount of necking took place in the rumble seats of the new Ford coupes, and every district had its lovers' lane.

But for the most part the pleasures were innocent ones. It was a gentle time; a time of Sunday School picnics, hockey and baseball games, fall fairs, and the annual "doing-down" of jams and jellies, pickles and relishes, when the wondrous odours drifted out from a thousand kitchens on hot, early-autumn days.

It was a time for moonlight excursions on board the last of the graceful, white steamers, a time for flashing paddles at summer regattas, a time for Sunday evening band concerts in Orillia's Couchiching Park and in Barrie, Midland, Collingwood, Stroud, and many other towns and villages, a time for fireworks on Queen Victoria's May 24 birthday, and on the July 1 commemoration of Canadian confederation. It was a very good time.

And then, in the dying weeks of 1929, time ran out. Late in October, the bottom fell out of the Winnipeg grain market; wheat prices plummeted dramatically within a few hours and continued to fall. "MILLIONS IN PAPER PROFITS ARE SWEPT AWAY AS PRICES CRASH" ran a headline in the *Manitoba Free Press*. "The wreckage was piled high, and thousands of small holders of wheat were among the flotsam," the front page story said. "They went out on the crest of the wave, to be strewn among the wreckage."

Meanwhile, in New York even more calamitous developments were taking place. On Monday, October 21, prices fell dramatically on Wall Street. They rallied briefly in mid-week, then resumed their toboggan-ride by Friday. The financial world sweated out the weekend, desperately hoping that the forty-eight-hour respite would give the stock market time to stabilize. But when Monday morning came, prices opened low and dropped steadily throughout the day.

Then came Tuesday, October 29, 1929, the day of the Great Crash. From the moment the gong sounded to open trading that morning, the orders were to sell, sell, sell. By the close of the day, 23 million shares had been traded, at ever-falling prices. The ticker fell hours behind. In the chaos no one could keep up with events, but by the time twilight fell over the financial towers of Manhattan, it was clear that a calamity of dreadful proportions had occurred. Thousands of shareholders, large and small, had been wiped out. Gone was all confidence, all faith in the future. Gone was prosperity. Ahead lay hard times, the Great Depression, the "Dirty Thirties."

In company with ordinary people everywhere, the citizens of Simcoe County had little real comprehension of what had happened or of what it would mean to them. It all seemed far away, as remote as a distant planet. Optimism was still the key word. In their year-end forecasts for 1930, at least two Simcoe County editors wrote of the "continuing prosperity" that lay ahead. At Barrie's annual motor show, in January, 1930, the new models shown included Hupmobiles, LaSalles, DeSotos, Durants, Marquettes, Reos, Overlands. At that time, few could foresee that, for every new model purchased, 10, 20 or 30 older cars would soon be put up on blocks because their owners could no longer afford to buy gasoline. (In Midland one inventive man took the motor out of his DeSoto and hitched it up to a team of horses.)

By the spring of 1930, factories in several Simcoe County towns were beginning to lay off men; there simply were not enough orders coming in to justify keeping on a full staff. Employees with many years seniority were given two weeks' pay and told that their services were no longer required. Able-bodied men who had worked hard all their lives suddenly found themselves with nothing to do but sit around the house or on a bench in the local park. NO HELP WANTED signs sprang up everywhere, like patches of poison ivy. There were simply no jobs to be had. For example, the Barrie *Examiner* of January 5, 1934 listed only one item under the *HELP WANTED* heading in its classified advertising section—and that was for an experienced cook to work in the kitchens at Camp Borden.

Some Simcoe County men, like thousands of others from all over the country, took to "riding the rods," drifting across Canada on freight trains in the vain hope of finding some kind of work. Midland, Barrie, Orillia and Collingwood all had their "hobo jungles" beside the railway tracks on the edge of town, where the "knights of the road" could heat their cans of pork and beans and wash their few clothes before moving on. Uneasily tolerated by local citizens, much as gypsy encampments would have been, they were populated by quite ordinary men trying to survive in quite extraordinary times.

Those lucky enough to keep their jobs had to get by on much smaller paychecks than they had enjoyed in the twenties. In public works, as well as in private industry, the word was to cut back on all expenditures. Faced with a serious reduction in receipts (down from $1,200,462 in 1931 to $998,127 in 1932), the Simcoe County Council was forced to reduce manpower and limit repairs to roads and bridges. To save money, a 1932 resolution provided that all hangings would take place in Barrie. That same year the Council also considered various ways of reducing the cost of education in the County. One way was to shorten the period of public school education, by raising the entrance age from five to six and lowering the age at which a child could leave school from sixteen to fourteen. In January, 1933 secondary school teachers had their salaries slashed by 10 to 20 per cent. And in June, 1936 it was decided to reduce educational levies to municipalities by the percentage of taxes that remained unpaid.

Prices fell drastically as the decade progressed. At Stover's Restaurant in Orillia, you could get a full-course meal—soup or juice, choice of liver and bacon or hamburg steak and onions or pork chops, potatoes, vegetables, rolls, dessert and beverage—for 35¢. D. W. Watson's Grill Restaurant in Beeton offered a hot beef sandwich, with plenty of lean meat, gravy, green peas and French fries for 20¢. Chocolate bars (twice as big as today's), soft drinks, chewing gum, potato chips, double-header ice cream cones were all a nickel. Pulp magazines like Doc Savage, The Shadow, Flying Aces, and Wild West—each containing a novel, two novelettes, and four or five short stories—sold for a dime.

Going to the movies was cheap. In a typical ad in January, 1933, Barrie's Capitol Theatre offered a double-feature of Ben Lyon in "By Whose Hand?" and Buck Jones in "South of the Rio Grande" for a quarter. An extra ten cents would buy a half-pound of freshly roasted Giant Redskins from the nearby Nut Shoppe to take with you.

Grocery and meat prices dropped to all-time lows, as in-dicated by this A & P ad in the Barrie *Examiner* in January, 1933: "Blade roast—12¢ lb., pot roast—10¢ lb., sirloin steak—18¢ lb., sausages—25¢ for 3 lbs., bacon— 25¢ for 2 lbs., salmon— 9¢ for large tin, butter—23¢ lb., Heinz Ketchup—29¢ for two large bottles, flour—35¢ for a 24-lb. bag, soap chips—15¢ for 2 lbs., graham wafers—29¢ for 2 lbs., fresh hams—10¢ lb., loin roast pork—12¢ lb."

Nor did it cost much to put clothes on your back and shoes on your feet. In June, 1934 a Midland department store offered the following bargains: "Boy's sweaters—79¢, men's work boots—$1.79, men's socks—15¢, men's four-piece suits—$10.95, women's dress shoes—$1.98, men's dress shirts—69¢, boy's windbreakers—49¢, boys' bloomer pants—98¢, women's aprons—25¢."

In the fall of 1934 General Motors introduced its Standard Six Chevrolet, priced at $710, and Hudson-Essex dealers in the County were displaying Terraplanes (from $898) and Hudson Eights, "embodying every worthwhile development of the automotive industry" (from $1056).

But low prices were small consolation to the majority of the people in the County, who had very little money with which to buy anything. It those dark days, every penny counted. Public Utilities Commissions were faced with ever-lengthening lists of delinquent accounts. For the most part, authorities were as lenient as they could possibly be. In Barrie, for example, many accounts were written off at 50¢ on the dollar, and the Public Utilities Commission of that town asked the Ontario Hydro Electric Power Corporation to waive the standard one dollar re-connection fee, pointing out that it was difficult enough for subscribers to pay their accounts up to date without tacking on a fine to restore service.

A former telephone lineman, who wishes to remain anonymous, tells the following story of the mid-1930s:

I remember this elderly couple. They lived in a kind of remote area, quite a long piece from their nearest neighbours. He'd been a good farmer all his life, but he was very sick then and couldn't work the land any more.

They fell behind in their phone bills—about a year and a half, as I remember. The company finally decided to cut them off, and I went out there to tell them the bad news.

But, when I got there, I just couldn't do it. You know, it didn't seem right for that old lady to be stuck out there, with no way of calling a doctor, and him likely to have an attack at any minute.

So I just went away and paid their bill, a bit at a time, out of my own wages . . . what little there was of them.

Never told anybody about that until now. People helped each other more in those days . . . had to, I guess. It wasn't anything much. Anybody else would have done the same thing under the circumstances.

Public Utilities Commission employees also suffered. To save

money, maintenance work was reduced to a minimum in
most communities. Many workers were laid off, and others
had their hours cut through a system of enforced three- and
four-day "work breaks." At the same time, hourly rates were
cut by ten per cent or more in most communities.

In spite of the good years of the twenties, few families had
been able to put aside any real savings, and prolonged unemployment soon brought real hardships and near-starvation
to many of them. Relief was provided by different levels of
government and by churches and other private institutions,
but it could do little more than maintain life at a subsistence
level. Worse than that, while appreciated, these handouts were
bitterly resented by men who had always provided for their
families, and who now, through no fault of their own, suddenly found themselves "on the dole." For most, it was a
harsh blow to pride, dignity and self-respect.

Many Simcoe County men and women remember one
particular aspect of Christmases during the early thirties. In
the words of one:

About the middle of December each year, we'd have a special
Sunday, when all the Sunday School boys and girls were asked
to bring whatever their parents could spare—a can of peas,
perhaps, or corn or tomatoes . . . sometimes a homemade plum
pudding, a jar of preserves, some cookies . . . maybe a bag of
potatoes, some candy canes, anything.

Then, two or three nights before Christmas, the women of
the Ladies' Auxiliary would get together, sort out the groceries,
and make up hampers the best they could. Sometimes the local
merchants contributed chickens or hams, and that helped a lot.

The hampers would be distributed to what we called 'the
needy' that same night. I've seen lots of men and women cry
when we knocked on their doors—partly from gratitude, and
partly from humiliation. They weren't any different from the
rest of us, of course, except that the men hadn't been lucky
enough to keep their jobs.

Those were hard times, all right, for everybody.

Many municipal bodies inaugurated make-work projects to
give the idle men something constructive to do and to remove
the stigma of having to accept relief money. In Beeton, for

instance, unemployed men were hired to cut weeds, repair roads and sidewalks, and remove dead trees. A similar program was set in motion in Hawkestone, where the first sidewalks were laid in 1931. The Simcoe County Council budgeted as much as it could afford for repairs to County roads and bridges. The going wage-rate was uniform in all municipalities: 20¢ per hour, 40¢ for a man and a team of horses.

The sad but simple truth was that the local, township and County Councils did not have enough money to provide adequate relief. Hundreds of area residents could not pay their taxes, and several communities were unable to meet their County levies.

All kinds of schemes, plans, resolutions and systems were tried in an effort to alleviate the situation. In January, 1933, the Barrie Horticultural and Town Improvement Society recommended that the unemployed men of the town raise vegetables for themselves and their families on vacant lots within the town limits.

In the same town, two years later, a Central Relief Committee, composed of citizens and members of the Town Council was established, including Mayor Blair, S. W. Moore, Charles J. Seitz, Thomas Sinclair, and Alderman H. J. Buchanan.

One of the most ambitious—and bizarre—approaches was the 1936 printing and issuing of "funny money" relief currency by Mayor Ben Johnston's Orillia Council. the "Co-operative Purchasing Relief Scrip," which bore a picture of the Champlain statute, was engraved much like regular Canadian bills and came in denominations of from 5¢ to $1. They could be redeemed at the Town Treasurer's Office or at the Royal Bank of Canada on the first day of each month, and carried a discount of one percent.

The Orillia "script money," as it became known, soon proved to be as unworkable as it was unpopular, and a few months later all $30,000 of it was reduced to ashes at a public burning in Orillia's Market Square.

Both the critical seriousness of the Great Depression, and

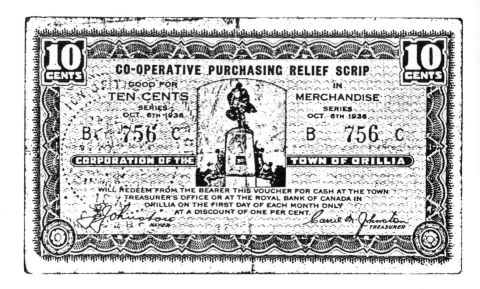

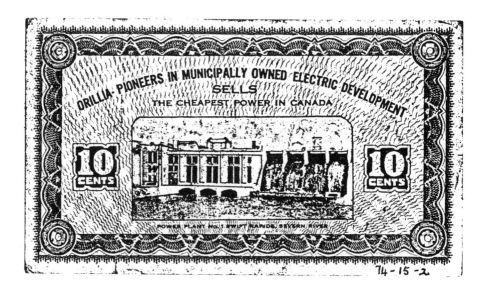

*1936 Orillia Relief Scrip showing the
Champlain Monument on one side and the power plant,
No. 1 Swift Rapids, Severn River, on the other*

the spirit with which citizens of the County rallied to meet it, were evident in Mayor John F. Craig's inaugural address to the Barrie Town Council, in January, 1933:

The task of any representative body in these serious times is one requiring the best thought and most careful judgement, if costly mistakes are not to be made. We must face the responsibilities that are ours with careful thought and courage; despondency or despair are particularly dangerous just now. . . .

The citizens are to be commended on their splendid response to the appeal of the Central Relief Committee for funds to be used for relief this winter. . . .

The work of the Central Relief Committee and those organizations that undertook the drive for funds are deserving of all praise. . . . The thanks of the citizens is due these men for the work they are doing and have done. I should like to say that the Central Relief Committee has not spent a single cent of the funds collected for any purpose whatever except for relief reaching those in need. No salaries are being paid, no expenses are being incurred, and the use of the Council room as an office eliminates any charges for rent. . . .

I wish to commend the strength of character of those out of work. They have borne themselves in these trying times with commendable restraint. Their respect for law and order and their bearing under great stress is one bright spot in the gloom of depression. . . .

We must endeavour to ease the burden of taxes as much as may be done, having in mind economy coupled with efficiency. . . . It should be our duty to endeavour to improve our position, and in this connection the reduction of the arrears of taxes must receive our special attention.

An oddity of the times was that, while unemployment was rampant in the towns, farm help was in short supply in most rural areas. Some men on the relief roles did go out at harvest time, when they worked a seven-day week, usually with every second Sunday off. In the main, however, the shortage continued, as Stewart L. Page, Agricultural Representative for North Simcoe, told the Barrie *Examiner* in August, 1935. "Despite the fact that farmers are paying $20 to $30 per month wages and board, help is still short in this district, and the farmers are having some difficulty in filling their requirements."

Further insight into the difficulties that were on every side during those years is provided by a study of the minutes of Simcoe County Council meetings. Matters connected, directly or indirectly, with the depression were on every Council agenda. In January, 1931, for example, by-laws were passed recommending the payment of various sums to County towns for civic improvement projects, designed to create jobs through the Ontario Government's "Unemployment Relief Act"—$31,500 to Midland, $30,000 to Orillia, $20,000 to Penetang and $13,000 to Barrie.

Like most citizens, Council had to scrimp in order to make the most of every available dollar. The annual grants to County libraries, routine for many years, had to be cut out of the annual budget. So did standard donations to many charities. Grants to hospitals were reduced. Free seeds could no longer be distributed for school fairs. Still, in spite of such economies, Simcoe County owed $63,000 by 1933.

At the core of the situation was the simple fact that a great many citizens were simply unable to pay their taxes. This, in turn, meant that many communities, Midland, Penetang, Collingwood, Tiny township and several others, fell in arrears on their annual levies, and County Council had less real revenue to spread over the many areas for which it was responsible.

In 1933 the Council agreed to guarantee $76,000 in debentures issued by the town of Midland, on condition that part of the proceeds would be used to bring delinquent 1932 and 1933 levies up to date. By 1935 both the Midland debentures and those arranged by Penetang were in default. In the main, such failures to meet commitments were due neither to bad faith, nor to bad management, so much as to the terrible reality that, wherever you turned, there just was not enough money to go around.

Of course, as is also always true in war time, some things went on pretty well as usual: soft ball games on hot summer evenings, fall fairs, church services and Sunday Schools.

180

Circuses came to town each summer. There were leaves to rake each fall. There was fishing, band concerts, the smell of lilacs and V's of honking geese coming north in the spring.

People were born, got married, raised families and died. Among the prominent citizens who passed on during the decade were Alphonse Arpin, the illiterate woodsman who had discovered the site of St. Ignace, where Brébeuf and Lalemant were put to death, in Tay township; and Robert A. Kent of Hillsdale, whose magnificent penmanship had been employed to write out the copy of the British North America Act that was sent to Queen Victoria in 1867.

There were diversions of many kinds: the cyclone that swept through Oro in 1934, causing widespread damage; the departure of James R. Ayling and Leonard G. Reid in their "Trail of the Caribou" biplane en route for Baghdad, from Wasaga Beach on the sunny morning of August 8, 1934 (adverse weather conditions and a shortage of fuel forced them down in London, after almost thirty-one hours in the air).

There was progress too. In 1933 Wallace Murdoch of Guthrie drove the first school bus in the County, taking pupils along No. 11 highway to the Barrie High School. In 1931 Wallace Hoover had enough faith in the future to buy a service station on Beeton's Main Street, a confidence which was subsequently justified by the fact that he operated it successfully until his retirement in 1973 at the age of eighty.

Similarly, in the spring of 1936 the congregation of the Shiloh Union Church at New Flos decided to go ahead with plans for redecorating. Even taking into account the fact that much of the labour was of a voluntary nature, it is still amazing to consider how little the project cost in those years of rock-bottom prices: hanging 60 rolls of wallpaper (@15¢) —$9.00; hanging border—$1.00; outside painting—$1.50; staining doors—$1.00; 1 gallon varnish for pews—$4.00; 5 quarts interior varnish—$4.40; 1 quart white paint—$0.85; 1 gallon stain—$2.25; 40 rolls wallpaper (@ 35¢)—$14.00; 28 rolls ceiling (@ 35¢)—$9.80; 41 yards border (@ 10¢)— $4.10; entrance doors $13.25. Total expenses—$65.15.

181

Mostly, the years of the Great Depression were years of stretching things out, doing without, making things last, saving a few cents here, a quarter there, getting from one day to the next. Winter was the worst time. It was harder for the unemployed men to get out then and easier for them to sit around the house and brood. With the shorter hours of daylight, more hydro was used in the towns and villages and more coal-oil in the lamps of the rural areas.

And there was the constant problem of keeping warm. Rural homes were heated by wood-burning kitchen ranges and potbellied stoves, city homes by monstrous cellar furnaces. In those days, before thermostatically-controlled, automatic heating, a lot of time was spent in stoking and banking fires, splitting kindling, and carrying out ashes and cinders.

If there was anything to burn. District farmers used to drive their sleighs to Saturday morning markets in Orillia, Barrie, Collingwood and Midland, and offer to deliver a cord of choice maple and oak, cut to stove-length and split, for $5 or $6. A half-ton of good coal cost about the same. Still, fortunate indeed was the homeowner who had more than two or three weeks' supply of fuel on hand at any given time. Every house had one particularly cold bedroom, the occupant of which was allotted the best eider-down quilts and thickest rugs.

Socks were darned. Clothes were stitched-up, patched, taken in and let out, and handed down from older to younger family members, until finally reduced to the status of cleaning rags. Worn-out soles were replaced by the shoemaker, if there was an extra half-dollar on hand, or worn with pieces of cardboard covering the holes, if there was not. In summer, most boys and girls went barefoot (as can be seen in any number of class graduation photos taken in the thirties).

In the strained circumstances of the time, the thought of major medical bills was a constant concern. The approach of most Simcoe County doctors was to supply whatever treatment was required first, and worry about payment later.

Many fees were settled according to the barter system: a quarter of beef for a broken leg, two dozen eggs for the treatment of a boil, and so on.

What many Simcoe County women who lived through the period remember most clearly, was the constant challenge of keeping enough wholesome, nutritious, satisfying food on the table for their growing families. Sirloin steak might be selling for just 18¢ a pound, but it was far beyond the reach of most families. "We learned how to use the cheaper cuts," one Stayner woman recalled recently, "like beef heart, kidneys, liver, stewing beef, sausages and peameal bacon. No one ever threw out soup bones in those days. And if you had any meat left over, you'd stretch it out, and make it into a shepherd's pie."

Homemade potato soup was a favourite, because the ingredients were cheap, and the results filling. So, for the same reasons, was rice pudding. "One of the best ways," an Alliston woman added, "was to make a white sauce, mix in anything you had on hand, and serve it on toast. That way, you could stretch a can of salmon, a few stocks of asparagus, some green peas, or a few bits of leftover ham to feed the whole family."

As the years passed, things gradually improved. Factories began to take on a few extra hands. The number of families on relief shrank with each passing month.

Mayor William James Blair of Barrie was probably a little premature in the optimism he displayed in his inaugural address to the 1935 Town Council. "The years of depression are apparently nearly past," he said. "Business conditions are gradually improving. . . . There is every prospect that there will be less misery and unhappiness in the coming year."

Still, the worst was over. A year later, the Collingwood *Enterprise* could be cautiously optimistic in its lead editorial on January 2, 1936:

Citizens of Collingwood have much for which to be thankful. . . . Mariners, on the whole, enjoyed a good season. Shipbuilding, unfortunately, has been at a standstill, only the occasional repair job bringing former employees back together again.

Still, many men have gone back to work in a variety of jobs. There are fewer on the dole, more in a position to pay taxes. . . .

But only continued courage, determination, industry and full co-operation can ensure happiness. . . . All must pull together if 1936 is to be better than the year over which the curtains have just been drawn.

1936 *was* better in Simcoe County. Here and there factories were hiring again, a few HELP WANTED ads began to appear in the newspapers, and—wonder of wonders—the occasional employee was even given a raise! In some homes lunch buckets that had been gathering dust on cupboard shelves for years were brought out, cleaned up, and once more packed with wax-paper-wrapped sandwiches, oranges, bananas, pickles, tomatoes and cookies. Hot tea and coffee was again poured into long unused thermos bottles. More and more men brought home paychecks; fewer had to line up for relief vouchers.

Times were still tough, but the worst was over. The backbone of the Great Depression had been broken, and confidence gradually returned to the land. For the first time since 1929, people began to plan for the future, to look ahead.

It was providential that they could not see too clearly, or too far into the future. Because just over the finally brighter horizon, the ugly, grey clouds of World War II were already gathering.

11 Ships in War and Peace

Although the calendar specifies September 21 as the beginning of autumn, Labor Day has traditionally marked the real end of summer for most Canadians. Over the last long weekend, boats are put away, cottages are boarded up against the coming winter, and families come home so that the children can get ready for the opening of school the following morning.

In Simcoe County the Labor Day weekend of 1939 seemed outwardly to be very similar to its predecessors. As in every other year, the sound of hammers nailing shutters over windows echoed along shorelines and out among the islands. As in every other year, boys and girls shrieked as they took their final swims in the already cooling waters, and hung their suits up to dry for the last time.

As in every other year, there were baseball and softball play-off games in various parts of the County; there were closing Saturday night dances in a dozen lake and riverside pavilions throughout the area; and there was a Sunday night band-concert in Orillia's Couchiching Park. In Barrie, those who stayed in town could take in a double-feature at the Granada Theatre—Wallace Beery in "Sergeant Madden," and James Cagney in "Angels with Dirty Faces," plus the opening instalment of a new series called "The Lone Ranger Returns."

But it was not, of course, just as in every other year; for Labor Day weekend, 1939, marked not just the end of another summer, but the end of many other things as well. It was the real end of the 1930s, the final end of the Great Depression, the end, in many ways, of innocence, and the end of twenty years of peace.

185

People sat by their radios to listen to the special bulletins, and the headlines of the newspapers were set in larger type each day, as they shouted out the growing inevitability of war:

Wednesday, August 30:

HITLER ELECTRIFIES EUROPE WITH MOSCOW NON-AGRESSION PACT!

Thursday, August 31:

HITLER DELIVERS WAR ULTIMATUM TO POLAND

Friday, September 1:

TIME RUNNING OUT IN EUROPE: ARMIES MASS

Saturday, September 2:

BRITISH PEOPLE SET FOR WAR

By Labor Day morning, Monday, September 4, Great Britain was again at war with Germany.

The grim reality of that fact was immediately brought home to the people of Simcoe County by the sinking of the *Athenia* by a German U-boat within a few hours of the declaration of hostilities. Among the survivors of the torpedoed British liner, which went down some 240 miles northwest of Ireland, were Margaret Childs of Barrie (later a noted artist and teacher) and Ethel M. Elgood, principal of Barrie's Ovenden College. After several hours of helping to row lifeboats the survivors were picked up by the freighter *Knute Nelson* and taken to Galway, Eire.

Within hours of receiving the news from overseas, Camp Borden went on an active wartime basis, and all entrances were sealed off by barricades and armed sentries. By Tuesday, September 5, all hydro-electric power plants in the County were being guarded by members of reserve militia units, Canadian Legion veterans of the Great War, and off-duty Provincial Police constables.

Although the Canadian House of Commons debated the matter for a few days, there was little doubt in Simcoe

County that Canada would once more go to the support of "the Mother Country" with every available resource. The lead editorial in the Barrie *Examiner* of September 7, 1939, accurately reflected the mood of most people:

This world is so constituted that all things come to an end in the regular course of nature, but in that same course, and by the same law, there is always a new beginning. The present summer is on the wane; the leaves will fall in due course, and the dead hand of winter will put an end to all vegetation—but the words of Shelley are eternally true: 'If winter comes, can spring be far behind?'

It is in this spirit that we have entered upon this struggle. Our world of peace—if it can be truthfully said to have been peace—has passed away. As men and women who value freedom, and will not bow the knee to a tyrant, there is nothing left for us to do but to fight. The words of Kipling ring in our ears at this time of peril:

In courage, keep your heart,
In strength, lift up your hand!

The response of the young men of Simcoe County to the call to arms was no less enthusiastic than it had been in 1914, but their participation turned out to be considerably different. In "The Great War," soon to become known as World War I, the vast majority of volunteers had gone overseas with the County's own Regiment, the Simcoe Foresters. In 1936 the Foresters had amalgamated with the neighbouring Grey Regiment, to become the Grey and Simcoe Foresters. On April 1, 1942, while in training at Camp Borden, the Grey and Simcoes were converted into an armoured unit, the 26th Army Tank Regiment.

Methods of warfare had become considerably more mechanized and technical in the two decades since the 1918 Armistice, and many recruits joined specialized units from outside the County in order to use, or acquire, particular trades and skills. By 1939, too, Canada had her own air and sea commands, and large numbers joined the Royal Canadian Air Force and the Royal Canadian Navy.

The net result was that Simcoe County men and women

fought and served in a much greater variety of capacities and in many more theatres of war than had been the case in the 1914-18 conflict.

Camp Borden, created to fulfil the needs of World War I, really came into its own in World War II. About half of the 185,000 Canadian soldiers who went overseas between 1939 and 1945 received at least some of their training there— thirty to thirty-five thousand of them at a time. The Air Force operation there became, not only "the Schoolhouse of the R.C.A.F.," but also one of the cornerstones of Canada's huge contribution to the British Commonwealth Air Training Plan. The B.C.A.T.P., an agreement between Great Britain, Canada, Australia and New Zealand, came into effect on December 17, 1939. The plan called for the training of 25,000 air crew a year.

The first group of trainees reported to No. 1 Service Flying Training School at Camp Borden on July 22, 1940, and the inaugural class of thirty-nine pilots received their wings eight weeks later, on September 30. By the time the British Commonwealth Air Training Plan was ended, on March 31, 1945, it had produced more than 130,000 trained air crew and was recognized as one of the outstanding success stories of the war.

At home, business and industry, church organizations, service clubs, all levels of government, and private citizens pitched in to support the war effort. As in the first war, the women of the County played a major role in turning out munitions and armaments. Many women went on active service with the navy (WRCNS), army (WAAC) and air force (WAAF).

Simcoe County Council voted full support to the federal government at its first meeting after the declaration of war, and through the years allocated substantial sums of money to such organizations as the Red Cross, the Navy League of Canada, Russian Relief and many others. It also played an active role in promoting the sale of Victory Bonds, as well as purchasing them.

Although the provision of food was a matter of vital importance, district farmers had to contend with a critical shortage of help throughout the war. Farm wives and daughters, servicemen on leave, high school students, even Italian prisoners of war—many volunteered or were conscripted: yet the problem of getting the crops in remained chronic. Pointing out that it was impossible to both fight and farm, the Council for Simcoe County played an active, and partially successful, role in trying to persuade the federal government that farm sons should be encouraged to stay on the land, and subjected to less pressure to enlist in the armed forces. Throughout the war, however, the balance remained an uneasy one, with the County providing more than its share of men and women in uniform, yet somehow managing to harvest each summer's yield.

One of the great contributions made by Simcoe County was in providing fighting ships for the Royal Canadian Navy. In September, 1939, the R.C.N. consisted of just 13 ships, including habour craft; by V-E Day, 1945, the Canadian fleet numbered over 900 vessels, about 400 of which were fighting ships, and the R.C.N. had assumed major responsibility for keeping the North Atlantic convoy lanes open to Great Britain.

The phenomenal growth of the Canadian Navy was based largely on two types of vessels, the Flower-class corvette, and the Bangor minesweeper. Later on, R.C.N. striking power was enhanced by the addition of frigates and Tribal- and River-class destroyers, but in the initial stages corvettes and minesweepers were the workhorses of the convoy system.

In December, 1939, the newly-formed Canadian War Supply Board asked for tenders for the building of corvettes and minesweepers in Canada. Two months later contracts were approved with twelve Canadian companies, including Collingwood Shipyards Limited, which was authorized to build three Flower-class corvettes in 1940 and another five the following year. The price per vessel was set at $528,000. Later in 1940, Midland Shipyards Limited was added to the group in time for the next corvette-building program.

The Great Lakes yards engaged in the construction of fighting ships were affiliated under a holding company, Canadian Shipbuilding and Engineering Inc., which had been organized by Roy M. Wolvin of Montreal. Collingwood

The launching of the H.M.C.S. Collingwood, *July 27, 1940*

Shipyards Ltd. and Port Arthur Shipbuilding Ltd. were the two most important members of this organization, since both had the facilities to build engines and boilers as well as hulls. When Wolvin died during the war, he was succeeded by John S. Leitch, who had been General Manager at Collingwood since 1912.

The very first corvette to be completed in this Canada-wide program was launched at the Collingwood Shipyards site on November 9, 1940. Appropriately, it was christened H.M.C.S. *Collingwood* and was to see long and distinguished service on the North Atlantic. Although the launching must have been a source of great local pride, it was not covered by Collingwood or district newspapers—a concession to wartime security.

In all, 13 corvettes were built at Collingwood between 1940 and 1945, and sailed down through the network of lakes and locks to the St. Lawrence and the North Atlantic:

Ship	Date of Launching
H.M.C.S. *Collingwood*	Nov. 9, 1940
H.M.C.S. *Barrie*	Apr. 4, 1941
H.M.C.S. *Galt*	May 15, 1941
H.M.C.S. *Orillia*	May 29, 1941
H.M.C.S. *Moosejaw*	June 19, 1941
H.M.C.S. *Battleford*	July 31, 1941
H.M.C.S. *Drumheller*	Sept. 13, 1941
H.M.C.S. *Halifax*	Nov. 26, 1941
H.M.C.S. *Woodstock*	May 1, 1942
H.M.C.S. *North Bay*	Oct. 25, 1943
H.M.C.S. *Owen Sound*	Nov. 17, 1943
H.M.C.S. *Guelph*	May 9, 1944
H.M.C.S. *Fergus*	Nov. 18, 1944

Between 1942 and 1944, the Midland Shipyards added another nine: *Brantford, Midland, Cobourg, Lindsay, Whitby, Parry Sound, Strathroy, Thorlock* and *West York*.

It would be impossible to estimate how many nautical miles these Collingwood- and Midland-built corvettes steamed during the war; how many depth-charge attacks they carried out; how many U-boat wolf-packs they helped to fight off; how many chill, grey dawns and early winter twilights they sailed through on the North Atlantic; how many merchantmen and tankers they saw go to their graves; how many survivors they picked up from the oil-slicked seas. But there can be do doubt that they played a very important part in winning the war at sea, so that Winston Churchill could have "the tools with which to finish the job."

Another important naval vessel during World War II was the Fairmile (or "M.L." for Motor Launch). Much smaller than corvettes and minesweepers, the Fairmiles were designed to detect and attack U-boats along Canada's coastlines. One hundred and twelve feet long and with a displacement of 79 tons, they were driven by two 650 h.p. gasoline motors, and equipped with depth charges, asdic and radar. Built of mahogany imported from South America, they had an emergency speed of 20 knots, and sailing in them was the approximate equivalent of going over Niagara Falls in a barrel.

In April, 1941, the War Supply Board let contracts for 24 Motor Launches with eleven Canadian firms, seven in Ontario, three in British Columbia, and one in Nova Scotia. Among the Ontario firms chosen were Grew Boats Limited, Penetang, Hunter Boats Limited of Orillia, and the Midland Boat Works—all of which had had long experience in building pleasure craft of similar construction. In all, these three companies turned out 21 Fairmiles during the war.

When the need came for fighting ships, it was not surprising that the Canadian Navy looked to the Simcoe County towns on the south shore of Georgian Bay, for they have been building vessels for more than a century. Since the beginning, Collingwood, Penetang, Midland, Port McNicholl, and Victoria Harbour have been sailing and shipbuilding ports on Ontario's great inland seas. Fishing fleets have sailed from them, as have naval ships of an earlier era, fast schooners, settlers bound for Fort William and the new west, tugs towing barges and tugs bringing in huge rafts of logs, and luxurious passenger liners.

As in sea ports around the world, the people who live there keep an eye to the weather, for their heritage includes a legacy of tragedy: of ships that sailed, never to return, and of good men lost to gales, blizzards, treacherous reefs, collisions at sea and fire.

That heritage extends back to include the loss of the *Mary Ward* in November, 1872, and the mysterious fate of the *Waubuno* in November, 1879. The *Mary Ward*, just purchased by new owners, foundered in a storm on her way from Sarnia to Collingwood, which was to have become her home port. The *Waubuno* went down on the Haystack Reefs off Moose Point, taking all twenty-four passengers and crew members with her in circumstances that have never been adequately explained.

The worst storms on the Great Lakes occur in November, just before the close of shipping, when terrible gales blow, snow squalls limit visibility to near-zero, and water temperatures drop to near-freezing. There still are people in Simcoe County's Georgian Bay ports who remember the dreadful blow of November 9 to 12, 1913, which they refer to simply as "the Great Storm." "The situation which existed on Lake Huron was unprecedented," the *Marine Review* reported in its December, 1913 issue. "Since the lakes have been commercially navigated, no such conditions have ever been met with before, and centuries may go by before such a phenomenon is again experienced."

For four days the wind howled and gusted without letup; the seas reached heights far beyond any ever before experienced, cresting to thirty-five feet and more; and heavy, driving snow made it impossible to see more than a boat-length in any direction. On Sunday, November 9 the wind blew at an average velocity of 60 miles an hour, gusting to 80 m.p.h. and more. When the storm finally abated on November 12, no fewer than eleven vessels had gone down in the Upper Lakes, eight others had been totally destroyed, and twenty more were left stranded on reefs and shoals. At least 250 seamen had lost their lives.

Over the years, many other ships were lost to fire—the *City of Collingwood* and the *City of Parry Sound*, to name but two. Both were luxurious passenger vessels, and both burned to the waterline while at dockside in Collingwood.

On November 14, 1940, in the second fall of World War II, two ships of special interest to Simcoe County's Georgian Bay ports were caught in a typical late-season storm. The large bulk-carrier *Anna C. Minch*, under the command of Captain Donald Kennedy (one of the most respected and best liked masters on the Great Lakes), foundered and sank in Lake Michigan, near Muskegon, Illinois. She went down

H.M.C.S. Collingwood, *September, 1943*

with all hands, including Captain Kennedy, seven seamen from Collingwood, and eight from Midland.

Not many miles away, the steamer *Novadoc*, upbound for Fort William with a cargo of coke, was driven aground, and for some time it was feared that all members of the crew, including five men from Collingwood and one from Midland, had been lost. But after many long, terrible hours of clinging to the hull in the icy water, all were saved when the tug *Three Brothers* managed to get a line aboard and haul them to safety.

Among the seaport towns of southern Georgian Bay, Port McNicoll was particularly famed as the eastern terminus for the fleet of great passenger steamers which linked southern Ontario with the twin cities of Port Arthur and Fort William at the head of Lake Superior. The route was seen as a short-cut and a change for rail passengers heading west for the Prairies and beyond.

At one time it was served by five luxury liners of the in-land seas, the *Alberta, Manitoba, Athabasca, Keewatin* and *Assiniboia*, and the carefully manicured lawns and well-cared-for flower beds surrounding the Port McNicoll docks were a familiar sight to hundreds of passengers who made the round trip every summer.

The *Alberta* and *Athabasca* were withdrawn from pas-senger service in 1916, although they continued to carry freight for another thirty years. The *Manitoba* was finally sold for scrap in 1949, the same year that the tragic fire on board the *S.S. Noronic* in Toronto harbour took more than a hundred lives.

The *Keewatin* and *Assiniboia* tried to abide by the more stringent safety regulations that came into effect after the burning of the *Noronic*, but ever-increasing costs of operation meant that their days were numbered. The last regularly scheduled departure from Port McNicoll occurred on November 28, 1965, when the *Keewatin* sailed under Captain Ernest H. Ridd; there were only two passengers, both mem-bers of the Great Lakes Historical Society.

Shipbuilding in Collingwood has a long history. It is not

known when the first vessel was constructed there, but as early as 1857-58 three ships were built on the Collingwood waterfront, the *Flying Dutchman*, *The Brothers* and the *Hope*. Two of these were launched at the north end of Hurontario Street, and the third probably at the east end of Ontario Street.

The barge *Hotchkiss*, capable of carrying a million feet of lumber was built in the harbour by Alfred Morrill in 1870. Other early shipbuilders included James Storey, W. Watts and Son, Pat Doherty, R. J. Morrill, and S. D. Andrews, perhaps best known for his famous passenger and freight steamers, the *Majestic* (1895) and the *Germanic* (1899).

In 1883, thanks to the approval by the Collingwood ratepayers of a by-law providing for a debenture of $25,000, the Queen's Drydock and Shipbuilding Company came into existence, with S. D. Andrews as its general manager. The drydock was opened on May 24, 1883, and its first customer was the steamer *Oneida* which had been damaged by fire during the previous winter's lay-up.

The period around the turn of the century was one of transition from the wooden construction of an earlier era to steel hulls. In 1900, Captain Alexander McDougall became convinced that the Georgian Bay area needed a steel shipbuilding industry, and that Collingwood was the place to start it. McDougall, a former resident who had become a shipbuilder at West Superior, Wisconsin, where he had devised the unique, round-shouldered hull called the "whaleback," approached the Queen's Drydock and Shipbuilding Company. The result was a merger of interests and the incorporation of the Collingwood Shipbuilding Company. A large steel construction plant was erected, building berths were constructed on the sides of the drydocks, and for the first time the staccato chatter of riveters' hammers disturbed the waterfront. From that year on a steady stream of vessels of many different types left the Collingwood yards for service in all parts of the world.

The first ship to be built by the new company was the

luxurious passenger steamer *Huronic*, the pride of the Northern Navigation Company. Launched in 1901, the *Huronic*
was soon to be familiarly known up and down the Lakes as
the "Huey" and was destined for a long and illustrious career,
primarily on the run between Sarnia and the Lakehead. Over
three hundred feet long from proud bow to graceful stern,
the *Huronic* incorporated the latest in accomodation, service
and passenger comfort: broad promenade decks, spacious
staterooms, a library, curving staircases, hot and cold running
water, and a magnificent, high-ceilinged dining salon that
would have done justice to the finest London or New York
hotels. Spotless white linen, gleaming silverware, the best
quality china, and fresh flowers graced the tables at every
meal. Passengers came back summer after summer, many
booking their annual cruises a year in advance. Later on, the
Huronic was joined by two sister ships, the *Hamonic* and the
Noronic, built in 1913 at Port Arthur; both were eventually
to go up in flames in the 1940s, the *Hamonic* at Sarnia, the
Noronic, with tragic loss of life, in Toronto harbour.

Among the other vessels built at Collingwood during the
early years were the smaller passenger steamer *Waubic*, and a
series of fine freighters, including the *E. B. Osler, Emperor,
Collingwood, Hagarty, W. D. Mathews*, and the ill-fated
James Carruthers, lost in the great storm of November, 1913
with all hands.

During the first World War, the Collingwood yards
turned to war production, building naval vessels of various
types for the British Navy, and ocean-going freighters which
sailed on most of the world's oceans and seas.

Collingwood had had grain elevators from as far back as
the 1850s, but the first large scale, modern storage operation
came into being in 1928 with the establishment of Collingwood Terminals Limited. Among those responsible for the
promotion and organization of the new company were Dr. J.
Robins Arthur, then the Mayor of the town, and H. I. Price,
who became its first president. Construction was completed
in September, 1929, and the first ship to dock there, the

S. S. *Munsing*, arrived with a cargo of corn a few days later.
In time, more than five million bushels of grain would be
handled by the Collingwood terminals each year.

Shipbuilding, shipping and grain storage all were hard hit
by the economic avalanche of the Great Depression, but they
experienced a sudden comeback in the early 1940s. Corvettes
and minesweepers were desperately needed in the early years
of World War II. Grain handling and shipping also revived
because of the critical need to get western wheat to a beleaguered and hungry Great Britain.

Full production: that was the story on the home front.
Meanwhile, both on the seas and overseas, the sailors, airmen
and soldiers from Simcoe County were paying a high price
for the victory that took almost six years to achieve. Each
week the newspapers of the County published lists of local
casualties. Each week the toll mounted. Chosen at random, a
single edition of just one weekly journal will serve to illustrate. On March 29, 1945, the Orillia *Packet & Times* printed
this resume:

Mrs. W. Tire of Waubaushene received word that her son,
Gunner E. Tire, had been wounded and was in hospital in Belgium;

Mrs. D. Isaac of Orillia was informed that her son, Burt,
had been wounded by shrapnel, and was in hospital on the
French-Belgian border;

Mrs. W. C. Orman heard that her husband, Private W. C.
Orman had been wounded in action;

Mrs. M. S. Pledger of Hillsdale received a telegram saying
that her youngest son, Paratrooper Kenneth Pledger, was missing and presumed dead [An older brother, Flight-Lieutenant
Oswald Pledger, D.F.C., had been reported killed in action
less than a month earlier];

Mr. and Mrs. Howard Brandon of Hillsdale were told that
their older son, Private Douglas Brandon, had been seriously
wounded;

Mrs. M. Shaw of Orillia learned that her son-in-law had
been killed in action.

That many dead or wounded from a single district in a

single seven-day period of a very long, and very terrible war!

It was much the same in every community, large and small, throughout the County. Innisfil lost five men; ten of the one hundred thirty young men and women who enlisted from Oro failed to return. So with Essa, and Medonte, and Matchedash, and all of the other townships, towns, villages, hamlets. In time there would be many more names added to the dead of 1914-18 on war memorials in parks scattered throughout the County.

World War II finally came to an end in the spring and summer of 1945: first with the defeat of Germany in May, then with the Japanese surrender in mid-August. Simcoe County rejoiced over the achievement of victory in Europe, but the celebrations were restrained, partly because the struggle had been so long and the costs so high, and partly because the war in the Pacific remained to be won. Many of the official ceremonies centred around church services, and there were more hymns played and sung than there were victory tunes and marches.

But when the news came over the radio that Japan had agreed to lay down its arms, on the evening of August 14, 1945, it was a different story. Then the war *was* really over at last, and Simcoe County, like the rest of Canada, pulled out all the stops and let joy be unrestrained. As described in the pages of the Barrie *Examiner*, this is the way it was in one community:

Within a few minutes cars were racing up and down the main streets, with horns blaring. By 7:30 the Barrie fire reels had joined the celebrating, and the screaming sirens were added to the din of the auto horns.

By eight o'clock, half a dozen members of the BCI band, travelling in a small truck, added their favourite tunes to the increasing volume of sound. All the time the raucous tooting of horns continued, while hundreds of shouting children and grown-ups jumped on passing vehicles, waving flags and shouting with joy. . . .

By nine o'clock, there were so many people on the main street that it was difficult to move along, and the traffic was such that it was practically impossible to cross the street. Boxes and packing crates were rounded up, and a huge bonfire started at a downtown intersection.

Alderman Grant Mayor with a trombone led a band of marching young people up and down the main thoroughfare.

Everywhere people were kissing—relatives, friends, sweethearts, and perfect strangers.

The war was finally over.

The following day, Wednesday, was declared an official holiday, with the daylight hours being mainly devoted to church services of thanksgiving, official parades, and speeches by politicians and other leading figures; but when darkness began to fall the mood of joy and revelry took over once more, and dancing in the streets, torch parades, bonfires, singing and shouting continued far into the early hours of the morning. Much the same mood prevailed in all communities, large and small, throughout the County.

In company with most other Simcoe County communities, Collingwood enjoyed relative prosperity in the years after the war. Its population, which had declined steadily from 1910 to the outbreak of hostilities in 1939, increased just as steadily from 1945 on:

Year	Population of Collingwood
1900	5,498
1910	7,708
1920	7,262
1930	5,728
1940	5,498
1950	7,027
1960	8,307
1970	9,150

Thanks to the progressive and aggressive campaign by the Collingwood Mayor and Council, aided by an active

Chamber of Commerce, many new industries began to locate in the Georgian Bay town. The influx began in the late 1940s and has continued up to the present time.

Over the same period there was a shift in the role of railroads, from small freight, mail and passengers, to bulk freight and the movement of grain. With the improvement of highways, trucking companies cut deeply into the express and carrier business, while daily bus schedules and increasing reliance on the family car drastically reduced passenger ticket sales. In 1955, passenger service between Toronto and Meaford was cut back to one train a day, and the following year the Collingwood-Beeton-Hamilton run was eliminated entirely. Further restrictions and deletions were soon to follow.

Among the new industries that came to Collingwood in the post-war years were Kaufman Furniture Ltd., Georgian China Ltd., Quinlan-Crawford Textiles, Canadian Mist Distillers Ltd. and L.O.F. Glass of Canada. In 1969, National Starch opened a plant off Highway 26 East. A subsidiary of Nacan Products Limited, it underwent several expansions and additions until, by the mid-1970s it occupied some 25,000 square feet and employed about seventy people.

Another major addition to the Collingwood industrial scene was the building of the Harding Carpets Ltd. plant in 1966. It was central Ontario's first carpet manufacturing plant, and originally provided jobs for about 150 Collingwood residents. The factory encompassed some 158,000 square feet, and was built at a cost of $5.6 million. Since then there have been four major expansions, almost doubling its original size. By the mid-1970s Harding was employing almost 600 in Collingwood.

Another major area of expansion came under the appropriate label of "Blue Mountain" and involved the unlikely combination of skiing and the making of pottery. In 1946, a Czechoslovakian refugee named Jozo Weider appeared in Collingwood. This native of mountainous central Europe arrived with little capital, but with boundless energy and enthusiasm, and with an infectious optimism. As a former Czechoslovakian skiing champion, it was natural that Weider should first turn his attention to the slopes of the Blue Mountains.

Organized skiing in the Collingwood area dates from the late 1930s, when the Blue Mountain Ski Club came into existence. The first trails were laid out by the great Fritz Loosli, and a somewhat crude tow called "the Red Devil" was installed. Jozo Weider saw the undeveloped potential of this operation, and eventually built it into Blue Mountain Winter Park, with a ski area of over 1,000 acres, poma-lifts, T-Bars and chair-lifts—one of the most modern skiing operations in North America. From this beginning evolved Simcoe County's flourishing winter recreation industry of the fifties, sixties and seventies. Over the years many other ski clubs and resorts came into being: Osler Bluffs, Georgian Peaks, Craigleith, Alpine, Devil's Glen, and Hidden Valley.

Then Jozo Weider devoted his energies to a second great interest, the making of quality pottery; an interest that was to make Collingwood the "Pottery Capital of Canada" with six factories turning out internationally known and popular products. Weider's success story is well summarized in the pages of the Collingwood *Enterprise-Bulletin* of November 26, 1970:

As with all of the Weider undertakings, the beginnings were small—and then followed rapid expansion. He pioneered the pottery business in the basement of the famous Ski barn about 1949, with Dennis Tupy making the first moulds. . . .

His (Weider's) experiments there, with the aid of European potters. Tupy and Hamablek, resulted in the unique qualities of texture and colour which have made Blue Mountain pottery so widely accepted.

The factory soon outgrew the Ski Barn, and expanded to larger premises four times within the next fourteen years, before finally taking a long-term home in the former Martin-Baker aircraft plant on Pine Street in 1963. "Today," the *Enterprise-Bulletin* article concludes, "the firm produces hundreds of models of pottery, and turns out several thousand pieces per day for the domestic and foreign markets."

Despite the healthy diversification into other types of industry, however, shipbuilding continues to be the economic, emotional and psychological heart of Collingwood. Regardless of other factors, the people of the town are confident and have a sense of well-being when a hull is being built and they can see the flames of welders' torches and hear the clang of rivets being driven home. Let there be silence along the waterfront, on the other hand, and there is an uneasy feeling, an acute awareness that the pulse of the community is not beating.

Down through the years many great ships have been built at the Collingwood yards: the *Huronic*, the great bulk-carrier *Agawa*, launched in 1902, the mighty *Rimouski*, the M.S. *Agawa Canyon*, Canada Steamship Lines' giant *Simcoe* (730 feet in length, with three anchors, each weighing 12,000 pounds, capable of carrying a million bushels of grain), and her sister ship, the *Feux Follets*, launched October 10, 1967. There were many others, including the tough, gallant, little corvettes and minesweepers of World War II—perhaps 200 steel ships in all, slipping away through the outer markers of Collingwood Bay to sea.

Richard Lowery, President of Canadian Shipbuilding & Engineering, summed up what might be called the Collingwood spirit, on the occasion of the christening of the motor tanker *Imperial Dartmouth* in November 1970: "This is a good shipyard, with good workers, building a good product," he said. "Every time we christen a ship, we have a sense of pride and achievement . . . but there is a bit of sadness, too."

12 The Women of Simcoe County

One of the most important factors in the development of Simcoe County during the twentieth century has been the role played by the Women's Institutes of many communities, large and small. This unique organization, dedicated to rural improvement, better educational, social and economic conditions, and women's rights, was founded by Adelaide Hoodless at Stoney Creek, Ontario in 1897. It quickly spread across Canada and around the world. Judge Emily Murphy became the first national president of the Federated Women's Institutes of Canada in 1919. Meanwhile, the movement was carried abroad by another Simcoe County woman, Mrs. Alfred Watt of Collingwood. Mrs. Watt went to Britain in the spring of 1914, where both she and the concepts adopted by the Women's Institutes were enthusiastically endorsed. It was almost two decades before the seeds she planted grew to fruition, but in May, 1933 the Associated Countrywomen of the World came into being at Stockholm, Sweden, with Mrs. Watt as its first president.

As the years passed, Women's Institutes were organized in almost every town and village in Simcoe County. A partial listing of the origins of some of the branches will illustrate the widespread importance of the movement, and point out some of the many important community projects it fostered.

The first Women's Institute in the County was organized on July 2, 1901 at Cookstown, and it has remained active to the present day. Other units were formed in 1902 at Thornton, Bond Head, Creemore, Duntroon, Nottawa and Singhampton, in 1903 at Churchill, and in 1905 at Ballycroy; some of these disbanded for a while when enthusiasm waned and were reorganized later.

The Minesing Women's Institute was founded in 1904, with Mrs. D. Wood as President, and Miss Ruth Standen as Secretary. One of its primary undertakings, begun in 1918, was the renovation and expansion of the Minesing Cemetery, with a new fence, entrance gates and a plaque inscribed: "In Memory of Our Pioneers."

In Essa, the local branch took on the responsibility of raising enough money to establish a library, which was officially opened by Sir Frederick Banting on February 14, 1924.

Beeton's Women's Institute was founded at a meeting at the home of Mrs. Henry Aitken (Kate Scott Aitken) on November 9, 1920. At that inaugural meeting it was decided that a fitting project would be the construction of a memorial entrance to the village park, in honour of the local men who had fallen in World War I. After an extensive and enthusiastic money-raising campaign, the Alliston Marble Works was commissioned to construct gates of granite to flank the approach. The unveiling took place on the bitterly cold, grey afternoon of November 27, 1927, with Earl Rowe acting as Chairman and the Beeton Citizens' Band providing background music. Four years later the edifice was completed with the addition of a wrought-iron archway, and the provision of around-the-clock electric lights.

In July, 1928 a group of Women's Institute members met at Midhurst to discuss the possibility of setting up a Simcoe County museum. Two years later the first displays, consisting mainly of pioneer and archaeological artifacts, were opened to the public in a section of the Barrie Public Library. The museum remained there until 1932, when it was moved to the old Registry building on Worsley Street. The collection of material grew and by the 1960s the project was beyond the resources of the Women's Institute. It was taken over by the County of Simcoe in 1962; land was bought near the site of the present Administration Centre at Midhurst and the main building of the museum was erected that year. Under the leadership of Ross Channen, who was Director of

Wyebridge Women's Institute ladies, 1910

the Museum from 1962 until his death in 1975, the museum became one of the best county museums in Canada. There have been several additions to the main building. The first wing, which houses the Archives, opened in 1966, a Canadian Centennial project of the County. The Victorian Wing was added in 1970 and the Cultural Wing in 1974. On the grounds behind the main building there are eight restored pioneer buildings and a large Agricultural Display Building. Over 10,000 people visited the museum in the first six months it was open and at present over 48,000 people visit the museum annually.

The Stroud Women's Institute was organized during an afternoon meeting at the home of Mrs. J. G. Patterson on January 19, 1909. The first president was Mrs. R. A. Sutherland. In this branch discussions and debates were particularly popular, and the early minutes refer to such topics as: The Incubator Craze, Canning and Preserving, Fattening Poultry for Market, Games and Home Amusements for the Young, Women's Suffrage, Spring Sewing, Salads, and the Place of Music in the Home. The Stroud group also established the village's first library, with each member being called upon to donate a volume. For the first nine years the library was housed in Chantler's store, after which it was moved to the Orchard home, then to the basement of the Municipal Building, and finally, in 1960, it found a permanent home in the renovated Community Hall. The Women's Institute also paid for the chairs and helped to provide the piano.

Other Women's Institutes sprang up in towns and villages throughout the County. The Crown Hill Women's Institute was organized in June, 1911, with Mrs. S. J. Dunsmore as first president. The Dalston branch came into being a year earlier, on January 27, 1910. The Hawkestone chapter was also launched in 1910, with Mrs. Cecil Wilson as president, and Mrs. Robert Kendall as secretary. The Jarratt Women's Institute held its first meeting in 1914, electing Mrs. Robert Ego as president, while the Shanty Bay group, one of the earliest, dates from January, 1910, when Mrs. Arthur Petersen was chosen as first president. And so it went, as the movement spread from community to community.

The Women's Institutes, which continue to flourish, have contributed so much to the progress of Simcoe County that it is difficult to do justice to their importance. Adhering to their motto, "For Home and Country," generations of members have dedicated countless hours to the enrichment of their communities. They have always stood ready to aid and comfort their less fortunate fellow-citizens: the elderly, the orphaned, the impoverished, the sick, the blind, the deaf and the mentally retarded. Through the two wars they supported the men overseas with parcels and other comforts. And they have sponsored untold numbers of worthwhile civic projects.

Necessarily, much of their work has been devoted to raising funds—a business which they have gone about with a maximum of good will and efficiency, and a minimum of fuss and notoriety. Bazaars, teas, bake sales, quilting bees, concerts, rummage sales, tag days, door-to-door selling campaigns—all have been used to finance the numerous causes they have championed.

But the Women's Institutes have also been active in things cultural, giving their support to such organizations and activities as theatre and dance groups, bands, musical competitions, art classes, literary discussion groups and creative writing workshops. One of the most important, long-term projects undertaken by the Women's Institutes has been the preparation of the "Tweedsmuir histories," a great boon to all students of Simcoe County's past.

Perhaps the best way to gain an appreciation of the amount of good work done by this organization over the years is to record in some detail the accomplishments of a branch, such as the Stayner Women's Institute.

The first meeting of the Stayner Women's Institute took place in 1912 under the auspices of Mrs. David Morrison, who was to become the local first president. The membership grew during the next half-dozen years, and one of the highlights of the early period came on October 19, 1919, when

Mrs. Alfred Watt was a guest speaker in Stayner. She told the members of her recent work in England, where she had succeeded in establishing over four hundred Women's Institutes.

Through various money-raising projects, the Stayner Women's Institute was able to send gifts each year to district patients in Toronto hospitals, and to those confined to the Gravenhurst Sanatorium. Annual donations were made to the local Horticultural Society and to the Fair Board to encourage children to become interested in gardening.

Like many other Women's Institutes, the Stayner branch took an active part in the establishment and maintenance of a town library. Among many other gifts, it paid for the front porch with its iron railing and a walk to the side door, when the library building was remodelled just after World War II. The Institute, which owned the building, also waived the final payment of $900, returning that money to the Library Board for the purchase of new books.

Down through the years the Stayner Women's Institute has participated in many other important community activities. The Institute:

— sponsored sewing classes;
— was active in the Simcoe County Arts and Crafts Association;
— sponsored youth leadership training courses;
— helped organize and assist at blood donor clinics;
— supplied playground equipment for the public school;
— sponsored Brownie and Girl Guide groups;
— helped organize immunization clinics;
— supplied first aid kits to the schools;
— organized T.B. clinics;
— helped to set up and staff Well Baby clinics;
— carried on a long campaign for improved garbage collection;
— donated tables and benches for the park;

— sponsored Department of Agriculture lectures and courses;

— sponsored swimming classes for children;

— and, as a Centennial project, donated a spinet piano to the Stayner library.

The making of fine quilts has always been a tradition in Simcoe County, and in the 1970s the pioneer skill not only survives but has become a legitimate and widely recognized art form. The basics of the craft are well summarized in the excellent volume *Pioneer History of Midhurst*, published by the Midhurst Historical Society in 1975:

Quilting was a craft of such importance that it has thrived to this day, especially in Simcoe County, well known for years for its Rug and Quilt Fair organized by the Simcoe County Arts and Crafts Association.

Quilting

Quilt patterns, like early songs and stories, moved from one pioneer community to the next, changing in detail, stitching and name. The names reflect the originality of the designer—Wedding Ring, Log Cabin, Around the World, Dresden Plate, Star Flower, Bear's Paw. The patterns could be varied to please the quilter. They could be separated by strips of cloth, set in groups of four, or the direction of the design changed. There was even an array of styles in the actual stitching. Tiny stitches made the quilt fluffier, and the stitches themselves made independent designs on the quilt bottom. . . .

Today quilts hang in galleries and museums—some as folk art, but others as outstanding examples of fine design.

Quilts were made for everyday need, or for special occasions by the ladies of the community—for a wedding, when a neighbor lost his home by fire, for a newborn baby, or just as a keepsake. These would sometimes be called 'Friendship Quilts,' with the names of the quilters embroidered on their own work. Especially fine ones were 'Sunday Quilts,' only to be used when company came.

One of the most famous of Simcoe County quilts is entitled "Northern Night," and hangs in the permanent collection of the Royal Ontario Museum in Toronto. It was designed by Ada Bruce Torrance, an Orillia artist, and features a jet black loon bobbing on the surface of a lake, while Northern Lights beam across the night sky. The pattern of the quilted border reinforces the idea of waves, and the stitching pattern itself adds to the dramatic effect of the Northern Lights. Several other beautiful quilts bear Ada Torrance's stitched signature, including an outstanding example of the art called "Trillium," which was sewn by the Warminster Women's Institute.

Among many other groups in the County, the women of Coulson Women's Institute also enjoy a reputation for fine quilting. One of the highlights in their long tradition was the winning of the $500 first prize in the 1957 Star Weekly Quilt Contest with a warm and original design called "Maple Syrup Time."

Another example of outstanding design in quilting was stitched by the Blue Mountain Group of the Simcoe County

Arts and Crafts Association. Entitled "Fall Fair," its central oval incorporates racing sulkies, sideshows, games and rides —all the fun, colour and excitement of the real thing.

The first Simcoe County Quilt Fair was held in 1949, and, as Adelaide Leitch points out in *The Visible Past*, the modern art of quilting achieved such high standards in Simcoe County that the big city daily newspapers began sending their art critics rather than their women's editors to cover the annual fairs.

The heritage of the County has also been enriched by the work of several fine women artists and sculptors. Barbara Perry grew up in Orillia and received her first training in art from Canon Greene, the Anglican minister who was also Franklin Carmichael's first teacher.

Miss Perry studied at a Toronto art studio for several years, but then temporarily gave up art for social work, which took her to Toronto, Winnipeg and Vancouver before she decided to return to the Orillia district. Much of her best work was done at the summer cottage at Orchard Point, which she had inherited from her parents. There, surrounded by the old things she loved, Barbara Perry lived year-round, untroubled by the lack of insulation and modern conveniences. Her landscapes, particularly her snow scenes, reflect her sense of affinity with nature, while many of her warm still-life paintings feature the onions, squash and other vegetables she grew in her well-cared-for garden.

For some years Miss Perry painted with four other district women of considerable talent: Katherine Day, Mrs. James Harvie, Mrs. J. E. Hinds and Miss G. M. Kidd. They became known locally as "The Group of Five."

Katherine Day, a member of that group, studied in Paris and London during the 1930s, before returning to her native district. In Paris she had been greatly influenced by the teaching of famed engraver and etcher Nick Eekman, whose wood cuts recaptured so much from the great period of Flemmish art.

For a while Miss Day toyed with the idea of remaining in

Europe, but came to the conclusion that art usually "draws one back to the place where one was born." Back home in Simcoe County, she had a house built to her specifications on a peaceful, fifty-acre piece of land between Price's Corners and Jarratt, which she called "Hawthorne." Then, in 1947, she moved to a new home, also built to her design, a short distance away. With its Gothic windows and cathedral ceiling, "Pax Cottage" resembled an old and beautifully designed country church, a place of retreat and seclusion, almost a shrine.

There Katherine Day developed her unique monotypes, created by painting with oils on glass (the oil paints diluted with kerosene). The prints were made by gently pressing art paper over the still-wet designs. The technique was capable of imparting an almost ethereal quality to the rubbings, but it involved extremely delicate and hazardous work—about eight out of every ten paintings being ruined in the process, even under the most gifted of hands.

Miss Day, who also designed many beautiful Simcoe County quilts, exhibited in New York and enjoyed the admiration of many art critics. But she was basically content to enjoy the privacy and security of her beloved "Pax Cottage," turning out a few exquisite pieces of work and leaving the highly competitive world of international art to others.

Undoubtedly the most widely recognized creative talent among the Simcoe County's women artists belonged to sculptor Elizabeth Wyn Wood. Born in Orillia, Miss Wood studied at the Ontario College of Art, under Emanuel Hahn, and at the Art Students' League in New York, under Robert Laurent. In 1926, she married her former teacher, Emanuel Hahn, although professionally she retained her maiden name throughout her long and brilliant career.

In spite of her delicate femininity, and restrained, basically shy demeanor, Elizabeth Wyn Wood made her mark as the creator of massive, monumental works in granite, limestone, copper and brass—many of them weighing tons and standing out against the sky like gigantic colossi.

She was amazingly prolific, yet every commission was completed with a patient eye towards perfection. The Niagara Peninsula is enriched by many of her finest creations. One of her largest works is the Welland-Crowland War Memorial which stands in Chippewa Park, Welland. It is just over thirty feet long, the platform rising to focus on the stark, dramatic figure of a Canadian soldier. In 1963, on a commission from the Ontario Goverment, she completed a majestic likeness of King George VI. Eight years in the making, the granite statute stands ten feet tall and is exact to the last bit of embriodery on the robes of the Royal Order of the Garter. She also did the fountains and wall reliefs at the Canadian entrance to the Rainbow Bridge, and the statute of John Graves Simcoe at nearby Niagara-on-the-Lake.

Her huge hammered copper mural (measuring eleven feet by fifty feet) was the show-piece of the Queen Elizabeth building at Toronto's Canadian National Exhibition. Other Elizabeth Wyn Wood works grace the Toronto head office of the Bank of Montreal, the Ryerson Polytechnical Institute, the clubhouse of New Woodbine Race Track, and the fountain at the Canadian National Institute for the Blind on Toronto's Bayview Avenue. She also did the Stephen Leacock Memorial in her native Orillia, and examples of her work are on display in the National Gallery in Ottawa, as well as in the Toronto, Winnipeg and Vancouver galleries.

Her enormous productivity is the more remarkable when one realizes that she was a full-time teacher at Toronto's Central School for almost a quarter of a century.

There was, however, one desirable commission that she did *not* get. The rejection came early in her career, and was tinged with humour. In 1924, the city of Winnipeg announced plans for a cenotaph to honour its citizens who had died in World War I, and solicited designs for the project. In November, 1925 the adjudicators announced their enthusiastic choice: a concept submitted by her husband, Emanuel Hahn, and described as having "great dignity . . . and outstanding architectural and decorative values."

214

That was fine until it came to light that, although he had lived in Canada for thirty-eight years, Emanuel Hahn was of German birth. The Canadian Legion, the Imperial Order of the Daughters of the Empire, and other organizations and individuals rose up in wrath; no "Hun" was going to be the designer of Winnipeg's war memorial!

So Hahn was paid off and a new contest announced. This time the winner, named on Armistice Day, November 11, 1927 was Elizabeth Wyn Wood, whose winning design was described by the judges as "remarkable for its originality and heroic proportions." But it was shortly revealed that she was the recent bride of the same Emanuel Hahn! Again a wave of indignation swept over the Manitoba capitol, capped this time by the fact that Miss Wood's design called for one or more nude figures!

The Winnipeg committee suggested a settlement of $500, which Miss Wood graciously accepted, thereby establishing a record for husband-and-wife commissions for statues not executed. (The Winnipeg war memorial was finally built in 1928, based on a design submitted by Gilbert Parfitt, an English-born architect who had emigrated to the banks of the Red River some years earlier.)

Above and beyond her own almost unparalleled contribution to Canadian art, Elizabeth Wyn Wood was extremely active in encouraging the work of others through her association with various professional groups. She was a founding member of the Sculptors' Society of Canada, a member of the Royal Canadian Academy, an executive of the Canadian Committee of the International Association of the Plastic Arts, and a Life Fellow of the International Institute of Arts, Letters and Sciences, centered in Zurich, Switzerland. Few Canadians have made a greater contribution to Canadian culture than the modest, retiring Elizabeth Wyn Wood.

Perhaps the most famous daughter of Simcoe County was Emily Murphy. Born at Cookstown, she married an Anglican clergyman, and moved with him to Edmonton, where she became a leading figure in the struggle for women's rights.

Compassionate, warm-hearted, brilliant, determined, Emily Murphy eventually gained the distinction of being appointed the first woman judge in the British Empire. As noted earlier she was also the first national president of the Federated Women's Institutes of Canada. And, under the pseudonym Janey Canuck, she was a frequent contributor to leading Canadian magazines and newspapers.

But Emily Murphy's most important role came as the acknowledged leader of the brilliant group of women known as "the Alberta Five." Together with Irene Parlby (Canada's first woman Cabinet Minister), the famed Nellie McClung (the first woman to be elected to a provincial legislature), and community leaders Henrietta Edwards and Louise McKinney, Judge Murphy fought a long and determined campaign to have women formally recognized as "persons" in Canadian constitutional law. Until then wives had technically been classified as mere chattels of their husbands. Recognition as full citizens proved surprisingly difficult to gain, but Emily Murphy and her cohorts doggedly pursued their cause through court after court, and eventually all the way to the Privy Council. There, in the court of final appeal, they at last gained a favourable verdict. The struggle, which extended over a five-year period, involved an enormous amount of work and considerable expense, but the eventual victory became one of the most important landmarks along the uphill road towards equal rights for women.

Several other Simcoe County women made significant breakthroughs on the political scene. Vera L. Johnson was born in Collingwood and graduated from high school there before moving to Port Huron, Michigan with her parents in 1912. Married to Judge Clair R. Black of the Michigan Probate Court, she became a court reporter and served in that capacity for thirty-two years before being appointed as the first woman judge of a United States county, St. Clair County, Michigan.

Mrs. William Todd of Orillia became the first woman ever elected to civic office in that town when she became a member of the Public School Board in 1918. Marjorie H. Hamilton was elected Mayor of Barrie in 1950—the first Ontario woman to hold such a post.

Mrs. Nelle Carter was Orillia's first woman Alderman, and the first of her sex to run for Mayor in Orillia (she was defeated by W. Cramp in 1953). Born in Port Rowan, Norfolk County, she moved to Orillia with her parents in 1907, and eventually became one of its best-known citizens. Her interests were many and varied, and her energy apparently boundless. She was, among other things, an expert carpenter, maintaining a fully equipped workshop and turning out numerous pieces of fine furniture. An accomplished bookkeeper and successful business woman, she operated a book store on Orillia's main street for many years.

She was also very active in club and church work, at various times holding important offices in the Orillia Quota Club, the Order of the Eastern Star and St. Paul's United Church. To focus on just one aspect of her busy life, Nelle Carter sang with the St. Paul's choir for over thirty years, was president of its Women's Missionary Society, headed up its Women's Auxiliary for eight years, and served as treasurer for the Simcoe County Presbytery for several terms.

But she was probably best known as the proprietress of the Carter Restaurant, which her husband, A. T. Carter, had originally founded as the "Candy Palace" in 1907—the year that Winnifred Nelle McGilvery arrived in Orillia. At the end of the 1950s, Nelle Carter still liked to help out behind the cash register of the restaurant during rush hours. "I just love meeting the public," she told the Orillia *Packet & Times* in June, 1959, and the public obviously enjoyed meeting her. In 1950, the same newspaper had declared Nelle Carter to be Orillia's "Citizen of the Year."

Another leading Orillia woman was Carolyn (Carrie) May Johnston. Born in Victoria County, she attended Orillia Collegiate and in 1926 accepted a position under long-time Clerk-Treasurer Charles E. Grant. When Mr. Grant retired early in 1929, she was named to succeed him, thus becoming

217

the first woman in Canada to hold that dual municipal role.

During her long term in office, her signature (Carrie M. Johnston) became well known as the co-signer, with Mayor Benjamin J. Johnston (no relation), of Orillia's famous Depression era "Co-Operative Relief Purchasing Scrip." In 1937, she became Mrs. Allan Ironside and, after extensive travel with her husband, returned to Simcoe County in 1963 when the Ironsides retired in Washago. She was very active with many clubs and organizations, including the Orillia Ski Club, Ontario Youth Hostel Association, Women's Canadian Club, Simcoe County Historical Association and the Ontario Historical Society, until her death in April, 1975. Allan Ironside continues to be a prolific and well-informed writer on Simcoe County's past, and a leader in the campaign to preserve the area's history and heritage.

The first woman reeve of the County was Mrs. Florence Belcher of Victoria Harbour. The daughter of the village's first clerk and treasurer, she was reeve from 1955 to 1957.

Simcoe County women have also been prominent in the field of writing. Perhaps the best known novelist from the area was Esther Miller MacGregor, who used the pen name of Marian Keith.

She was born at Forest Home in 1876, the daughter of John Miller, who taught school on the 2nd Concession of the old Barrie Road, and Mary Johnston. The Millers later moved to Edgar and then to Orillia, where Esther taught school and Sunday school. She was educated at Rugby and Erin public schools, and then graduated from Toronto Normal School. Her teaching career spanned the period from 1899 to 1906. It was at this time that she began her long and prolific literary career. Her first novel, *Duncan Polite*, was published in 1905; her seventeenth and last book, *The Grand Lady*, in 1960.

In 1910 she married Dr. G. C. MacGregor, the tall, handsome minister of the Presbyterian church in Orillia. His work eventually took them to Toronto, London, Calgary and Brantford. In 1928 Rev. MacGregor was seriously injured in a train accident near Hamilton, from which he never completely recovered. He retired in 1939, and the couple moved to the Owen Sound area, where they lived in a large house on Bay Shore Road.

Through all of these changes "Marian Keith" continued with her writing. Her books were strongly influenced by her Presbyterian background, and many of them are about ministers and churches. All of her novels have a pronounced moral flavour. She usually wrote about a subject she knew well— the Scottish settlers who came to Central Ontario in the late nineteenth century. In many of her books, for example, *Duncan Polite* (1905), *Silver Maple* (1906), *Treasure Valley* (1908) and *Elizabeth of the Dale* (1910), she provided an accurate and sensitive picture of life in rural Simcoe County in the early days. Although most of her plots were derived from Victorian melodrama, she was an able chronicler of the times she wrote about—the general stores, church socials, one-room school houses, Scotch-Irish rivalries, building and harvesting bees, sleighrides, and so on.

Several of her stories depict life in the Orillia area around the turn of the century: *Treasure Valley*, *'Lisabeth of the Dell*, *In Orchard Glen*, *Little Miss Melody* and *The End of the Rainbow*, to name a few. Some involve real-life characters; "Aunt Flora," the central figure in *The Grand Lady*, for example, was Miss Keith's aunt, Grace Johnson of Oro.

Her later novels, such as *A Watered Garden*, *Yonder Shining Light* and *Lilacs in the Dooryard*, are set in the area northeast of Owen Sound. With the exception of three books, that was as far afield as she wandered from Simcoe County in her writings. She did make an extensive trip to Palestine, which experience she used as the basis for two novels, *Under The Grey Olives* and *Glad Days in Galilee* (later published in the United States as *The Boy of Nazareth*). And, towards the end of her career, she wrote a biography, the life of George Leslie MacKay, which she entitled *The Black Barbarian*.

Marian Keith did not gain any lasting place in Canadian literature. Her books have been out of print for many years, and she is largely forgotten outside of Simcoe County. It is probably fair to say that she was not a great writer, although some of her best passages are reminiscent of Ralph Connor, and at least one of her novels (*Gentleman Adventurer*) was highly praised by the *New York Times*, which called it "a stirring tale, stirringly told."

In addition to providing a valuable picture of the times and its people, there is a warmth and gentleness in her novels which make them a delight to read. She had a lively sense of humour, which comes through in many of the anecdotes she narrates. In *The Silver Maple*, for example, she vividly describes an incident that takes place on the 12th of July. While the Protestant Irish members of the district Orange Lodges are parading with their fife-and-drum bands, members of the Clan MacDonald, led by Highland pipers, arrive at the village's only hotel and commandeer every place at the bar, every seat at the tables, and the complete stock of liquor and beer. When the thirsty marchers turn up shortly afterwards, their indignation and horror is apt to make a reader laugh out loud.

In her last novel, *The Grand Lady*, in which she narrates the life of her much admired "Aunt Flora," the author writes with great tenderness and affection and with a deep appreciation for the importance of sights, sounds and feelings, as is evident in these paragraphs:

I can see her yet, standing out there at the cookhouse door, washing the old churn dasher, and singing 'Over the Water and Over the Sea' . . . and quoting Shakespeare or the Psalms . . . and with a half a dozen or so children underfoot.

We owe any progress we have made in life to her influence. . . . no wonder we were all in love with her. . . .

From the door of the log shanty, where her girlhood had been spent, she watched the little clearing around her widen, saw the great elms and maples come crashing to earth under the pioneer axes, saw the smoke of neighbouring clearings rise in a ring around her own, until they merged in wide, sunny fields.

But there was no corresponding widening of her horizons; she moved only once, from the first log shanty to the new log house, the width of a field. Two brothers and a sister went out

220

into the world, father and mother went down the narrow farm road to the churchyard, but she toiled until she was left alone, and her work was done.

Marian Keith—Esther Miller MacGregor—died in 1961, in her eighty-fifth year.

Among other Simcoe County women who made their marks as writers were poets Edna Jaques and Mrs. Charles Hudson, and novelist Phyllis Griesback Primmer.

One famous woman writer to whom the County does not appear to have much claim (although a tenuous one has occasionally been made) is Mazo de la Roche. True, the author of the renowned *Jalna* series attended high school in Orillia in the early 1890s; a high school registry now in the collection of the Orillia Public Library shows that Maizo Roche, 13, daughter of Wm. Roche of Coldwater Road, gained admission on August 29, 1892. (At that time the "de la" which became part of her literary signature had apparently not yet been added.) But the Roches only stayed in Orillia for some four or five years. Mazo's father was a commercial traveller who frequently changed his base of operation, and the family soon moved on to another town.

She never wrote about Orillia, nor did she mention her stay there in her autobiography, *Ringing the Changes*. It was, apparently, just a case of "passing through," one stop of many along the way, which left little impression on her youthful mind.

Simcoe County women played an important role in the care of the wounded and the healing of the sick. One of the best known was Eleanor J. Johnston who was Superintendent of Orillia's Soldiers' Memorial Hospital for more than a quarter of a century. Soldiers' Memorial was built as a tribute to the young men of the town who had fallen in the War of 1914-18, and under Miss Johnston's supervision it gained the reputation of being one of the best hospitals in Ontario. By the time of her retirement in 1933, she had seen 140 nurses graduate through the training school she operated there.

Miss Helen J. Shanahan of Oro Township served the

Royal Victoria Hospital in Barrie for forty years, first as nurse (from 1925) and then as chief administrator (from 1946 to 1965). She was particularly concerned with nurses' training and saw to it that the hospital was provided with an excellent nursing staff.

Dr. Helen MacMurchy of Collingwood was one of the first women to graduate in medicine from the University of Toronto; she became internationally known for her work in child welfare. Miss Catherine Ford, who was born in Roche's Point but raised and educated in Collingwood, became Director of Professional Training at Belleville's Ontario School for the Deaf. Nurse Ethel May Dawson, who came to Collingwood from England as a child, helped to deliver more than 2200 Simcoe County babies in a career that spanned more than fifty years. And there have been many other dedicated Simcoe County women who worked for the good of their communities in the general field of medicine—usually unsung, but seldom unappreciated.

In the field of education, a high percentage of the teachers down through the years have been women, and most modern-day residents of Simcoe County look back with appreciation and deep respect at the beneficial influence some woman teacher has had on their lives.

Then, too, there are the tens of thousands of mothers and wives who never aspired to prominence as writers or artists or pioneers in the professions and political arts. These "ordinary" women, no less than the public figures of the period, contributed their talents and energy to the development of Simcoe County.

13 Into the Fifties and Beyond

The period following World War II brought sweeping changes to Ontario, many of which combined to greatly increase the pressure on Simcoe County as a vacation and recreation area.

After the long, bitter, austere years of the war, there was a general restlessness and an impatience to enjoy once more the pleasures that peacetime life had to offer—including cottages and camping, swimming, fishing, boating, sun-kissed days and moonlit nights. Gas rationing was a thing of the past, and all of North America was anxious to be on the move once more.

The unprecedented post-war tide of immigration brought hundreds of thousands of citizens from many countries to Canada—the great majority of whom settled in the major cities. Before long the newly constituted area of Metropolitan Toronto claimed more than two million citizens. Beyond it the mighty industrial complex known as the "Golden Horseshoe" stretched along Lake Ontario all the way from the American border in the southwest to Oshawa in the east. With the increasing density of population, an ever-growing number of urban dwellers sought free-time escape into more rustic and rural areas, where there were fewer people, more space, more air to be breathed, and more freedom. For the most part, that meant looking north—toward Simcoe County and beyond.

Despite some economic setbacks and a slight depression in the early 1950s, there was a general trend toward increasing affluence. More people could afford to own cars, to travel, to buy camping equipment and mobile trailers, to make down

Trent Waterway, Lock 42

payments on waterfront properties, and to purchase the lumber, shingles, cement blocks, plumbing and electrical equipment necessary to build summer cottages.

The cottage-building phenomenon was aided by two factors which carried it to feverish, land-office proportions: the wholesale opening-up of Crown land by the Ontario Government, which made attractive lots available at miniscule down payments, and the quick-buck promotions of real estate entrepreneurs, who cut service roads through the bush, dredged swampy bays, blasted rock outcroppings and trucked in tons of fill to convert marginal shoreline into fast-selling, 100-foot frontage, pseudo-wilderness subdivisions. By the seventies there was scarcely a weedy bay, a nearly submerged island, or a precipitously rocky promontory in the whole County that did not have a vacation property of some kind attached to it.

The situation was aggravated, too, by the fact that the adjacent urban dwellers had more and more free time in which to enjoy the pleasures offered by the relatively unspoiled, "natural" atmosphere of Simcoe County. The standard work-week in the cities dropped from 44 hours, to 40 hours, to 35 hours. Annual vacations stretched from one week to two, then to four, five or more, depending upon seniority and/or the bargaining power of the unions involved.

Another important factor was that the recreational resources of the County were increasingly used on a year-round basis. In earlier times the cottage and resort season had extended only from about the 1st of July holiday to Labour Day. Then, with the coming of the family car, it was expanded to stretch from Queen Victoria's birthday in May to Thanksgiving in early-October. Finally, after World War II, it became a 12-month phenomenon. More and more cottages were insulated for winter use, and service roads were kept open by township snowplows, as people discovered that the joys of being outdoors were not limited to the hot weather months. Snowmobiles became the wintertime equivalent of pleasure boats and provided similar opportunities for socializing, family fun and getting close to nature.

Skiing became more popular with each passing winter. As early as 1946, Judge Harvie recommended to the Simcoe County Council that this sport be developed as a major attraction in the Collingwood area. Ten years later, on January 29, 1956, a magnificent 113-foot ski jump, said to be the finest in Eastern Canada, was officially opened near Midland.

Meanwhile, ski resorts sprang up in several parts of the County, especially in the Collingwood-Blue Mountain area, and the influx of skiing enthusiasts increased year by year. Devil's Glen, Hidden Valley, Georgian Peaks—these and several others soon gained a reputation for their fine slopes, excellent facilities and pleasant hospitality. Sports cars with ski racks became as familiar a sight in January as canoes on car-top carriers had long been in July.

Later, cross-country skiing gained more and more adherents. The *Toronto Telegram's* Harvey Currell described the attractions of this sport in his column, "Town and Country Trips," on February 26, 1964. Currell had just returned from a solitary skiing hike near Bass Lake in Oro Township when he wrote:

At least once each winter, I like to head across country on my skis, to explore the country of untrodden snows and winter silence.

Here, I gain new respect for the hills by climbing them on my own muscle power, before gliding down the other side. I find myself taking time, too, to observe things like the little ridge a meadow mouse leaves on the surface as it tunnels under the snow.

I remember for days afterwards the flash of snow buntings' wings as 20 or 30 of them rise in a flock ahead of me.

Ice fishing, too, really began to come into its own in the years following World War II. The waters of Lake Simcoe and Lake Couchiching had provided superb summertime angling for more than a century, but the taking of fish in wintertime had generally been left to the Indians and to a few commercial fishermen who stretched their nets from hole to hole with half-frozen fingers. Then sport fishermen began to take to the ice—first a scattered few, then hundreds, and finally droves. Less than an hour's drive from Toronto, Lake Simcoe soon became the ice-fishing centre of Ontario. Catches of lake trout, whitefish, pickerel, perch and fresh-water herring were generally good, and sometimes phenomenal. Catering to this new mania provided employment and important off-season revenue for many local residents. Fish hut rental operations sprang up all around the lake. The anglers required transportation to and from the fishing spots by bombardier or snowmobile. There was a demand for fresh and salted minnows to use as bait. Overnight accommodation was in short supply, and restaurants and snack bars had to take on extra help. The big lake was no longer left to sleep under its protective coating of ice.

These changes did not, of course, happen in any one year; it was a gradual process, and the cumulative effect of them was not readily apparent. Tourism and the development of recreational resources had been important elements in the economic life of Simcoe County since the late nineteenth century.

But, if things seemed on the surface to be going on more or less as usual, fundamental changes were occuring in the social, economic and political life of Simcoe County. Prior to World War II it had been predominantly a rural area, invaded by welcome hordes of cottagers, campers and fishermen on nine or ten summer weekends. From the late 1940s on, it gradually became a full-time playground for the hundreds of thousands of urban dwellers who were jammed in along the shores of Lake Ontario just over the horizon to the south. The escapees from the big cities—the cottagers, campers, summer anglers, ice fishermen, skiers, party-seekers, bird watchers, hunters, farm owners who did not farm—were ever present, and the longest respite local lovers of peace and quiet could look forward to was from Sunday evenings to Friday afternoons. As Dr. Roy I. Wolfe pointed out in a 1952 edition of *Canadian Geographer*: "At no time in

history have so many people been able to choose so freely
what they want to do with their leisure time, nor has leisure
time itself ever been so widely and abundantly distributed.''

Both the County and the province contributed to this
development, as did many municipalities. Winter carnivals,
designed to attract visitors, and featuring such highlights as
parades and sleigh-rides, became annual events in several
towns and villages. A tourist bureau was set up near Barrie in
1958 to provide information for those entering the district.

Beginning in 1955, a series of provincial parks were
opened in various parts of Simcoe County. These offered a
considerable variety of facilities and attractions, ranging from
picnic and camp sites, to swimming and fishing, to museums
and displays of wild animals and birds. By 1967 six County
sites were in operation: Bass Lake, Earl Rowe, Wasaga
Beach, Devil's Glen, Springwater, and Mara, and two were
located nearby: Sibbald Point and Sixmile Lake. The parks
were large—Sibbald's, for example, provided 725 camp sites,
and Springwater sometimes had 2500 picnickers at a single
sitting. With their low prices and clean, attractive surroundings, they were highly popular from the beginning. Bass
Lake (one of the smaller parks at 87 acres) drew 132,249
visitors and 18,357 campers in 1966.

According to the minutes of the Simcoe County Council,
that same year set new records for tourism: more visitors,
more employment, more revenue than ever before. The up-
swing was to continue; by the late 1960s Tiny Township, for
example, with more than five thousand summer homes lining
its Georgian Bay shores, estimated that 70% of its tax revenue
was derived, directly and indirectly, from cottagers, vacationers and sportsmen.

If a single development could be said to symbolize the
great post-war recreational invasion of Simcoe County it
would be the building of Highway 400, from Toronto to just
beyond Barrie. It is sometimes called "Ontario's Vacation-
land Freeway."

"Originally," William Fulton, then Ontario's Deputy

Minister of Highways, said in 1959, "we only planned to siphon off some of the traffic that was jamming the two main routes running north from Toronto, the old Number 11, or Yonge Street, and the newer Highway 27. But 400 kept growing out of its breeches and nowadays, although we highway engineers don't really approve, we have to admit that it has become more than just a means of getting cars from one place to another; it's also an elongated public garden, a pleasure drive, a playground and picnic area, an institution and conversation piece."

Extending from the northern outskirts of Toronto to join Highway 69 near Coldwater, 400 closely follows the route taken by Etienne Brûlé in his explorations into Huron territory more than 350 years ago. By the mid-1960s it was one of Ontario's—and Canada's—busiest highways. In 1975 the average traffic volume at the Highway 7 interchange just north of Toronto was about 40,000 motor vehicles a day, but even that impressive figure is deceiving: Highway 400's peak loads come on weekends, a phenomenon which has earned it the nickname of "the busiest temporary one-way street in the country."

Although it carries a high volume of other traffic, Highway 400 is primarily the highway of weekenders. According to 1974 figures, almost four thousand cars an hour stream northward towards Ontario's cottage country on Friday evenings in summer, against a mere trickle of traffic heading south. The process is, of course, reversed at the end of each weekend.

On both legs of the weekly exodus from Toronto, the Golden Horseshoe, and neighbouring U.S. states, the traffic is usually bumper-to-bumper and can be brought to a complete standstill by the slightest of rear-end accidents. Radio station helicoptors, hovering overhead, take pleasure in describing the hopelessness of such traffic jams to those caught in them. Enterprising roadside residents sell cold drinks, sandwiches and home-baked goodies to the fuming and frustrated motorists.

Planning for the new super route (originally called the Toronto-Barrie Highway and given the number 400 because it was Ontario's first four-lane highway) got underway in 1945. By 1947 grading had been completed from Toronto to the junction with Highway 27, just south of Barrie. It took three more years to complete the overpasses and cloverleafs, to extend the grading to connect with Highways 93 and 11 north of Barrie, and to complete the paving. On December 1, 1951, one lane each way was opened to traffic, but it wasn't until July 1, 1952 that the mammoth project was officially finished and declared fully operational at a ribbon-cutting ceremony.

From then until 1960 little work was done on Highway 400, apart from routine resurfacing. An exception was the extensive rebuilding program required in the Holland Marsh area after the Hurricane Hazel disaster in the fall of 1954. In the mid-1960s a two-lane extension was completed north of Barrie to join Highway 103 near Coldwater.

By the beginning of the 1970s it was apparent that 400's four lanes had become inadequate, with worse and worse traffic jams. Plans were announced for widening it to six lanes, and the work was carried out during 1971 and 1972. Over most of the route the expansion was achieved by reducing the original 30-foot centre median to ten feet, and by taking four feet from the shoulders on each side. A new steel box-beam median barrier, which had proven successful on New York State freeways was installed—the first of its kind in Canada.

While the building of Highway 400 was important to all of Simcoe County, its impact was most strongly felt in Barrie. Just as Orillia is often said to be the heart of the County, so Barrie has always been the gateway to the north (via historic Highway 11). The opening of 400 added significant new dimensions to that role. Barrie became less than an hour's drive from the sprawling urban metropolis to the south.

Barrie was an important community even before the interior of Simcoe County was opened for settlement. It was originally called Kempenfelt, but was later given its present name in honour of Commodore Robert Barrie, R.N. who commanded His Majesty's ships on the Great Lakes in the early 1800s. Many of its streets commemorate the lives of other Royal Navy officers. These include Dunlop, Collier, Blake, Worlsey, MacDonald, Bayfield, Clapperton, Sampson, Napier and Codrington.

The town has always been one of the most bustling, exciting places in the County. It was the "County Town"—a favourite spot for parades, circuses, and celebrations of all kinds, as well as being the County Seat. Queen Victoria's Jubilee in 1897 was celebrated there in style, and the whole County turned out there for the Duke of York's visit in 1900. The Raceway, where the Queen's Plate was run in 1873, drew its crowds, as did the Grand Opera House and the Fair Grounds. The Market Square was the start of many a parade.

Barrie was the County Seat until the new Administration Centre at Midhurst opened in the latter part of 1973. The Court House, the jail, the Registry Office and other County buildings are located there. Barrie has also been the centre for specialized medical services in the County.

It was incorporated as a town in 1853 and became Simcoe County's first city on January 1, 1959, with Willard L. Kinzie its first mayor. Its steady growth in population accelerated in the years following World War II:

Year	Population of Barrie
1901	6,024
1914	6,555
1920	6,775
1932	7,480
1939	8,310
1945	10,633

Simcoe County: *The Recent Past*

1950	12,833
1960	21,050
1970	26,019
1976	34,050

It has had to accommodate this steady growth by increasing its land area several times: in 1899, Allandale was united with Barrie; when Barrie became a city it annexed 2537 acres (making a total of 4781 acres); and in 1964 another 1752 acres from Vespra Township were annexed.

Further proof of its growth is provided by the fact that its use of electricity climbed from 522 kilowatts in the early 1920s to over 30,000 kilowatts by the late 1960s.

The Lake Simcoe city has enjoyed a healthy industrial climate, encouraged by progressive civic administrators and active community leaders throughout most of its existence. In the early years of the twentieth century, when Barrie's population was just over six thousand, some of its leading industries were:

Simcoe Brewery Limited,
  founded in 1843 by Robert Simpson:
Dougall Brothers' Furniture Factory;
Barrie Tanning Company,
  established in 1850 by Andrew Graham;
Wilkinson Woolen Mill;
Ball Planing Mill;
Barr & Henry's Carriage Factory;
Butterfield's Foundry;
Barrie Milling Company;
Dyment Foundry Company;
Carley's Boatworks;
Imperial Soda and Water Works,
  established in 1890 by J. T. Walsh;

Simcoe Marble Works,
   also established in 1890;

Simcoe Bicycle Works;

Barrie Wickerworks Manufacturing Company;

Barrie Brewing Company,
   which turned out 25,000 gallons of ale and porter
   per week;

Spencer Industrial Company Ltd.;

Barrie Carriage Works;

Barrie Shoe Manufacturing Company;

Barrie Iron Works;

Olympia Candy Works;

C.N.R. yards at Allandale.

Barrie was anxious to attract still more industrial plants. In 1918 Alderman William Adamson prepared a booklet called "19 Reasons Why Barrie Should Be the Leading Manufacturing Centre of Canada." It was published and widely distributed soon after the end of World War I. Among the reasons given were these:

The town encircles Kempenfelt Bay, one of the most beautiful sites in the world, a complete horseshoe on Georgian Bay.
   The town has a closer connection with the great prairie provinces (that soon will house 25,000,000 people) than either Toronto, Montreal, Hamilton or London.
   The streets are paved and trees shade the walks.
   There are many families settling in Barrie and the probability is that we will have a large influx of Europeans here; therefore, the labor market will be crying for employment.
   The Town would be willing to make suitable terms in regard to leasing town lands for factory sights for bona fide industries.
   We also have one of the best Collegiate Institutes in Canada. . . . our education system is perfect.

For the most part, however, Barrie gained few new industries during the 1920s and the Depression years of the 1930s. Two industries which did start up in this period were Clarke and

Clarke (later Robson-Lang Leather) and Copaco. The Clarke and Clarke leather firm moved to Barrie from Toronto in 1927, setting up business in the old Barrie Carriage Works Factory. Copaco (Co-operative Packers of Ontario Limited) was established by 1,565 area farmers in 1931. It processed pork and other meats and was renowned throughout much of Ontario for its fine sausages.

Most Barrie plants were busy, mainly with war production, from 1939 to 1945, but the emergence of this city as a major industrial centre dates from the end of the war. The first and most important step in this development came in 1945 when Canadian General Electric decided to establish a plant on the site of the old Barrie Fair Grounds on Bradford Street. In 1946 it had 110 employees; by the early 1970s C.G.E.'s payroll was over 900.

A steady stream of other industries opened up in Barrie after 1945, including such manufacturers as Lufkin Rule, Canada Dry Bottling, De Vilbiss, Mansfield-Denman, Seven-Up, Canadian Tampax, Imperial Eastman, Chrysler Outboard, Bombardier Ski-Doo, Formosa Brewery, Corah, Woolen Industries, Diebold and General Tire.

The 1974 Industrial Services Directory, published by the Barrie Chamber of Commerce, listed forty-one local plants, employing approximately 5400 people. In addition to those mentioned above, the major employers included Plastomer Ltd., Cooper Tool Group Ltd. (formerly Lufkin Rule), Kolmar of Canada Ltd., and Canadian Tyler Refrigeration Ltd.

Further expansion was encouraged by the development of fully serviced manufacturing sites by the municipality, including such large scale operations as Cloverleaf Industrial Park and Bayview Industrial Park.

Many citizens should share in the credit for Barrie's impressive industrial growth since 1945. These include: those who served on the Industrial Committee of the Chamber of Commerce down through the years; Mayor Willard Kinzie, who campaigned for better industrial land and services during the 1950s; Reg Welham of the Chamber of Commerce;

John Mitchinson, former manager of the Canadian General Electric plant; Harold Bairstow, former Industrial Commissioner; Robert Hollywood, Mayor Dorian Parker, Mayor Heber E. Smith, and Alderman O. J. Perri.

The rapid growth in population placed a heavy financial burden on the town. New streets had to be built and older ones resurfaced; more schools were required; water mains and sewage systems needed to be extended. But by the mid-1950s, thanks to the expansion in manufacturing, over 40% of the local taxes were being paid by industry and business— to the considerable relief of the residential tax assessment.

While the industrial boom created an ever-increasing number of job opportunities in Barrie, many of the city's newer residents were former Torontonians who chose to raise their families in a smaller community, while commuting to and from their big city offices. Thus, to some extent, Barrie became an exurban satellite of Toronto. Highway 400 provided the original avenue for these commuters, to be supplemented later by a network of GO trains and buses.

During the same period, Orillia, Midland and Collingwood also experienced dramatic growth in population and in industrial and business activity. On the other hand, many of the County's smaller communities were declining in size and economic importance. Above all, they were becoming less self-sufficient and more dependent. Just as Barrie was drawn increasingly into the Toronto sphere of influence, so the smaller towns tended to become residential satellites of the County's cities and larger towns. More and more the people who live in the villages and hamlets have become commuters: the breadwinners go outside to work, the women do their buying at district shopping plazas and supermarkets rather than at local stores, the children and young people are bussed to large district schools.

It was an evolution which had been going on for a long time. In his *History of Churchill Village*, written in 1937, Walter S. Reive already lamented this trend: "Like other

Rural scene in Vespra Township

villages, Churchill has seen business leave and go to the factories in towns and cities. Once it was a busy spot, with extensive carriage-building and blacksmith business, harness shops, dressmaking, shoemaking, photograph gallery, even pottery-making. . . . Two hotels were there, too."

Like many others, New Flos was declining as a business centre by the 1930s. The post office was closed down; the general store was replaced by a smaller one; and blacksmiths and harnessmakers went out of business as farming became steadily more mechanized. By the beginning of World War II New Flos had less than half the population it had claimed in 1900. A similar pattern can be seen in the fate of several churches in the New Flos area:

Crowe's Corners—closed in 1955;

Tenth Line, Flos—one service a year after 1936;

Allenwood—closed in 1965;

Edenvale Presbyterian—closed in 1966;

Ebenezer—one service a year since 1965;

VanVlack Presbyterian—closed in 1930, sold 1933.

In the mid-1950s the New Flos rural school shut its doors and the local children were thereafter transported to a central school in Elmvale. In Tecumseth township, twenty-four rural schools disappeared in 1960, replaced by two large central schools which, together with schools in Beeton and Tottenham, were operated under a single school board.

Down through the years more than one Simcoe County village became a ghost town or simply disappeared from the map of Ontario. Keenansville, for example, once a thriving centre in Adjala Township, had only a single resident family by the 1960s.

An interesting case history, showing the changes that have taken place in many smaller Simcoe Country communities, is provided by the story of Cookstown. A paper, based on the Tweedsmuir history of that village, by Donna McLean, tells the story. Cookstown, located at the junction of Highways 27 and 89, is also the hub of four townships, Essa, Innisfil, West Gillumbury and Tecumseth, and was once a busy place. An appreciation of the transformation that has taken place can be gained by comparing two maps of the main street business section—one made in 1928, the other in 1974. At the end of the 1920s it was a complete community with all the essential stores and services. A 1928 stroller along Queen Street (Highway 89) and King Street (Highway 27) would have passed these establishments: a bakery, a shoe store, a drug store, a furniture store and funeral parlour, two hotels, three barber shops, a newspaper office, a grocery store, a meat market, three general stores, two hardware stores, a shoe repair shop, a Chinese laundry, two garages, two dry goods outlets, a dentist's office, two doctors' offices, a lumber yard and mill, a bank, a telephone office, an insurance broker's, the post office, the United Church with its parsonage, and the village jail.

In 1928, too, Cookstown was well equipped to serve the farming district surrounding it. In its business section or along the CNR tracks that crossed Queen Street were: stock yards, a flour mill, a creamery, grain elevators, feed storage bins, a seed mill, a cheese factory, an evaporator, an apiary, two blacksmiths and a harness-making shop.

By 1974 the scene had changed drastically. Gone were almost all connections with the farm industry—only the flour mill, long unused, was still standing. Gone was the newspaper; gone the hotels; gone the cheese factory, the Chinese laundry, the meat market, the dentist, the apiary, and the telephone office. Several buildings along main street were empty, and others had been torn down, leaving vacant lots. A smattering of establishments remained from the 1920s, most changed in location, in ownership or in other ways; there was still a bakery, a bank, the library, the post office (still run by the Coleman family, as it has been for over a hundred years), a funeral home, the United Church with its parsonage, and two other churches. The lumber yard had actually expanded its operation, due to the cottage- and home-building boom of the 1950s and 1960s.

There were more service stations and auto-repair shops than there had been in 1928. There was a jug milk store and three or four snack bars. And, to cater to the summer and weekend tourists, there were a number of smart boutiques and antique shops—a curious blending of the ultra-modern and nostalgia for the past.

There had been other important changes. The last passenger train to stop at Cookstown had passed through on July 2, 1960, and the CNR station had shut down in 1967. As the older residents died, more and more of their stately brick homes were purchased by ex-Toronto commuters. Commuters also built split-level bungalows on the outskirts of the village. More and more younger members of the village left, seeking higher education and the professional and business futures that could no longer be found at home. Thus the population of Cookstown, though changing dramatically in sociological terms, has remained at around seven or eight hundred from the turn of the century to the present day.

As Miss McLean pointed out in her paper, Cookstown has experienced a transition "from an economically self-sufficient community to one of almost total dependence on the surrounding larger centres."

This does not mean that there is no longer any community spirit in Cookstown. It is true that by 1973 more Cookstown residents worked in Toronto, Barrie, Camp Borden and Alliston than were employed within the village, but the annual Cookstown fall fair is still one of the best in Simcoe County. The Women's Institute, which celebrated its 75th anniversary in 1976, remains active. The village has held an antique steam-engine festival every summer since 1966. Curling is popular with both young and old. There are minor hockey and baseball leagues, active service clubs and church groups, boy scout and girl guide troops, carnivals, and community dances. Yes, Cookstown is alive and well and living in Simcoe County; but it is a quite different place than it was in what many life-long residents refer to as "the good old days."

In broad terms, what has happened is that large and small communities everywhere have become more and more interdependent. Since the middle of the century, farm and rural people must increasingly look to the cities for many things— higher education, career opportunities, the best of medical care, advanced technology, and much more. At the same time citizens of the overflowing urban centres rely on the farmers to meet their ever-increasing need for food, and they look more and more to the rural and wilderness areas to provide the clean air, space and recreation that is missing from their day-to-day environment.

At best, this evolution broadens horizons and encourages mutual understanding and willingness to share; at worst, it exposes conflicting interests and may lead to hostility. Under pressure, tourists and other visitors can quickly change from welcome guests into arrogant invaders, and local residents from obliging hosts into gouging exploiters.

Nowhere in Simcoe County did these counter-forces come into more intense conflict than at Wasaga Beach.

This magnificent strip of fine, clean sand curves in a beautiful, seven-mile-long crescent around the southeastern corner of Nottawasaga Bay. Just inland, and paralleling it, is the Nottawasaga River, so that Wasaga Beach is in fact a long, slender slit of land between the ocean-like bay and the quietly flowing river. A dozen miles away, the Blue Mountains, rising a thousand feet above the water, provide an impressive backdrop.

Well before the turn of the century, nearby residents went to Wasaga Beach by horse and buggy to picnic and swim. As the years went by, the beach attracted ever more visitors. With the coming of the automobile, it became accessible to people who lived much further afield, and the weekend crowds soon became a matter of concern. By 1925 the Simcoe County Council was informed that, while there were only about a hundred cottages on the beach, three to four thousand cars, and almost 15,000 people, were turning up on sunny summer Sundays. Just two years later, the Council was told that the influx on long weekends—the 1st of July, Civic Holiday, and Labour Day—had passed the 40,000 mark.

The popularity of Wasaga Beach increased even during the Great Depression, but it was not until the war years that the real invasion began. "Canada's greatest military establishment, Camp Borden, provided thousands of soldiers who used its dance halls, its honky-tonks, and its tourist cabins for a bit of weekend fun," Dr. Roy I. Wolfe wrote in his 1952 article in *Canadian Geographer*. "These soldiers gave to Wasaga Beach a new character, a character that it has retained." Weekend crowds were often estimated at between 75,000 and 100,000 during the war, and, if anything, increased after the return of peace.

To cater to this huge transient population, hundreds of commerical establishments, many of them tacky, smelly and noisy, sprang up along the beach. Today the village is one continuous midway, several miles long, lined by innumerable garishly decorated, large and small emporiums: bowling alleys, tourist cabins, motels, taverns, amusement arcades, souvenir stands, rides, miniature golf courses, Go-Kart tracks, places selling tacos, take-out chicken, hamburgers and hotdogs, corn-on-the-cob, pizzas, soft ice cream, submarine sandwiches, Chinese food, and everything else imaginable. It is Coney Island, Atlantic City, and Toronto's old Sunnyside, all rolled into one.

It is little wonder that friction has from time to time developed between the swarming hordes of weekend visitors on the one hand, and the beleaguered permanent residents and peace-and-quiet-seeking cottagers on the other. To quote Dr. Wolfe again:

To sunbathe, to gambol on these soft, hot sands, to dash into the cooling, but not cold, waters; these are the activities one may dream of for the rest of the year. But not at Wasaga. To gambol on the beach is to court death; for it is no longer a beach, but a hard-packed roadway. All day and far into the night a noisy, stinking parade of cars separates the would-be bathers from the water, and every year people who brave the onrush of cars are killed.

Various steps have been taken to control the huge weekend crowds and to counteract the all too prevalent vandalism and rowdy behaviour of the transient summer population. The Museum of the Upper Lakes, built on an island in the Nottawasaga River which was created by the silt that collected for more than a century around the sunken H.M.S. *Nancy* (lost in the War of 1812), was one such attempt. The Museum houses a handsome collection of models, artifacts and pictures which tell the story of navigation on the Upper Great Lakes. The Ontario Zoological Park, displaying lions, tigers, bears, deer, bison, rhino and many other animals, is another popular feature, especially among visiting families with small children.

In 1959, following representations to the provincial government by the village of Wasaga Beach, the area was established as a provincial park, which grew to include over 3,000 acres by the 1970s. Under the jurisdiction of the Ontario Department of Lands and Forests, a plan was put into effect in 1962 which limited access to the park and beach area to four controlled entrances.

In spite of such measures, an uneasy truce between the few residents and the many weekend invaders is probably the best than can be hoped for in the foreseeable future.

This confrontation of conflicting values remains as a demonstration of the sociological changes which have taken place in Simcoe County, as in many other places, since the great upheaval brought about by World War II.

14 Agriculture

The history of farming in Simcoe County goes back further than in many other parts of Ontario, because the Huron Indians were primarily an agricultural people who grew such crops as corn, squash, pumpkins and sunflowers.

When the first settlers came in the early nineteenth century, they did mixed farming because they had to be self-sufficient. But from the early days there were always some cash crops, and as time went by farmers started to specialize—a trend which has continued to the present day. The crops selected varied according to soil composition, temperature and rainfall. Today many districts in the County are widely known for their production of a particular agricultural commodity.

Few, if any, parts of Ontario have a wider range of soil conditions than exist in Simcoe County. In 1967, Stewart L. Page, Agricultural Representative for North Simcoe, wrote a series of articles for the Barrie *Examiner*. In one of them Page, who retired that same year after forty-three years with the Department of Agriculture, had this to say:

Simcoe County, due to its location and unusual geological history, is a land of extremely variable soil drainage and climatic conditions. In North Simcoe in particular, we find most of the soil types that are to be found throughout Ontario, and it is not uncommon to find a dozen different soil types on one farm.

Drainage may vary from water-logged fields to arid sand plains. The climate and soil may by suitable for tender crops such as tobacco, corn and many fruits and vegetables in some areas, but hazardous frost pockets in other areas limit production to more hardy crops. As to topography, some land is as flat as old lake bottoms, which many areas once were, and some

243

areas so hilly that the trees have difficulty standing upright.

By reason of these variables, no common pattern of agricultural production is possible in North Simcoe. . . . each farmer must choose the crops, soil treatment and management to suit his particular farm, or even particular fields.

Mr. Page went on to point out that of the tillable farm acreage in North Simcoe, about one-third is first class, one-third is second class with relatively minor soil problems, and the remainder is marginal with severe soil deficiencies. South Simcoe is also varied, with the rich, black soil of the Holland Marsh, the sand hills and plains of the central region, and the orchard-growing region of Collingwood.

One of the main trends in agriculture in this century has been toward more and more mechanization. Among the earliest machines was a treadmill which was a flexible, inclined platform upon which a dog walked, providing power to run a cutting box. About 1880 the portable steam engine came along. Hooked up to a thresher, one of these units would serve a whole district, with the men of the neighbourhood providing the work force as it moved from farm to farm.

The first tractors appeared in 1917, when the Department of Agriculture sent five of them to Simcoe County—three Case 9-18's, one Titan 10-20, and the fifth of unrecorded manufacture. Twenty-two young farmers were trained in how to operate them, and about 780 acres were plowed to demonstrate what they could do. The tractors operated mainly on kerosene and were capable of turning over about an acre per hour—*if* they could be kept going for an hour. They were subject to frequent breakdowns and, since the Agricultural Representative was the only maintenance man in the County, much time was lost in waiting for repairs to be made.

The tractors improved with time, of course, but until the outbreak of World War II in 1939 most of the work was still done with horses and horse-drawn equipment. According to the Department of Agriculture, probably not more than 10% of the farms in the County at that time could have been called "mechanized."

The situation changed rapidly during the war, however, and the process of mechanization continued at a rapid pace into the 1950s. A survey conducted in North Simcoe in 1956 showed that 96% of the farms depended on tractor power, and less than 50% still kept horses (few of them having more than one or two). By then rural electrification had reached 95% of the farm homes, providing a great boon for farm women, as indicated by the same survey:

Equipped with Each	Per cent of North Simcoe Farm Homes (1956)
Radios	100%
Home freezer, or rented freezer space	97
Electric washing machines	96
Refrigerators	90
Water on tap in kitchen	70
3-piece bathrooms	53
Television	42
Electric sewing machines	24

By the mid-1950s the following types of mechanical equipment were in fairly general use (no one farmer had all of the listed equipment; many of the larger, more expensive machines were owned and used on a co-operative basis):

Tillage equipment: two- and three-furrow tractor plows, cultivators, harrows, double-disc, one-way disc or tiller, roller or packer, row-crop cultivator, manure loader and spreader;

Seeding equipment: combination grain drill with grass seeder and fertilizer attachment, corn planter, potato planter;

Spraying equipment: potato sprayer, weed sprayer;

Haying equipment: power take-off mower, dump- and side-delivery rakes, hay-loader, buck rake, forage harvester, hay-blower, hay and straw balers;

Harvesting equipment: grain binder, windrower, combine, threshing machine, corn picker, potato digger and grader;

Maple syrup gathering, Elmvale

Barn equipment: milking machines, milk coolers, electric pump and pressure water system, feed grinder, lights and heaters, stable cleaner, automatic ventilators.

In his article in the Supplementary Edition to the *Innisfil Historical Review: 1850-1950*, Brian Baker describes some of the changes that took place between 1950 and 1967:

Into the 1950's most farmers here still used the picturesque method of binding grain and wheat and stooking the sheaves. Then, with the help of ten or more neighbours, each farmer would have a 'threshing bee', and the sheaves were hauled to the barn by teams and wagons and threshed, the grain being blown into the granary, the straw into mows or stacks in the yard. To-day, most farmers own tractor-drawn or 12-foot self-propelled combines, the latter harvesting 25 or more acres a day.

Haying methods have changed vastly. Into the 1950's, horse-drawn mowers and sulky dump rakes were used. Loose hay was built onto four sling ropes, making quarter-ton bundles that could be pulled up into the mows with a horse-pulled rope, pulley and car-track system. Then came first round, then square tractor-pulled balers and forage harvesters. Self-propelled windrower conditioners are already replacing the hay mowers. Field baling was such a novelty in the early 1950's that many custom operators earned the $1200 cost of their bailers in a single season. . . .

The forage harvester, first used by George Faris, Concession 2, for cutting in corn ensilage, put an end to the heavy, dirty job of loading corn sheaves by hand onto a wagon and hauling it to a blower-chopper at the silo, where the sheaves had to be hand-fed. Now three men can put 130 tons of corn a day into a silo without touching a fork. Scores of new silos, with sizes up to 25 feet by 70 feet high, have recently been built in concrete.

The modern farmer is faced with many decisions as to what equipment he needs—and what he can afford to buy. His dilemma is that he needs modern labour-saving equipment to keep down operating costs, but he will go broke if his capital investment gets too high. It is a matter of balancing —sometimes on a very thin wire. During the fifties the wise farmer used co-operative equipment wherever possible, buying only what machinery he had to have. He also adjusted his production to make the most profitable use of it. This was an important factor leading to increased specialization, to larger farms, and to more intensive farming.

The Agricultural Representative Service began in 1907, on an experimental basis. Simcoe was one of the original six counties to participate in the new plan, which was administered jointly by the Department of Agriculture and the Department of Education until 1912, when the former assumed full responsibility for it.

The Simcoe County office was located at Collingwood until 1920, when it was moved to Barrie. The following year the County was divided into two zones, North and South, for purposes of agricultural administration. A new office was established in Alliston to serve South Simcoe, while Barrie assumed responsibility for the Northern division (consisting of the nine townships of Sunnidale, Vespra, Flos, Tiny, Tay, Medonte, Oro, Orillia and Matchedash). Later the Barrie office was moved to Elmvale, where it remains to the present day (in 1974, Mara and Rama were added to the Northern Division).

While touching on almost all facets of farm and rural life, the role of the Agricultural Representative has from the beginning focussed on two major areas: 1) interesting and educating boys and girls in the various aspects of farming, and 2) helping farmers by providing up-to-date information, giving advice, and making available the technological and scientific resources of the Department of Agriculture.

One of the earliest ventures at Collingwood was the establishment of experimental plots within the town limits, where some forty-eight tests of various field and garden crops were conducted. In 1911, Agricultural Representative James Laughland conducted a demonstration orchard project. It produced high yields of No. 1 grade apples, which sold at the then unheard of price of $3.00 a barrel.

Stock and seed judging classes conducted by the Agricultural Representative were a popular feature during the early days of the Extension Service. In 1911 they were held at Creemore, Nottawa, Alliston, Cookstown, Elmvale and Orillia. Supported by young and old alike, they drew large crowds—over 400, for example, turned up for the Orillia meetings.

Beginning in 1911, one-month short courses in agriculture for young farmers were conducted each winter until 1941, when the teaching of vocational agriculture was established as part of the curriculum in high schools and collegiates throughout the province.

Another important cornerstone of the Agricultural Representative Service was the School Fair Program. It was conceived by F. C. Hart, one of the six original Agricultural Representatives, in Waterloo County in 1909. The scheme involved educational meetings each winter, the distribution of high grade seeds and eggs through the schools in the early spring, and the inspection of student's plots and poultry flocks throughout the summer, and culminated with the school fairs, where judging was done, in September.

The idea spread rapidly. The first Simcoe County school fairs were held at Stroud and Nottawa in 1913. The next year, three more were added: Creemore, Ivy and Minesing. In 1915 Beeton, Oro and Moonstone had fairs. Then they were started in Orillia Township, with Uhtoff and Ardtrea alternating (1916), in Essa (1918), Tay (1919), and Bradford (1920). Later on, Severn Bridge, Waubaushene, Sunnidale, Wyevale and Lafontaine followed suit.

School fairs continued to flourish throughout the 1920s, and even during the "Dirty Thirties," but, for reasons never clearly explained, the program was dropped by the Department of Agriculture in 1939. However, many were continued on a local basis, usually under the sponsorship of agricultural societies, with the continuing support of the Agricultural Representatives.

Farmers' Institutes, first organized in 1904, were later called Boards of Agriculture and helped to spawn the Farmers' Clubs which were created for both educational and social purposes. During World War I many of these Clubs served

as buying and distributing agencies for such farm requirements as fertilizer, salt, feeding concentrates and binder
twine on a wholesale basis. Out of this grew the United Co-
operatives of Ontario.

By 1919, sixty-eight Farmers' Clubs were active throughout the County, and their increasing political interest led to
the election of the Farmer's Government in Ontario, with the
Hon. E. C. Drury of Simcoe County as Premier of the province. Shortly thereafter, however, the political movement
began to lose its momentum, and many of the clubs folded
during the mid- to late-1920s.

In company with most of their fellow-Canadians, Simcoe
County farmers were hard-hit by the Great Depression. In
1932 top-grade bacon hogs were selling (or not selling) for
$5.00 each; No. 1 potatoes brought 10¢ to 20¢ a 90-lb. bag;
and other prices reached similar disastrous lows. As one result, there was a great revival of almost-forgotten pioneer
skills: weaving, knitting, the making of homemade bread,
the putting down of preserves, the salting of pork, and so on.
Barter often replaced cash trading. Old-style co-operation, in
the form of "bees," sharing, mutual help, and unselfishness
helped them all to survive.

During these lean years substantial progress was made in
the improvement of agricultural products. The Agricultural
Representatives introduced Farm Management courses,
which were well attended. Various steps were taken to up-
grade the quality of swine, sheep and cattle. For example,
with the assistance of the Simcoe County Council, 253 sows
and 50 boars of inferior quality were replaced with selected
stock; bull bonuses were paid to improve dairy and beef cattle; and Lamb Fairs were held to encourage the breeding of
higher grade market lambs.

From 1936 until the outbreak of war in 1939, a campaign
was conducted to improve the quality of potatoes grown in
the County. This eventually led to the formation of the
North Simcoe Seed Potato Growers' Co-operative, which
built up an important export trade in seed potatoes to the

United States. Simcoe County potato producers won top honours at Toronto's Royal Winter Fair on three occasions. A key factor in the program was the establishment of the Lafontaine Restricted Seed Potato Area, a development which probably saved the unique, French-speaking community from economic disaster.

The Junior Farmers' Club program flourished during the 1930s. For example, 125 to 150 Juniors exhibited at the Barrie Junior Fair each year, with from 600 to 800 entries, and the Orillia Boys' and Girls' Sheep Club had over 90 members.

The coming of war in 1939 changed the agricultural picture dramatically, turning the situation completely around. During the Great Depression, there had been an excess of available labour, but only a very limited market. Abruptly, with the departure of hundreds of young farm people, there was a severe labour shortage coincident with an unprecedented demand for farm produce.

The role of the Agricultural Representatives became a quasi-military one, as they negotiated with the wartime authorities for the postponement of military service for essential farm workers and for harvest leaves for military personnel with agricultural experience.

Two organizations, the Simcoe County Federation of Agriculture and the Wartime Production Committee, were very effective in helping to maintain agricultural production and in sustaining the morale of the hard-pressed rural people of the County. Co-operation between the Simcoe County Federation of Agriculture and the Ontario Department of Agriculture led to an extensive program of night classes during the war and postwar years. From this beginning came such important organizations as the following:

Ontario Cream Producers, Simcoe branch;

Ontario Hog Producers, North Simcoe branch;

North Simcoe Seed Potato Growers' Co-operative;

Simcoe County: The Recent Past

Soft Wheat Growers' Committee;

Simcoe County Recreation Service;

Simcoe County Library Co-operative;

Bass Lake Co-operative Park;

North Simcoe Farm Supply Co-operatives;

Simcoe County Health Unit.

Simcoe County farmers made an outstanding contribution to the war that was finally won in 1945. "In spite of a depleted labour force, and with worn-out machinery and equipment, they met this challenge," Stewart L. Page, retiring Agricultural Representative for North Simcoe, wrote in the Barrie

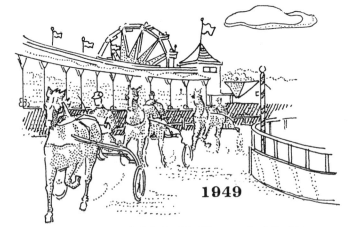

97th ANNUAL
FALL EXHIBITION
OF ORO AGRICULTURAL SOCIETY

1949

TOWN HALL, ORO
"The Home of the World's Fair"

Examiner of June 30, 1967. "They met the continuing demand for food supplies overseas by more than doubling production, many by working from dawn to dusk in the fields, and often doing the chores by lantern light. We should also give due credit to the farm women, who went a long way towards replacing lost manpower by taking over work in the fields and in the barns."

Since the war, breed organizations have played an increasingly important part in the improvement of livestock. By the mid-1950s, these breeder groups were active in Simcoe County:

Simcoe County Holstein Club;

Simcoe County and District Ayrshire Breeders' Association;

Simcoe County and District Jersey Breeders' Club;

Simcoe County Shorthorn Breeders' Club;

Simcoe County Hereford Breeders' Club;

Simcoe County Yorkshire Breeders' Club.

The role of the Agricultural Representative continues to be an extremely important one in Simcoe County, the more so because modern farming becomes steadily more complex. Today it requires a knowledge of advanced agrarian technology and science, marketing, cost accounting, business administration, and the financing, operation and maintenance of very expensive and highly sophisticated machinery and equipment.

Fall fairs and school fairs are still important annual events in the rural life of Simcoe County, although they have changed considerably since the early days. The Oro Fair—much later dubbed the "Oro World's Fair" by E. C. Drury and Henry Tudhope—is one of the oldest in the County, dating from 1842. Here is how novelist Marion Keith described it:

It was as much a social as an agricultural event—the hall containing the products of the women's deft fingers stood near the gate. At one side was a long shed, devoted to the display of farm produce—a grandstand, formed by nature from a grassy knoll covered with sweet smelling pines, rose at one side and made a convenient and delightful resting place. . . . Now it was thronged with people, and resounding with a joyous bedlam of all the noises that all the farms in Oro joined together could produce.

In the early years of the Oro Fair, tugs-of-war and oxen-pulling competitions were annual highlights among the men, while the women vied for honours in butter-making and the products of spinning wheels and looms. Many years later, on a hot, late summer day in 1952, with the parking area filled with cars and trucks in place of oxcarts and horse-drawn buggies, the Hon. Leslie Frost, then Premier of Ontario, officially opened the 100th consecutive "Oro World's Fair."

Because of varying soil and climatic conditions, agriculture in Simcoe County involves many different kinds of produce, and hence many different types of farming.

Livestock

In the early years, mixed farming was the rule. Most pioneer homesteads raised some dairy and beef cattle, a few pigs, chickens and some sheep for their own use. With the growth of the Toronto milk shed, and the increasing requirements of the towns of the County, more farmers developed dairy herds.

In the dairy industry, a change has been made from dual-purpose Shorthorns to Holsteins, Jerseys and Guernseys and from cream production to fluid milk. Only a small percentage of milk now goes to cheese factories.

The market for beef has increased. The quality of some producers' livestock has become widely recognized. For many years Copaco, a co-operative meat-processing plant in Barrie, served County beef- and swine-producers well. Today a few local slaughter houses remain in operation, but most animals are shipped to the Toronto stockyards.

There have also been important changes in the kinds of beef cattle raised. In Innisfil, for example, Herefords became the chief breed, with Shorthorns, Polled Angus and Holsteins also popular. A recent arrival from France, the Charolais, is growing in favour.

Among pig-producers, the long-backed Landrace breed began to challenge, though by no means to replace, the well established Yorkshires. Many hog barns were equipped with automatic self-feeders and drinking bowls, as the process of mechanization continued.

Field Crops

Oats and barley have always been important coarse grains in Simcoe County. They are grown primarily as livestock feed, with the straw for bedding. Fall wheat, though falling off in acreage planted, is still important as a combination cash crop and feed source.

New and improved varieties of grass and clover are continuously being developed as forage for livestock. Birdsfoot trefoil has played an important role in renovating some pasture lands.

Since about the mid-1950s, grain corn has become a crop of mounting importance, with yields of 100 bushels per acre not uncommon in many parts of the County. In fact, in 1976 Alan Scott, Agricultural Representative for North Simcoe, described it as the predominant crop in his district. Modern pickers, driers and other mechanized equipment have increased the efficiency and profits of well-organized growers. The heavy, dirty job of loading corn sheaves by hand onto a wagon, and hauling it to a blower-chopper at the silo, where the sheaves had to be hand-fed, is largely a thing of the past.

Fruit

The Collingwood area has always been the fruit belt of Simcoe County. For a great many years most of the produce of Nottawasaga township was bought and processed by Smart

Brothers cannery in Collingwood. Today, apples are the principle fruit crop, while the acreage devoted to cherries steadily decreases.

Potatoes
Potato acreage in Simcoe County increased markedly during the late 1950s, especially in the Alliston district, where the sandy loam soil was ideal for the growing of this crop. This trend was considerably encouraged when Salada Foods established a potato-processing plant at Alliston. By the 1970s almost one-fifth of the potatoes grown in Ontario were produced by Simcoe County farmers.

As in many other sectors of agriculture, the trend is toward fewer growers with larger operations. At the present some 50 to 60 growers manage more than 10,000 acres of potatoes.

Vegetables
Holland Marsh—or, as it is often called, Bradford Marsh—is the major vegetable-producing area in the County (and one of the largest in Canada). Here, in the rich lake-bottom land, enormous quantities of carrots, celery, onions, cabbages, beets and other market garden vegetables are grown each year.

In addition, smaller "muck land" pockets throughout the County have been brought into vegetable production.

Asparagus has been grown extensively in the Collingwood area for many years. In the 1950s, a few large farms started to grow it in the district around Alliston. Some is sold fresh to Toronto-based wholesalers and chain stores, but the great bulk goes to processing plants for canning or freezing.

Tobacco
Like corn, tobacco was grown by the Petun Indians at the time of the Jesuit missions. No tobacco plants were cultivated in Simcoe County for more than three centuries.

"Curly" Deshepper, on Highway 90, was the first planter in the County. By 1946 some 3,500 acres were planted on a commercial basis under permits issued by the Ontario Flue-Cured Tobacco Marketing Board.

With the discovery that smoking is dangerous to health, and with a cut-back in the acreage authorized for planting, tobacco has decreased in importance during the past few years. However, it still remains an important cash crop for some Simcoe County farmers, particularly in the area between Alliston and New Lowell.

Nursery Sod
The great urban building boom of the fifties and sixties produced an almost insatiable demand for nursery sod. Millions of square yards of sod were required to cover over the clay and marginal fill surrounding thousands of hastily constructed suburban homes in Toronto, Hamilton and other mushrooming urban centres.

The growing of this specialized crop began in Simcoe County during the early 1950s, and the high quality of the sod produced was soon recognized throughout Ontario. As a result, thousands of acres are grown annually, and Simcoe County growers are recognized as among the best in North America.

Other Farm Products
A number of large ranches raising mink and foxes have sprung up in Simcoe County in recent years, particularly in the Alliston district. Their production of pelts and raising of breeding stock has had an important impact on the fur industry.

Christmas trees, which can be grown on scrub or marginal land, have been harvested by the tens of thousands in Simcoe County and shipped to urban markets in Canada and the United States. Besides producing significant revenue for some area farmers, this enterprise has played a subsidiary role in the overall reforestation program of the County.

Poultry

Long gone are the days when every farmer kept a flock of hens to provide eggs and an occasional Sunday dinner. Poultry-raising today is a highly scientific and mechanized operation, in which thousands of birds are confined to double-tiered, well lighted, automatically cleaned cages from birth to death, never seeing the light of day. Sustenance is provided by automatic, self-serve feed troughs and waterers, and the eggs roll into pick-up trays for easy gathering. In Innisfil Township, the pioneers of modern poultry raising included Ray Lougheed, Frank Lockhart and Hunter Farms Limited of Stroud.

Figures from "Agricultural Statistics for Ontario, 1973," issued by the Department of Agriculture and Food, show the relative importance and value of various types of farm prod-

Steam-driven portable threshing machine, 1880s

uce to Simcoe County in the 1970s. Among the field crops, the leader in terms of *farm value* is potatoes, representing just over $11 million in 1973. This is of particular interest in view of the fact that potato-growers seeded only 14,760 acres, the second smallest acreage of all the field crops listed by the Ministry of Agriculture and Food.

The total corn crop—shelled and fodder combined—was second, accounting for close to $9 million in 1973. Hay, with a farm value of well over $6 million, was third. Mixed grains, barley, winter wheat and oats follow in that order.

Simcoe County, 1973	Acreage Planted	Total Farm Value
Potatoes	14,760	$11,341,100
Corn (shelled)	28,000	5,420,000
Corn (fodder)	29,800	3,296,000
Total Corn	57,800	8,716,000
Hay	129,700	6,649,000
Mixed grains	56,000	4,536,000
Barley	27,000	2,480,000
Winter wheat	12,000	1,257,600
Oats	17,000	1,190,000
Grand Totals	314,260	$26,169,700

The 1973 information also shows how completely the raising of beef and dairy cattle has come to dominate the livestock picture in Simcoe County. Although almost half as many pigs as cattle were sold, the farm value of the latter was almost fifteen times as great. The sale of sheep and lambs has dwindled to the point where its accounts for only a minor share of the total livestock market.

Simcoe County, 1973	Number Sold	Total Farm Value
Beef cows and heifers	44,000	$15,392,000
Milk cows and heifers	29,400	12,650,400
Steers (1 year & over)	31,000	9,920,000
Calves (under 1 year)	30,100	4,605,300
Total Cattle	136,310	43,440,100
Pigs	68,500	3,940,700
Sheep and lambs	13,600	435,000
Grand Totals	218,410	$47,815,800

Despite these impressive farm value totals, the overall acreage devoted to agriculture in Simcoe County has decreased over the last quarter of a century, after reaching a peak in the mid-1950s. According to the latest available figures, this decline was most dramatic in the five-year period from 1966 to 1971.

Simcoe County	Total Acres	
	Improved Land	Improved Pasture
1951	498,164	93,690
1956	504,005	122,795
1961	485,235	121,947
1966	481,356	114,591
1971	481,793	80,733

In the future, because of the high capital investments required for successful modern-day farming, the trend toward larger farms will inevitably continue. Land and mechanization costs grow year by year, and it is now virtually impossible to make an adequate profit with less than 100 acres in production—with 150 acres being a more realistic minimum. A

typical dairy farm might have 450 acres. Because of the high
cost of this land, Alan Scott, Agricultural Representative for
North Simcoe, is pessimistic about this aspect of farming:
"It may soon be virtually impossible for a young man to be
a farmer, unless he inherits substantial land holdings, or is
content to manage someone else's land as a business."

Concurrent with this evolution is the ever-growing tendency towards agricultural specialization. Just as urban industries have long prospered by turning out a limited selection
of mass-produced items, so farmers must more and more con-
centrate on mastering the technology and business practices
involved in growing or raising a particular crop or type of
livestock. In the modern agricultural world, the general prac-
titioner is on the brink of becoming an endangered species.

But the most important change, and the one that most
concerns agriculturists, is the steady shrinking of the acreage
available for farm production. As the cities and larger towns
spread out, shopping centres, suburban housing developments and high-rise apartment complexes usurp more and
more of the arable land of the County.

At the same time urbanites are buying up marginal farms
in the County at an ever-increasing rate. A few take on their
mortgages as potentially lucrative, long-term investments,
but most are simply looking for a quiet "country place" to
which they can escape on weekends and annual vacations.
Some rent their properties to active farmers in the community, so that the land is not taken out of production. Many
others, however, are content to let the weeds grow and the
land lie fallow, as they either commune with nature or wait
for the zoning by-laws to be changed so that they can cash
in on real-estate developments. Whatever the motivations,
there is, every year, less and less land available for legitimate
farmers to farm.

The quiet, peaceful, rural way of life is fast disappearing
—just as the old split-rail and root fences are being bulldozed
aside in the inevitable, and in many ways sad, evolution towards much larger, but fewer, farms.

15 Past and Present

The mid-1960s were years of great activity in reclaiming and recapturing the County's historic past. The Museum started by the Women's Institute got new life as a County project in the new location at Midhurst in 1962. The reconstruction of Sainte-Marie among the Hurons began in 1964. The building of the Museum of the Upper Lakes at Wasaga Beach was started in 1967. That same year an encouraging start was made toward restoring the early naval and military establishments at Penetanguishene.

In 1967, the year of Canada's 100th birthday, many Simcoe County municipalities and communities turned to history for their Centennial projects. The County sponsored the publication of a pictorial history, *The Visible Past*, by Adelaide Leitch, and established a County Archives in a new wing of the museum at Midhurst. Nottawasaga restored the century-old schoolhouse at Duntroon and made space for township offices in the interior. Other communities chose conservation or beautification projects. Innisfil acquired a site for a new park and Orillia constructed Centennial Park. Essa built a new library at Angus. Staynor built a flood-lit ball park.

There are several active and high calibre historical societies throughout the County, whose members have researched and written some outstanding papers on various aspects of the County's past. The County Archives provide a rich source for students of the history of the area. Libraries, too, are important repositories of information regarding bygone days, and many County librarians, past and present, have found time apart from their regular administrative duties to collect, compile and catalogue important papers, books and

262

documents.

One of the first museums to be established was the Collingwood museum, which was founded as the Huron Institute in 1904. Thousands of articles were donated, and through the years the Collingwood museum built up outstanding collections of pioneer tools and equipment, Indian artifacts, and ship models and marine photos.

One of the great contributors was Dr. David Williams, publisher and editor of the Collingwood *Enterprise-Bulletin*, whose years of unstinting support are recognized by a large bronze plaque in the lobby of the present museum.

Until 1964 the Huron Institute was housed in the basement of the Collingwood Public Library. In April of that year a disastrous fire totally destroyed the building, but most of the contents of the museum survived and were restored by months of patient, careful work.

Many people contributed to the survival and success of the Collingwood museum, including R. W. Thom, J. N. Bourrie, John Saunders, Professor Gilbert Patterson, John A. MacLean, Donald H. MacKay, Jozo Weider and Mrs. Ruth Gibbons.

In 1964, Reeve Mel McKean supported a bid to purchase the obsolete CNR station and surrounding property as a Memorial Park and new home for the Collingwood museum. The official opening took place on May 20, 1966, with the Hon. J. C. Auld, Minister of Information and Tourism, acting as presiding dignitary. Today, the Collingwood museum is recognized as among the best of its kind in the province.

Many private citizens have also contributed in important ways to the preservation of the Simcoe County heritage. At Wyevale, to cite one instance, Harry and Phyllis Hunt operate an "Outdoor Education Centre," which features a beautifully preserved, water-driven grist mill that dates from the nineteenth century. Many groups of students from Tiny township and beyond come each year to learn more about how their pioneer ancestors conquered hardships, persevered, and established communities in the wilderness of Upper Canada.

It seems probable that no region of Ontario is more bedecked with historic plaques than Simcoe County; they are there because the citizens are genuinely and legitimately proud of their heritage. If a stranger were to spend a week or ten days driving around the County, to locate, read and contemplate them, he would gain a deep appreciation of what the County is all about.

Take, for example, the one that stands at the corner of the old cemetery, on Highway 24, just north of the hamlet of Duntroon—the inscription reads:

This plaque stands at the centre of seventy-nine five-acre lots, laid out by the government in 1833 for the use of needy immigrants. Pioneer families—Islay Scotch, some Irish and German —settled here, but soon found these 'free' lots to be too small, and moved to other farms. Many of them and their descendants are buried in this cemetery.

Or the bronze plaque that is situated on the 13th Concession line in Innisfil township—under the heading "Mast for a Great Ship," it bears this legend:

Here grew some of the largest pines ever found in Ontario. In 1853 a 120-foot log was cut on the farm of Thomas Webb, Lot 23, Con. 12, one of three large pines whose stumps still remain. Hauled to the water by ten teams of horses, the log was shipped to England to become a mast for the *Great Eastern*. This epic iron vessel, the first with both sail and steam, launched in 1858, was for 40 years the largest ship in the world.

The plaques touch upon many aspects of the County's early and recent history, ranging from the African Episcopal Church at Edgar, where the freed slaves worshipped, to the site of the 1967 International Plowing Match, just south of Holly.

As well as reporting the events of the day or week, the newspapers of the County are also chroniclers of the past. From time to time, usually in conjunction with an anniversary of some kind, they print informative and interesting articles on various aspects of the early history of their part of the County.

264

Their "morgues" (where single copies of all past issues are kept) provide an incredibly rich fund of information for the historian. In some cases this is neatly preserved on micro-film, a process by which the newspapers for several months can be stored on a reel no larger than a saucer and only two inches thick; in others, the actual newspapers, yellowing with age and their dried edges crumbling, are filed in heavy, dust-covered volumes—stacked, according to some mysterious law of physics, so that the one you want is inevitably at the bottom. Many newspapers (for example, the *Northern Advance* (1854-1940), are indexed and available to the public at the County Archives. Whatever the circumstances, the story of the community is there in the words written and set in type by generations of editors, reporters, and printers.

Simcoe County's first newspaper was the Barrie *Magnet*, which began publishing on August 6, 1847. Its English-born publisher, Thomas Fox Davies, brought his press and trays of type from Toronto by ox cart, a trip that required two days to complete. It became the *Northern Advance* in 1852 and eventually was purchased by the Barrie *Examiner* in 1940.

In the later years of nineteenth century, most County towns had at least two weekly newspapers, and often more. But, as publishing costs increased and the competition for advertising became more crucial, only the most viable survived. Many of the early newspapers ceased publication and closed up shop; others were absorbed by more successful rivals, as the amalgamated names of many of today's journals show. For example, the Orillia *Packet and Times*, and the Collingwood *Enterprise-Bulletin* well illustrate the journalistic evolution that has taken place over the past century and more.

The *Enterprise*, Collingwood's first newspaper, was launched in 1857 by editor and publisher John Hogg. Thirteen years later, in 1870, the first edition of the *Bulletin*, established by David Robson, hit the street. In 1880, a third paper, the *Messenger*, began publication. The following year,

Barrie Examiner *office, 1890*

the building that housed the offices and printing facilities of the *Enterprise* was completely destroyed by fire. Mustering his resources after the calamity, John Hogg bought out the *Messenger*, and for many years he and his son published the *Enterprise-Messenger*, before shortening the name of the masthead to the original *Enterprise*. Other newspapers came and went: the *Collingwood Journal*, established in 1858 by Joseph H. Lawrence, and the *Free Lance* and the *Independent*, both of which began publication in the 1890s. None survived for more than a few years.

For more than half a century the *Enterprise* and the *Bulletin* continued in keen rivalry, the *Enterprise* being staunchly Conservative in its political outlook and the *Bulletin* as unwaveringly Liberal. Hence every issue of government, from local to federal, was enthusiastically debated on the editorial pages of the two weeklies. For most of this long period, the highly respected David Williams presided over the *Bulletin's* editorial page, in addition to filling many important journalistic and civic posts, ranging from president of the Canadian Press to mayor of Collingwood.

Finally, in the deep Depression year of 1932, the two journals buried the political hatchet, joined forces, and became the Collingwood *Enterprise-Bulletin*, which survives and prospers as a first-rate weekly newspaper to this day.

By 1967, there were a dozen newspapers in the County. Two, the Barrie *Examiner* and the Orillia *Packet and Times*, had become dailies; the ten weekly papers were the *Alliston Herald*, Barrie *Banner*, *Bradford Witness*, *Beeton World*, Collingwood *Enterprise-Bulletin*, *Creemore Star*, *Elmvale Lance*, Midland *Free Press Herald*, Orillia *News-Letter*, and *Stayner Sun*.

In the early years, editors (who were usually publishers and owners as well) showed great individualism and wrote about anything that struck their fancy or aroused their ire. This was especially true of the *Beeton World*. "It was written in a racy style, and with little regard for the Queen's English, but packed a real punch," Kate Aitken said of it in her book,

Never a Day so Bright.

In 1915, this different and fascinating item appeared in the *World*: "Gordon Nichol saw an aeroplane speeding south at a great height on Wednesday night of last week. It was equipped with powerful lights." In the primitive aviation world of 1915, it is highly unlikely that an aircraft would be flying after dark—least of all "at a great height." With runway lights, direction-finding equipment, and air traffic controllers still undreamed of, where and how was that aircraft to land? And, since planes of that time were never intended to fly at night, why was this equipped with "powerful lights"? It is enough to make even a skeptic wonder if what Gordon Nichol witnessed that night in 1915 could have been an early appearance of a "Flying Saucer" or a UFO. Unfortunately, subsequent issues of the *Beeton World* make no further reference to the mysterious phenomenon.

Among the luminaries of the academic world, Arthur R. M. Lower has been one of the most highly respected historians of the last several decades. Lower grew up and received his early education in Barrie and vicinity. He went on to become the esteemed head of the History Department at Queen's University and Douglas Professor of Canadian History at Queens (1947-1959). His published works include *Colony to Nation*, a fine general history of Canada, *My First Seventy-five Years*, an autobiography published in 1967, and *History and Myth*, a work on Canadian nationalism, published in 1975.

Simcoe County has contributed many outstanding successful businessmen. Among them are T. P. Loblaw, F. K. Morrow, Jack McCague, and another who achieved enormous success, Eric Harvie. Harvie, who was born in Orillia in 1892, was described by Peter Newman in *The Canadian Establishment* (Vol. I):

He amassed a greater personal fortune from petroleum than any other Canadian, yet was not an oilman, stayed in the industry only eleven years, and exhibited none of the free-wheeling traits that characterize the breed.

Harvie seemed totally indifferent to power, casually abandoning the opportunity of becoming the only Canadian to put together a fully integrated major oil company, and even though he went on amassing a fortune of well over $100 million, he used little of the money for himself. Instead of going about Calgary in one of those burnished-arc Cadillacs oilmen seem to prefer, he drove an old Studebaker, so banged up that its undercarriage was a sheet of solid bronze.

In 1944 Harvie purchased the Alberta mineral and oil rights owned by the London-based British Dominion Land Corporation for an estimated $110,000. Two years later he leased 480 acres southwest of Edmonton to Imperial Oil, and early in 1947 the great Leduc strike was brought in on this property. The Vermilion and Redwater fields that were subsequently discovered were also mainly on land he controlled.

By 1951 Harvie's various companies held shares of 82 producing wells and had increased the land they owned to over two million acres. In the mid-1950s he sold Western Leaseholds, his exploration company, to Canadian Petrofina for about $50 million, and by the early 1970s had disposed of his remaining assets and retired an extremely wealthy man.

Harvie, as *The Canadian Establishment* points out, "may be the only rich Canadian who leaves behind a popular legacy. His magpie instinct for collecting anything and everything he happened to see endowed his foundation with the finest collection of western artifacts and general trivia anywhere." His astonishing accumulation included: a pair of Queen Victoria's royal bloomers, ten thousand mounted butterflies from the Duke of Bedford's collection, a complete bar-room from Keremeos, B. C., paintings by A. Y. Jackson and A. J. Casson, and bullets found at the site of Custer's last stand on the Little Bighorn.

Simcoe County has produced several outstanding writers, apart from those already mentioned. One of the most prolific and informatively entertaining, is Kenneth McNeill Wells, who was born at Mitchell, Ontario in 1905, but who moved to Orillia when still a child. Wells was a successful journalist with the Toronto *Telegram* but, following service in World War II, raised goats and kept bees on a farm in Medonte Township. He continued to write, however, and his often humorous newspaper articles provided the basis for four popular books, which were illustrated by his wife, Lucille Oille: *The Owl Pen, By Moonstone Creek, Up Medonte Way* and *By Jumping Cat Bridge*. An ardent yachtsman, Wells also wrote several books about freshwater navigation and the joys of water travel in Ontario: *Cruising the Georgian Bay, Cruising the Trent-Severn Waterway, Cruising the North Channel, Cruising the Rideau Waterway, Trailer Boating* and *The Moonstruck Two*. Several of these have become "bibles" in their field and are studied and enjoyed by hundreds of small boat skippers each summer.

Music has always played an important role in the life of Simcoe County. Most towns and villages had bands which played when the young men went off to war, for parades, patriotic occasions, and Sunday evening bands concerts, and at fairs. Church congregations were proud of their choirs. Music festivals were popular into the 1950s, with school groups practising for weeks before the annual competitions.

Among the towns, Beeton and Stayner were long noted for having fine brass bands; the Stayner band played for moonlight excursions on Georgian Bay in summer, and for evenings of skating at the Clark and Turner rinks each winter. The Barrie Collegiate Institute has had a very famous band, under the direction of W. A. Fisher. It has won international acclaim and many awards over the last two decades.

In recent summers, there has been considerable musical activity, particularly in the Collingwood area, with its annual Blue Mountain Summer School of Music and Dance. In 1976, this program—jointly sponsored by George William College and Georgian College—ran from June 22 to August 16. In residence as part of the faculty, were the members of

Lighthouse, one of Canada's top rock concert attractions. Performances by students and faculty were put on in the new outdoor shell, and there were weekly concerts by the Blue Mountain Symphony Orchestra.

It would be difficult to think of anyone who is more a part of the modern scene in the mid-1970s than singer Gordon Lightfoot. Born in Orillia in 1938, Lightfoot's interest in music became evident at an early age. Throughout his high school days in Orillia he played in the school band, sang in music festivals and operettas, studied piano, and experimented with writing lyrics.

After graduation from high school in 1957, he went to Toronto to begin a professional career that would soon earn him national and international acclaim. Today he is recognized as an outstanding singer, song writer, poet, musician and author. His lyrical and imaginative book for children, *The Pony Man*, was greeted with critical approval and popular enthusiasm. And, in the late spring of 1976, impatient with the hesitant financial support that was being extended to Canada's Olympic athletes, he organized a benefit concert in Toronto's Maple Leaf Gardens. It was an artistic triumph and it provided thousands of badly needed dollars for our athletes at the Montreal Games.

Though Gordon Lightfoot's music is for today, and his success contemporary, his lyrics frequently reveal an awareness of his roots in Simcoe County and a strong appreciation of the past.

In art, the members of Canada's famed "Group of Seven" did much of their early painting in the Georgian Bay area, which A. Y. Jackson described as "painter's country," and two of them, Franz Johnston and Franklin Carmichael, were closely linked to Simcoe County.

Johnston lived in the Midland area and painted many of his later canvases there; Carmichael was born in Orillia in 1890. Today a plaque outside the public library on Orillia's main street commemorates Carmichael's great contribution to Canadian art:

FRANKLIN CARMICHAEL, 1890-1945

Born Orillia—studied Ontario College of Art and L'Aca-
demie Royale des Beaux-Arts at Antwerp—worked
with Lismer and Varley in commercial art—in Toronto
in 1914 shared a studio with Tom Thompson—youngest member of Group of Seven—participated in all
Group's exhibitions—graphic style and sense of design
led to distinguished career as artist, industrial designer
and teacher—some of his best known works: *Autumn
Woods, Lake Superior, North Tundra* and illustrations
for Grace Campbell's book 'Thorn-Apple Tree'.

Carmichael's two favourite painting locales were the rugged
Pre-Cambrian Shield terrain along Georgian Bay and Lake
Superior, and the gently rolling farm county of central On-
tario. Among the many fine pieces he produced in Simcoe
County were *Farm Buildings, Severn Bridge* and *Hilltop,
Severn Bridge.*

Another artist who knows the country from the perspec-
tive of many generations, is Arthur Shilling, an artist from
the Rama Indian Reserve, just east of Orillia. In the mid-
1960s, while still shy of his 25th birthday, Shilling began to
attract attention as a painter of exceptional talent, and his
career remains in the ascendancy as this is written a decade
later.

Bridget Teufel wrote about Arthur Shilling in a series of
excellent articles she did about the Indians of Simcoe County
for the Orillia *Packet and Times* in 1965:

If there is such as thing as 'the typical painter,' Arthur is it. At
24, he transforms feelings and impressions into art as long as his
paints last. The tubes gone, and no money in the house, he will
grab a hunk of clay, and shape it after somebody's face. He
would paint on the walls, if necessary—and it *is* necessary at all
times for an artist to put out somehow, somewhere, the pictures
that are in himself.

Shilling started drawing as a small child. Later, he carved
totem poles. He made his first oil painting in 1960. . . .

In 1962, he was awarded a $1,500 scholarship from the

Indian Affairs Department, to study at the Ontario College of Art. . . .

'Everything has a soul' he said when he was 22, 'This plant, that tree trunk, that child. Unless an artist searches for it, his work is flat, meaningless.'

This 'laying bare of the soul' shows in all of his paintings— mainly portraits of children or old people. A touch of tragedy —or melancholy—lingers over most.

His models—the little boy next door, his sister Glenna, an old uncle. In light and in shadow, he captures their 'souls'. . . .

Now and then he sells a painting to have the funds for new materials, but he is a bad advertiser for himself. 'This painting isn't finished.' 'That one is not good enough.' 'This here is just a study'. . . .

Many would say that Shilling works under 'ideal' conditions for an artist. No money, no television, no distractions—just his visions and sometimes some Chopin or Brahms on the record-player. As he paints with the intensity that drives him now, he gives the impression that he may fly up to that lonely mountain where the good Thunderbird has its huge nest, and from there look over the world at his feet—and paint it.

Now, a dozen years after Bridget Teufel wrote her article about him, Arthur Shilling has gained the acclaim of critics and much greater popular interest. Like most Canadian artists, however, he still finds it a constant struggle to keep food on the table and tubes of paint on the tray of his easel.

Yet, by comparison with most of his Indian brothers and sisters, Shilling is lucky; his skills and his perserverance have earned for him a measure of acceptance in the world beyond the boundaries of his Rama reserve, some independence, and the right to feel pride in his talent and in his heritage.

In general, the Indians of Simcoe County have fared little better—though certainly no worse—than the survivors of the original population have fared in the rest of Canada. In their struggle to adapt to the realities of twentieth century and to envelopment by the white people, while still preserving at least the roots of their own culture, they have had some successes. But the way has not been easy, nor is it easy now.

The great majority of them live on reservation land, in

scattered, small and dwindling pockets—in Rama Township, on the eastern shore of Lake Couchiching; on Georgina, Snake and Fox Islands in Lake Simcoe; and on Christian, Beckwith and Hope Islands, lying to the north of Penetang peninsula in Georgian Bay. Almost all are Ojibways, or descendants of other, closely related branches of the once widespread and powerful Algonquin people.

For local government, each band has an elected chief and several councillors (about one for each one hundred residents). The councils meet once a month, and during the early years of the twentieth century the meetings were well attended. In more recent times, however, interest in community affairs has declined considerably, and, for the most part, only those having matters to bring before the council attend. This growing apathy is a source of much concern among the Indian leaders of Simcoe County. It stems from a

Ojibwa

feeling of frustration among the native people—a belief that, for a variety of reasons, they can do little to help themselves.

In part, this frustration grew out of the fact that every decision taken by chiefs and councillors, including the expenditure of band funds and the use of reservation land, was subject to veto by the Department of Indian Affairs (later the Indian Affairs Branch of the Department of Citizenship and Immigration). Control of revenue is necessary for effective government, but such control has never been granted to the chiefs and councillors of Canada's Indian people, including those of Simcoe County.

For much more than a century, the affairs of the Indians of the County were controlled by a succession of resident representatives appointed by Ottawa. It was they who presided over the monthly meetings of the band councils, and they who recommended or rejected the proposals made for the expenditure of band funds.

The first Indian Agent assigned to the Rama reservation was S. P. Jarvis, who took up his post in June of 1837; the eleventh appointee to fill that role, F. W. Purser, assumed his duties on December 6, 1960. Since the late 1960s, the administration of the Simcoe County Indians has been handled locally by a branch of the Department of Indian Affairs and Northern Development located in Orillia, and the emphasis has been somewhat more on co-operation and slightly less on control. But the Indian people and their leaders are still a long way from enjoying any real political autonomy. It was not, in fact, until 1960 that Canada's Indians were given the right to vote in federal elections.

"Very few run for chief here now," said Irwin Douglas, elected head of the Rama Indian band, in 1965. "Under present conditions, only a fool does." Douglas, a disabled veteran of World War II, worked hard for his people (on a meagre salary of $180 a year), but he found that his efforts were eroded at every turn.

Lack of adequate housing has always been a major problem among the native peoples. At Rama, it was common to find from six to sixteen people living in a single dwelling, with inadequate sanitary provisions, no privacy and no quiet space in which young students might do their homework, "We need six new houses each year," Chief Douglas said. "Instead, we get two." This was true despite the fact that half of the building costs for new homes was supplied from band funds, to be paid back later by house owners. To this day, over-crowding remains a major sociological problem among the Indians living on reservation land.

Meanwhile, bands funds, accumulated mainly through the sale of reservation holdings in the 1800s, diminished drastically with the passing of the years. "Around 1948-49, there was about $164,000 in our account," Chief Douglas said in 1965. "In June of 1960, this had shrunk to exactly $101,611.95. Now we have some $68,000 left."

The economic situation continues to deteriorate. Most Simcoe County Indians survive quite well, and even prosper, relatively, in the summers. Then there are fish to be caught, berries to be picked, minnows to be sold as bait, fishing parties to be guided, and odd-jobs to be had, and tourists are eager and able to buy Indian handicrafts. But the winters are an entirely different story. In 1965, only eighteen people from the Rama reserve found work in Orillia during the cold months; almost all of the other families were on welfare. This assistance, based on provincial standards, provided from $25 to a maximum of $39 per week, regardless of how many children there were in a family. On Simcoe County's Indian reserves, where households commonly numbered eight, nine, ten or more, hardships and hunger were chronic conditions of life.

Inadequate nutrition, over-crowded living accommodations, and substandard sanitary conditions have all contributed to a high rate of illness among the Indians. "Poor diet is the cause of many of their health problems," Dr. T. L. Torrance of Orillia, who administered medical care to Rama for more than twenty years, said in 1965. "They eat a lot of fat pork, potatoes and bread, but far too few fresh vegetables."

Diphtheria and smallpox used to frequently reach epidemic proportions on the reserves, but have now been almost entirely eliminated through immunization. Measles, chicken pox and mumps are still fairly common among the children, while respiratory infections strike many adults each year. "The Indians have poor resistance to these," Dr. Torrance said. "It may be because their ancestors did not have these illnesses, and therefore did not build up immunity against them."

Poor hygiene has been another important cause of health problems among the Indians—not because they are any less interested in keeping clean than their white neighbours, but through a lack of facilities. As late as the 1940s, there were only four or five wells on the Rama reservation, and many women had to walk up to a half a mile to fetch water. By the mid-1960s, no more than a dozen families had running water —and none had a bathtub. The situation has improved since then, but it still leaves a great deal to be desired.

The popular conception that there was unrestricted use of liquor and resultant social ills among Indians was, to a large extent, exaggerated. Sergeant Ray Williams of the Brechin detachment of the Ontario Provincial Police agreed that alcohol was a major factor in some cases, but he pointed out that most liquor offenses involved a small number of chronic repeaters. "Our records show that over a period of time, crime and liquor incidents involving Indians are not excessively high," he said.

Nor did he believe that the teenagers from the reserves were particularly irresponsible or delinquent. "The juvenile problem is not any worse with Indians than with whites," he told Bridget Teufel—and it was an opinion based on first hand knowledge and experience as a law enforcement officer in Simcoe County.

Although the lot of the Indian residents of the county remains harsh, with poverty and unemployment still endemic, there have been some encouraging developments in recent years. They have shown considerable initiative in taking steps to improve their situation: they have developed a camping park, they constructed and operate a marina and they market native crafts to summer tourists. At least in some cases, the government authorities have seen fit to lend meaningful support to such ventures. Not all succeed, of course, any more than all new enterprises prosper on the downtown streets of Barrie, but in counteracting the apathy that many Indians have been conditioned to feel, the attempt is worthwhile.

Although not all would agree, most people—Indians and whites alike—regard the integration of Indian children into the general educational system of the province as having been a step in the right direction. It began in 1957, and was completed by 1964. In the early stages there were a few scattered incidents of racial tension, but it soon became apparent that the young people of both cultures tended to be considerably less prejudiced than their parents.

Prior to 1945, it was almost unheard of for an Indian boy or girl to enter high school, let alone graduate. By 1960, only one student from Rama, Marie Ste Germaine, had earned a Grade XIII certificate. She subsequently trained at St. Michael's hospital in Toronto and went on to a successful career in nursing. Two others had passed into Grade XIII but failed to complete it.

In recent years more and more young Indians from the Simcoe County reservations are earning high school diplomas, but it remains harder for them to graduate than it is for their white classmates. This is so for several reasons: because of the hours spent on buses going to and from school; because, coming from one culture, they must succeed in an entirely different one; because of less nutritious food; and because the crowded living conditions at home are not conducive to sound study habits.

They deserve all the help and encouragement that can be extended to them; for, in a mixture of the old and the new that is Simcoe County, their roots lie centuries deeper in the soil than those of the earliest white settlers.

16 The County Government

Each winter, on the Monday before the third Tuesday of January, an important and impressive event takes place in the chambers of the Simcoe County Council in the Administration Centre at Midhurst. The spacious parking areas, hedged by neat rows of tall reforestation pines, fill up quickly in the early afternoon. Inside, the visitors' gallery of the Council chambers just as rapidly reaches capacity—with a few left to sit in the aisles, or stand in the entrance ramps. There are television cameras, representatives of local press and radio, ex-Wardens of the County, relatives of the Council members, specially invited guests, and interested members of the public.

There is a subdued but real sense of excitement and expectancy, for this is the first County Council meeting of the new year, and, for many newly elected members, it is their first official appearance as representatives of their towns, villages or townships. It will also see the election of the next Warden of the County, the man who will fill the most important role in County government for the coming year.

The new Administration Centre at Midhurst, which was opened November 27, 1973, by Provincial Treasurer, John White, is a somewhat angular, brick and stone building, which incorporates some very modern architectural concepts, while retaining a sense of tradition. A tribute to its designers, it seems to *belong* where it is, and to be appropriate for the County.

While not ostentatious, the decor of the chambers is very pleasant, achieving an effective balance between comfort and efficiency. The dais, tables and chairs are of light, well-

279

Simcoe County Administration Centre

polished wood. The floors are attractively carpeted to reduce noise. Sunlight filters through the windows, even on a mid-January afternoon.

When the County Clerk calls the meeting to order, the first order of business is the selection of the new Warden. Nominations are made from the floor; here and there a member rises to propose a candidate of his choice, giving a brief summary of the nominee's qualifications. Each nomination is seconded by another member, who adds his own laudatory comments.

The slate of candidates having been determined, the County Clerk, who acts as chairman for this part of the proceedings, calls for a voice vote, and each member in turn announces his or her choice. The overflow audience is hushed and the atmosphere tense, as the votes are recorded by the County Clerk. There is a sense of competition, although the rivalry between the candidates is a friendly, rather than a bitter, one.

When the voting is completed, the County Clerk reads out the results, and the new Warden is declared elected. The swearing-in and installation ceremonies follow, highlighted when the successful candidate leaves the chambers for a few moments, to return wearing the black, wide-brimmed, three-cornered "Warden's Hat" and the Warden's Gown. Deeply rooted in tradition and worn by generations of Wardens, this mark of office dates back to at least the eighteenth century, and was no doubt brought over from England, under circumstances that are now lost in the mists of time.

During the inaugural proceedings and throughout the remainder of the first Council meeting of the year, a feeling of friendly dignity prevails. This is grassroots democracy; there is little of the pomp and circumstances which attend the openings of federal and provincial parliaments, and certainly there is no pomposity or putting on of airs. The members of Council are "ordinary" men and women, rather than image-conscious politicians. They see their service as a duty and a privilege, rather than as a stepping stone to positions of greater power. For the most part, they know and respect each other and, while honest disagreement will add spice to many a future meeting of Council, there will almost never be acrimony or hostility. All of them are concerned with doing a good job for their electors and for Simcoe County.

Apart from the cordiality, however, there is an air of seriousness about the first meeting of Council each year, because the members are aware of the trust placed in them, and of the importance and difficulty of the many problems and challenges they will be called upon to consider during their term in office.

The Simcoe County Council is composed of fifty-three members, making it one of the largest governing bodies in Ontario. It includes reeves and deputy reeves of the municipalities; members are elected for two year terms. At present the composition of the Council is as follows:

	Number of Members
Townships	32
Towns	13
Villages	8
Total Members	53

As outlined in legislation of April, 1972, representation is according to the number of municipal electors. A municipality of less than 2500 municipal electors is represented at the Council by a reeve with one vote. One of from 2500 to 5000 municipal electors is represented by a reeve and a deputy reeve, each with one vote. A municipality of from 5000 to 7500 municipal electors is represented by a reeve, who has two votes, and a deputy reeve, who has one vote. Those of over 7500 municipal electors are represented by a reeve and a deputy reeve, each of whom has two votes.

As autonomous political entities, the two cities, Barrie and Orillia, are governed by elected mayors and aldermen, and are not represented on County Council.

The only territorial increase to the County in this century occurred on January 1, 1974. The townships of Mara and Rama (on the east side of Lakes Couchiching and Simcoe) were transferred by mutual agreement from the former County of Ontario, when the Regional Municipality of Durham was formed. There are now eighteen townships in Simcoe County: Adjala, Essa, Flos, Innisfil, Mara, Matchedash, Medonte, Nottawasaga, Orillia, Oro, Rama, Sunnidale, Tay, Tecumseth, Tiny, Tosorontio, Vespra, and West Gwillimbury. The total population of the County in 1977 was 208,063.

At the beginning of each year the Council, sitting as a committee of the whole, elects several standing committees and boards, each of which deals with a different area of administration. In the mid-1970s the standing committees are: Finance and Administration, Roads, County Property and Printing, County Planning, Agriculture and Reforestation, Social Services, Tourist and Industrial, Recreation, Warden, and County Land Division. This list gives some idea of the broad scope of the Council's responsibilities. In addition to the committees, there are four boards, on which Barrie and Orillia are also represented; these are Children's Aid Society, Health, Library, and Museum and Archives.

Special, temporary committees may also be appointed from time to time when the need arises. Each committee and board holds its own meetings, with a chairman and a secretary, and reports to the Council as a whole. Most by-laws originate in committee, and then are presented to the Council, where they are given three readings, and voted on by all members. Decisions are made by majority vote.

Since the Council members are joint custodians of the public funds, a large proportion of their time is taken up with the consideration of money grants. All applications for such grants must initially be recommended to the Finance and Administration Committee by the committee in whose jurisdiction it falls. If approved, payment is made by the County Treasurer, on instructions from the County Council.

The largest area of expenditure in recent years has been for social services: general welfare, Children's Aid, and Recreation Service, public health, homes for the aged, and day care for the children of working mothers. Various departments of the provincial government contribute to the financing of these essential agencies, but the bulk of the revenue at the disposal of the County Council comes from the municipalities. Towns, villages and townships collect their own taxes, a portion of which is passed on to the County Council to defray the cost of county-wide services.

Each year, before the first day of July, the County Council must pass an Equilization By-law, the purpose of which is to ensure that each municipality pays a fair and equitable share of the operating budget. On occasion (such as during the Great Depression), some municipalities have been unable to meet their levies; in such cases, the County Council has always co-operated with local administrators in working out mutually acceptable arrangements.

The County Library Board has played a very important role, both in the provision of reading material and in the collection and preservation of important historical information that has to do with the County's past. (The latter, of course, has also been the concern of the Museums and Archives Board.)

Libraries have received support from the County Council since before World War I. By the mid-1960s the Library Board was supplying books to more than 20 public libraries, and to some 260 school libraries. The cost of the library service was covered in part by the Ontario Department of Education and in part by Simcoe County Council.

By the beginning of the 1970s, the servicing of school libraries had been taken over by the Simcoe County Board of Education. In 1977 the County Library Board is responsible for thirty-one public libraries and depot stations. In the cities and larger towns, the libraries are large-scale, modern facilities staffed by professionals; in some remote areas, as few as 214 books are loaned in a year.

An important, non-elective, career member of the Council is the County Clerk. He is responsible for Council correspondence, for a host of administrative details, for organizing Council meetings, for the drafting of all by-laws, and for keeping an accurate and full account of all proceedings at each Council session and later publishing them as official minutes.

A study of these minutes, dating back to the early years of the twentieth century, provides an appreciation of the enormous variety of problems, challenges, issues, crises, and routine administrative chores with which County Council has had to deal over the years. Its responsibilities have ranged from the purely local (fall fairs) to the international (World Wars I and II).

The following selection of items from the minutes of past meetings of County Council illustrates that diversity. It is not a capsule summary of the Council's activities, most of which have been concerned with such major, perennial matters as health, reforestation, the construction and maintenance of roads, agricultural problems and the provision of social services. Some of the items listed are weighty concerns; others are more trivial; many now simply reveal the passage of time. They show that a member of Council has to be a person for all seasons, capable of dealing with widely diverse concerns. County Council:

1909 granted a loan of $5000 to the Tudhope Carriage Company;

1910 raised the fine for horse stealing to $50;

1910 agreed to the reshingling of the County Jail at a cost of $295;

1911 considered R. H. Webb's request for compensation for a broken spring on his automobile, due to rough roads in Vespra (later it was established that, except in cases of clear negligence, government agencies are not responsible for such damages);

1913 granted $1,000 towards construction of the Champlain Monument in Orillia;

1915 granted $250 for comforts for the County's soldiers, and $1,000 to the Belgian Relief Fund, the Red Cross, and the Canadian Patriotic Fund;

1917 voted to support the Conscription Bill, introduced by Sir Robert Borden, then before the House of Commons;

1918 set the salary of the County Clerk at $800 per annum;

1920 agreed to pay $108 to John Lister, for damages caused when his horse shied because of some galvanized pipes at the roadside, just south of Bond Head;

1922 voted $2,850 to buy Lot 1, Con. 6 in Vespra, to be used for reforestation;

1923 voted to give mail carriers the day off on Christmas Day and Dominion Day;

1924 authorized a $50 reward for information leading to the conviction of anyone setting a fire in a wood lot;

1925 voted not to buy new chairs for jurors, but approved the purchase of 12 new cushions for existing chairs;

1926 voted to oppose any legislation compelling owners of horse-drawn vehicles to carry lights;

1926 voted $200 towards the raising of the *Nancy* (substantially larger amounts were voted later as salvage work progressed);

1927 debated the merits of trucks vs. horses for road work;

1930 recommended that each municipality pay a $10 reward for capturing or killing any dog worrying sheep;

1932 discussed various means of cutting costs of education because of the Depression;

1933 inaugurated a campaign to eradicate TB among cattle in the County;

1934 agreed to turn over the old Registry Office to be developed as a museum;

1936 sent a letter to Queen Mary, expressing sympathy on the death of George V;

1938 granted $50 to each of 12 County fairs; approved the use of chemicals to control weeds along County roads;

1939 supported the establishment of a Simcoe County Library Association;

1942 established a Simcoe County Agriculture War Production Committee;

1943 heard a report that $126,000 in Victory Bonds had been purchased in a current campaign;

1945 sent a letter of congratulations to Prime Minister Mackenzie King, following victory in Europe;

1947 heard that the cost per patient per day in Collingwood hospital was $6.71;

1950 voted to purchase and plant 550 acres per year to speed up the reforestation program;

1951 approved the purchase of a photo-stat machine for $6,549 (the first in the County);

1954 asked the federal government for disaster-area status, following the devastation caused by Hurricane Hazel;

1958 voted to establish a tourist and Information Centre on Highway 400 near Barrie:

1962 voted $29,796 for construction of a County Museum and for landscaping the grounds;

1966 voted $2500 to Wasaga Beach zoo;

1969 passed a motion expressing opposition to the legalization of marijuana.

The agendas dealt with by County Council grow longer and more complex with each passing year. As one indication of this, annual budget estimates have increased steadily since early in the century, from $97,423 in 1909 to $8,193,394 in 1977.

A feature of Simcoe County administration has been the unusually long terms of service of many who have held public office. J. S. Drinkwater, for instance, who was Warden of the County in 1936, spent forty-two of his more than ninety years in Orillia municipal politics. J. R. Coleman, who gave thirty-nine years of service to the County, began as Assistant Treasurer and Clerical Assistant to the County Engineer in

January, 1934 and progressed to Deputy Treasurer (1948) and Treasurer (1952). He retired at the end of 1972.

In Oro township, to cite another example, George Tudhope was appointed Clerk when the first township council met in 1835, a position he held with a few interruptions until 1892. He was then succeeded by his son, Henry, who was Clerk of Oro until 1919, when he in turn was replaced by his son, Wesley. On June 4, 1969, Wesley Burt Tudhope died, just two months short of celebrating his 50th anniversary as Clerk and Treasurer of the township. With his death, an astonishing record of family public service came to an end.

Education in the County has always been of prime concern. In the 1960s the elementary school system underwent extensive changes. While municipal areas, such as Barrie, were growing and were building new schools, rural areas were experiencing crises of declining enrollments and inability to provide broad educational advantages to their far-flung schools. Townships began to consolidate their schools, although this meant daily bussing for young children. In a short period of sixteen years, the number of public elementary schools was reduced to one-third as many. The total number of elementary schools (including the Separate Schools) decreased from 238 to 102, while the total enrollment increased.

Elementary Schools

Year	Number of Public Schools	Number of Separate Schools	Total Enrollment
1961	216	22	28,344
1968	96	25	32,724
1977	76	26	33,775

The administration of the schools was changing too. Before the sixties, each local area or "section" had its own school board which was autonomous. Gradually school sections began to unite into township units. This system, in which the township unit was the smallest administrative unit, became mandatory in 1964. Eight inspectors (two of them for the Separate Schools) supervised County elementary education. In January, 1969, this plan was superceded by a new system in which there is one large unit of administration, the Simcoe County Board of Education. It is responsible to the Ontario Ministry of Education. At present, local levies pay about 45% of the education budget and provincial grants about 55%.

In the mid-1970s, Simcoe County and its Council and other administrators of local government face very serious problems and challenges. Perhaps the most basic and most difficult of these is the threat posed by the environmental pollution and ecological decay that have become apparent during the past dozen or more years. For at least a century, Simcoe County has derived much of its character, and earned much of its revenue from its bountiful natural resources. Generations of cottagers, picnickers, tourists and fishermen have enjoyed its clear waters, its beaches, its forests, and the peace and quiet of its rural countryside.

Now, all of these assets, so long taken for granted, are in serious jeopardy, imperilled by pollution on the one hand, and ever increasing demands for recreational space on the other.

In various ways the County has been taking steps to meet this double-pronged threat for many years. The reforestation program, dating back to the early 1920s, has been a continuing and largely successful attempt to restore one great natural resource.

The goal of making maximum use of available recreational land, both for residents and visitors, has been advanced by the development of township parks and picnic areas, as well as by co-operation with the provincial government in the establishment of the several fine provincial parks that now serve hundreds of thousands each year.

The Nottawasaga Valley Conservation Authority, established in 1960 as an autonomous, corporate organization, is committed to a comprehensive program of natural resource management within the area of its jurisdiction—the combined watersheds of the Nottawasaga River, Pretty River, Black Ash Creek and Silver Creek. Twenty-eight Simcoe County municipalities lie either wholly or partly within this area, and each appoints a member of the Authority.

The lands acquired by the Authority and turned into conservation areas are developed for forestry and land-use improvement demonstrations, education in conservation, and recreation. Technical advice is provided for such things as tree planting, pond construction, erosion control, wildlife conservation and general improvement of the land.

Among the fine parks developed by the Nottawasaga Valley Conservation Authority for public use are those at Utopia, New Lowell and Tottenham. The description of the New Lowell Conservation Area, furnished by the Authority, will illustrate the excellent facilities and services being developed:

The New Lowell Conservation Area comprises 140 acres of open wooded and wetland areas, each harbouring many different types of wildlife.

Picnic tables, fireplaces, comfort stations, and an excellent beach are provided for the picnic and camping enthusiast. Wilderness camping may also be enjoyed by the hardy canoeist.

A wide variety of native trees, as well as many types planted by the Conservation Authority, provide homes and protection for many species of wildlife, and at the same time serve to beautify the area.

The site was once that of an old mill pond, the original dam built to supply water power to a grist mill, which was later used for chopping livestock feed. Today, a large, modern dam creates a 50-acre reservoir, encompassing one-half mile of Coates' Creek.

Rainbow trout are stocked in the reservoir yearly, and provide excellent opportunities for some exciting fishing.

Wood duck boxes have been placed in the upper reaches of the reservoir to encourage the residency of this wildfowl.

Another, earlier step in the same general direction was the

establishment of the Simcoe County Community and Recreation Service in 1945, as a project of the Community Life Training Institute of the University of Toronto. Its purpose was to help Simcoe County residents to appreciate, develop and enjoy the potential of their natural environment and sociological heritage. From the beginning, it provided a clearing house for ideas and training opportunities for a wide range of county groups; rural and urban committees, teen clubs, farm clubs, senior citizens' organizations, art and historical societies, sports leagues, cottagers' associations, and church clubs. Many volunteer leaders received their first training through the workshops, courses, seminars and conferences conducted by the Community Service.

Under its first director, Miss Louise Colley, a county-wide organization was established for arts and crafts, music, drama, day camps, swimming instruction and various other activities. The Recreation Service provided a great variety of assistance—from clinics for minor league baseball umpires to garden projects—with a very small staff and at very low cost. Its 1966 budget, for instance, ran to only $39,964.22, or about 23¢ per annum per County resident.

As part of this program, Simcoe was the first county in the province to employ a full-time recreation director.

By the 1970s, the Simcoe County Recreation Board was composed of four members of Council and three others appointed by the Council. Its work was financed by a grant from the County Council, with additional support coming from the Ontario Department of Education. Its object continues to be to assist residents in using their leisure time constructively, for the benefit of the community as a whole, as well as for their individual fulfilment.

These various activities demonstrate clearly that Simcoe has been a vanguard county in coping with the problems of the present, and in taking steps to meet the challenges of the future. But evidence revealed during the early- to mid-1970s made it all too obvious that the time available for making such adjustments was drastically less than had previously been assumed.

Late in 1976, scientists and technicians employed by the Ontario government discovered that Lake Simcoe was suffering from a serious pollution problem. The Ministry of Health announced that the lake's walleyes (pickerel) were contaminated with mercury; fifty fish tested had been found to contain up to 1.70 parts per million, several times the .50 p.p.m. that authorities consider the maximum safe level. The fish should be eaten only occasionally, the report warned, and pregnant women should not eat any.

The news stunned the people of Simcoe County, officials and ordinary citizens alike. The great lake was such a unique and dominant feature of the county, that it was hard to accept the gravity of its sickness.

For centuries it had reliably yielded up bountiful catches of fish: to the Indians who built their weirs and strung their nets, to the pioneers who speared suckers and spawning muskies with their pitchforks, to generations of cottagers, to tourist anglers from New York, New Jersey, Michigan, Ohio, Pennsylvania, and to resident fishermen who, year after year, carried their catches home along quiet town and village streets.

Historically, it had offered an incredible variety of fish: huge, carnivorous muskies, weighing up to forty pounds and more; heavy-bodied lake trout, sulking in the deep, dark canyons; lunker bass, hovering warily around a thousand points and shoals; tender-mouthed whitefish; succulent pickerel; savage pike, with teeth like barbed wire; schools of silver herring; fat perch; ugly ling; and teeming swarms of minnows.

For a great many years a flourishing commercial fishery existed in the lake, as the following table from *Fishing in Lake Simcoe* (by H. R. McCrimmon of the Department of Lands and Forests) demonstrates:

Reported Commercial Catch In Pounds

	1900-1909	1910-1919	1920-1929	1930-1939	1940-1949
Herring	28,640	11,211	4,501	10,265	135
Whitefish	174,500	71,266	58,014	92,681	5,074
Lake trout	40,815	73,427	199,469	215,528	24,870
Pickerel	20,200	12,991	1,100	0	0
Bass	104,200	0	0	0	0
Pike	0	0	0	0	0
Muskie	23,000	0	0	0	0
Sturgeon	0	0	0	0	0
Perch	145	97,092	32,770	29,595	0
Catfish	6,390	1,253	10,446	4,295	4,200
Carp	0	1,607,406	1,819,927	523,712	236,039
Dollar Value	19,965	85,171	130,421	19,859	6,473

Clearly, the peak for commercial fishing was reached in the 1920s. The zeros generally indicate when each species was declared to be a "game fish," and could no longer be netted and sold. After 1950, to protect and preserve the dwindling fish populations in the lake, no commercial fish licenses were issued, except for the taking of minnows for bait, and the removal of carp and other coarse fish. From then on, the emphasis was on sport-fishing for pleasure, rather than commercial fishing for income.

Above and below its surface, the ecology of a great lake is an evolutionary process, one in which yesterday's patterns are today's history, and today's data provides tomorrow's scientific analyses. There have been four major changes in the life-cycle of Lake Simcoe since the end of the 19th century.

Chronologically, the first was the introduction of carp into the Lake Simcoe watershed in the 1890s. These undesirable, coarse bottom-feeders were originally imported from

Europe in the early 1890s to stock garden ponds on the summer estates of well-to-do Simcoe County residents. It is believed that the original carp in Lake Simcoe found entrance through the lower Holland River, following the breeching of a dam at Dyke's Pond, near Newmarket, during spring flooding in 1896. Although they contributed substantially to the commercial fishing of the first half of this century, their presence has been deplored by most authorities, local residents, and visiting fishermen ever since their first appearance.

There was also the coming of the pike. Until about 1930, the muskie was the king (or queen) of sport-fishing in Lake Simcoe. For decades, they had lured anglers from all over North America and had provided summer employment for scores of lake-wise guides, who knew where they could be found. The pike had always been there, but in small numbers and generally scorned as a "trash fish," easy to catch and of inferior eating quality. But from about 1930 on, pike began to appear in greater numbers. The increase was first apparent at the north end of the lake, around Smith's Bay and the Atherley Narrows, but Cook's Bay was eventually to become the principal pike habitat.

Coincident with this development, the muskie (or muskelunge) population declined drastically. By 1956, according to McCrimmon (*Fishing in Lake Simcoe*), it contributed "practically nothing to the sports fishery" of the lake.

There is still, of course, some fine muskie fishing to be enjoyed in Simcoe County—particularly in the Port Severn area, off Waubaushene and Port McNicoll, and in Midland Bay. And Lake Simcoe continues to host a few giants of this species, as guides such as Bruce Park of Keswick are well aware.

But to a great extent the pike have taken over as the dominant "big fish" of Lake Simcoe, earning increasing recognition for their fighting qualities and increasing acceptance as desirable food for the table. Many of these fish grow to great size; the second largest pike ever caught in Ontario, a 42-pounder, was taken from Cook's Bay in the early 1970s.

The third major change that has taken place in the ecology of Lake Simcoe has been the increasing popularity of ice fishing since the end of World War II. Some fish had always been taken through the ice, the first settlers adopting the custom of the Indians and standing over open holes with three-pronged spears. But, where it had been an occasional and practical occupation in earlier years, ice fishing became a highly popular sport during the 1950s and later. And, largely because of its proximity to Toronto, Lake Simcoe became the most popular ice-fishing lake in Ontario. The number of ice-fishing huts on the lake increased from about 800 in 1950 to well over 4,000 by the mid-1960s. In the winter of 1970-71, more than 70,000 anglers tried their luck on the ice of the lake, and they caught almost 300,000 fish—mainly whitefish, lake trout, smelt, herring and perch.

Yet, by the mid-1970s, it was clear that fishing in Lake Simcoe, particularly ice fishing, was in a state of drastic decline. "The fishery is in trouble, make no mistake about it," Paul Hethrington, past president of the Lake Simcoe Fish Hut Operators Association, told Bob Rife of the Toronto *Globe and Mail* in December, 1976.

Catches of lake trout dropped sharply during the early 1970s, but it appeared that the whitefish were most severely endangered. These figures, submitted by Ron Desjardine, biologist with Ontario's Ministry of Natural Resources, made the picture all too clear:

Year	Total Lake Simcoe Whitefish Catch (in Pounds)
1968	100,000
1973	40,000
1974	20,000
1975	10,000
1976	7,000

"According to our catch figures, the bottom has fallen out of the whitefish population," Charlie Weir of the Ministry of Natural Resources said, late in 1976. "We're making an attempt to hold onto some of the fish, while hopefully something happens to clean up the lake."

And Desjardine, who provided the figures, described the situation as "ominous." While no one could be sure of the cause, it seemed likely that the decline was because of poor success in the hatching of whitefish eggs—probably due to increasing algae and silt in the lake.

Closely related was the fourth major change in the lake's ecology—the contamination of its fish. "Most of us have viewed the mercury pollution in Lake St. Clair and the English-Wabigoon systems with detached concern," John Power, outdoor columnist for the *Toronto Star*, wrote in January, 1977. "Distance dulls the impact of ecological catastrophes, which don't hit home until they occur on the doorstep; like the shocking news that Lake Simcoe's walleyes are contaminated by mercury, and the larger fish unfit for human consumption."

Reluctantly, Simcoe County came to accept the fact that its great inland sea was seriously, perhaps critically, ill; and that, unless drastic measures were taken, the malady could cost millions of dollars in lost revenue, and an inestimable loss to the thousands of people who might have enjoyed the lake in the future.

Yet, however sobering, the threat to the lake is just one of the major problems facing the county and many other sections of Ontario. There is an ever increasing need for local governments to co-operate and co-ordinate efforts with a wide variety of provincial and federal agencies, since it is abundantly clear that no county is an island, entire unto itself.

In fulfilling their administrative responsibilities, today's County Councillors must assimilate a staggering amount of economic, sociological, scientific, technological and ecological data.

Since the early 1960s, a great many planning studies have been carried out in Simcoe County and the southern Georgian Bay region. Conducted by various government departments and private groups, they deal with many different aspects and factors, as this partial list will illustrate: *Georgian Bay Region Economic Survey*, Ontario Department of Economics and Development, 1963; *Barrie-Simcoe County Highway Planning Study*, Ontario Department of Transportation and Communications, 1971; *Nottawasaga Valley Conservation Report*, Ontario Ministry of Natural Resources, 1973; *Optimum Recreational Development in the Lake Simcoe-Couchiching Area*, Canadian-Ontario Rideau-Trent-Severn Committee, 1973; *Georgian Bay Regional Plan*, Georgian Bay Regional Development Council, 1973; *Draft Master Plan for Minesing Swamp*, Ontario Ministry of Natural Resources, 1975. Together they provide an imposing volume of maps, charts, statistical tables, graphs, projections, conclusions and recommendations. To sift through this great body of confusing, and sometimes conflicting information, in order to determine the best possible courses of action, places a growing burden on those who govern Simcoe County in the mid-1970s.

By no means, of course, is the outlook entirely bleak and gloomy. There is promise and potential in what lies ahead, as surely as there are problems; but the latter must be dealt with before the former can be realized.

The major questions were well summarized in a report entitled "Prospects for the Georgian Bay Region," issued by the Ontario Ministry of Treasury, Economics and Inter-governmental Affairs, in September, 1972:

Where should future urban growth take place, and how should it be accommodated?

If Barrie grows considerably, what would discharge of its treated waste do to the ecology of Lake Simcoe? Similarly, what would growth in Orillia do to Lake Couchiching?

If Barrie, Orillia, Collingwood and Midland are all encouraged to grow, what should their target populations be?

What kind of transportation system should be designed to serve the region's future needs?

How much more of the demand for cottages, ski-slopes, chalets and snowmobile trails can the region meet without despoiling the environment?

How much should the region rely on tourists to provide a desirable degree of growth and development?

To what extent can the region's traditional occupations —agriculture, fishing and forestry—provide a reasonable standdard of living?

With the growing number of city-oriented people moving into the rural areas, how can additional urban sprawl be prevented?

There are no easy answers to these questions, nor are there apparent short-term solutions. Meeting the challenges of the present and future will require resourcefulness, determination, adaptability, willingness to compromise, and dedication. Fortunately, these are qualities which have been abundantly evident in Simcoe County's recent past.

Acknowledgment

We wish to thank the Simcoe County Archives for supplying background material for the sketches that appear on pages 16,40,60, 128, 178, 210, 252, and 258.

Notes on Sources and a Short Bibliography

History is where you find it. The collected materials from which this work was fashioned include government documents published by many different federal and provincial departments; local histories of towns, villages and townships, especially Centennial booklets and the Tweedsmuir histories; written replies to specific inquiries; unpublished university theses; magazine articles; learned society papers; private collections; maps; promotional brochures; reports and studies of many kinds; and books on specific topics.

The files of the newspapers of the County were a mother lode of information—particularly the "morgues" of the Barrie *Examiner*, Orillia *Packet & Times*, Collingwood *Enterprise-Bulletin* and Midland *Free Press*.

The research included first-hand observations made while travelling throughout Simcoe County. Also important were personal interviews with many officials and older residents. J. Keith Mc-Ruer, Agricultural Representative for South Simcoe, was especially helpful in gathering information on agriculture.

The libraries in the cities and towns contributed valuable data that they keep on file. The articles on Orillia area women by Sally Gower, on file in the Orillia Public Library were most useful. The many museums scattered throughout the County and the Simcoe County Archives provided valuable assistance.

Of the numerous books and articles, published and unpublished, consulted in the preparation of this volume, the following should be singled out for special mention:

A Century of Progress, the Centennial Review of the Township of Essa, 1850-1950. 1950.

Coldwater Canadiana. *Huronia: A Glance Into the Past*. n.d.

Collingwood Centennial Committee. *The Story of Collingwood, 1858-1958*. 1958.

Department of Lands and Forests. *A History of the Lake Simcoe Forestry District*. 1963.

Drury, E. C. *Farmer Premier: The Memoirs of E. C. Drury*. Toronto: McClelland & Stewart, 1966.

Frost, Leslie. *Fighting Men*. Toronto: Clarke, Irwin & Co., 1967.

Hunter, Andrew F. *A History of Simcoe County*. Barrie: The Historical Committee of Simcoe County, 1909.

Innisfil Township Council. *A Record of 100 Years of Progress*. 1951 (updated in 1967).

Kidd, Bruce. Report to the Community Programs Division, Ontario Department of Education. 1967.

LeGear, Richard, and Kearns, John. *History and Development of Industry in Barrie*. Unpublished, n.d.

Leitch, Adelaide. *The Visible Past*. Barrie: The County of Simcoe, 1967.

McCrimmon, H. R. *Fishing in Lake Simcoe*. Department of Lands and Forests, 1956.

Midhurst Historical Society. *Pioneer History of Midhurst*. 1975.

Ontario Ministry of Transportation and Communications. "Highway 400." 1976.

Orchard, Joseph. *The Land I Love: Minesing, Ontario*. 1971.

Oro Historical Committee. *The Story of Oro*. 1972.

Osler, W. Edmund. "The Oslers of Ontario." *Chatelaine*, Dec., 1969-Feb., 1970.

Paterson, Gilbert C. *The County of Simcoe*. Education Committee, Simcoe County Council. 1968.

Penetanguishene, 1875-1975. 1975.

Phillips, William J., and Pecsenye, John. *Alliston: A Study of an Ontario Town*. Unpublished, n.d.

Platt, Bert. *Beeton 1874-1974*. Published privately, 1974.

Rawson, Mabel. *Port Severn: Crossroads Community*. Simcoe County Press Limited, 1976.

Shaw, J. G. *Saints Lived Here*. Martyrs' Shrine, Midland, 1975.

The Story of Stayner, 1867-1967. Unpublished, 1967.

Train, Gladys. *Memorial History of Shiloh Union Church*. 1970.

White, Geoffrey. *History of the Barrie Public Utilities Commission*. Unpublished, n.d.

Index

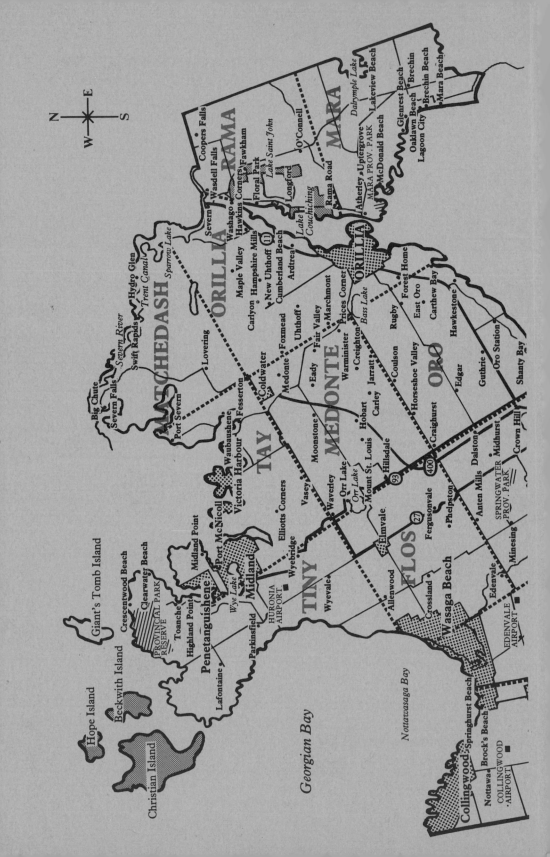